Crime Prevention
The Law Enforcement Officer's
Practical Guide

Richard L. Arrington

Criminal Justice Program Analyst
Commonwealth of Virginia, Department of Criminal Justice Services
Richmond, VA

JONES AND BARTLETT PUBLISHERS
Sudbury, Massachusetts
BOSTON   TORONTO   LONDON   SINGAPORE

World Headquarters

Jones and Bartlett Publishers
40 Tall Pine Drive
Sudbury, MA 01776
978-443-5000
info@jbpub.com
www.jbpub.com

Jones and Bartlett Publishers Canada
6339 Ormindale Way
Mississauga, Ontario L5V 1J2
Canada

Jones and Bartlett Publishers
International
Barb House, Barb Mews
London W6 7PA
United Kingdom

Jones and Bartlett's books and products are available through most bookstores and online booksellers. To contact Jones and Bartlett Publishers directly, call 800-832-0034, fax 978-443-8000, or visit our website www.jbpub.com.

Substantial discounts on bulk quantities of Jones and Bartlett's publications are available to corporations, professional associations, and other qualified organizations. For details and specific discount information, contact the special sales department at Jones and Bartlett via the above contact information or send an email to specialsales@jbpub.com.

Production Credits

Chief Executive Officer: Clayton E. Jones
Chief Operating Officer: Donald W. Jones, Jr.
President, Higher Education and Professional Publishing:
    Robert W. Holland, Jr.
V.P., Sales and Marketing: William J. Kane
V.P., Production and Design: Anne Spencer
V.P., Manufacturing and Inventory Control: Therese Connell
Publisher, Public Safety Group: Kimberly Brophy
Acquisitions Editor: Jeremy Spiegel
Associate Editor: Janet Morris

Production Editor: Jenny L. Corriveau
Manufacturing Buyer: Amy Bacus
Director of Marketing: Alisha Weisman
Interior Design: Anne Spencer
Cover Design: Kristin E. Ohlin
Composition: Publishers' Design and Production Services, Inc.
Cover and Interior Image (blue siren): © Comstock Images/
    Alamy Images
Cover Image: © Stephen Morton/AP Photos
Text Printing and Binding: Malloy, Inc.
Cover Printing: Malloy, Inc.

Library of Congress Cataloging-in-Publication Data

Arrington, Rick.
    Crime prevention : the law enforcement officer's practical guide / Rick Arrington.
        p. cm.
    ISBN-13: 978-0-7637-4130-3 (pbk.)
    ISBN-10: 0-7637-4130-2 (pbk.)
    1. Crime prevention—Handbooks, manuals, etc. 2. Law enforcement—Handbooks, manuals, etc. I. Title.
HV7431.A74 2006
363.2'3—dc22

2006010094

6048

Printed in the United States of America

10 09 08 07 06   10 9 8 7 6 5 4 3 2 1

This book is dedicated to my family and to all Crime Prevention or Community Resource Officers who are thrown into the position with little direction or training and have proven that prevention works.

Chapter 4: Crime Prevention in Practice and Theory   33

Chapter 5: Crime Prevention Community Programs   38

Chapter 6: Crime Prevention Campaigns   54

Chapter 7: Preventing Property Crime   59

Chapter 9: Frauds Against the Individual   102

Chapter 10: Violence Prevention   113

The Origins of Crime Prevention and Community Policing

"We have found a strange footprint on the shores of the unknown. We have devised profound theories, one after another, to account for its origins. At last, we have succeeded in reconstructing the creature that made the footprint. And lo! It is our own."

—Sir Arthur Eddington

■ Introduction

We were promised that it was a fad, a passing experiment that wouldn't last long enough for the officers to learn how to spell SARA, much less understand the problem-solving concept behind the acronym that stands for Scanning, Analyzing, Response, and Assessment. Well, the promise was not kept, and it appears that some forms of community-oriented services are in place in almost all law enforcement agencies today. Notice that I called it "community-oriented services" and not "community policing." Why? Because, since its growth in the 1980s, federal grants have abounded for community policing programs. Therefore, any number of programs have been named, or renamed, community policing. Some programs identified as community policing are as akin to it as a skunk is to a lap cat. I have witnessed uniformed vice or hit squads being included as part of such programs; K-9 units being written up in national magazines as the core to a community policing effort; and other such absurdities. Those claiming that these programs are community policing are not being intentionally deceptive, they just have been misled themselves. In order to understand community policing one must look at its roots and the thought processes of its founders.

■ The History of Crime Prevention and Community Policing

Specialized units designed to put a positive spin on negative interactions with police grew out of the civil rights and war protests of the 1960s. These special public relations units spent most of their time making presentations about the good that their respective agencies were doing. Soon the officers staffing these units became familiar with the idea of making it more difficult for criminals to carry out their acts by employing locks and mechanical devices. The officers began to educate the public in "target hardening," and agencies began to see a positive impact from the educational campaigns. As a result of the decreasing need for public relations, these units began to concentrate exclusively on preventing crimes, and thus the primary role of the crime prevention unit became one of education. In 1971, the National Crime Prevention Institute was created at the University of Louisville to provide training in crime opportunity reduction programs. Crime prevention has expanded to include mechanical approaches such as target hardening, community activism approaches such as those associated with Neighborhood Watch programs, and environmental approaches such as opportunity reduction through environmental changes. When crime prevention was new, funding flowed freely into research and development of such programs, but when community policing became the newest thing, funding for prevention programs began to dry up. Among crime prevention practitioners, jealousy led to a popular refrain that they had been doing community policing for years and that there was nothing new about what was being done. Many agencies called their crime prevention unit something different, but they continued to work the same as always. Many still contend that crime prevention is community policing.

The Community Policing Practitioners

The community policing camp insisted that what they were doing was not business as usual, but an entirely new way of addressing crime—an improved way of policing. Even the so-called experts cannot agree as to what, exactly, community policing is. Some contend that Herman Goldstein's problem-oriented policing, originating in 1983 in Newport News, Virginia, or a planning strategy are at the heart of community policing. Others believe the high-visibility patrols and organizing communities, as was modeled in Baltimore, Maryland, in the 1980s, is more what is meant by community policing. Regardless of what process is favored, all community policing programs point to Sir Robert Peel's principles of policing as the basis for their program. Crime prevention practitioners also refer to Peel for their origins and tenets, which are as follows (Mayhall, 1995, p. 297):

1. The basic mission for which police exist is to prevent crime and disorder as an alternative to the repression of crime and disorder by military force and severity of legal punishment.
2. The ability of the police to perform their duties is dependent upon public approval of police existence, actions, and behavior and the ability of the police to secure and maintain public respect.
3. The police must secure the willing cooperation of the public in voluntary observance of the law to be able to secure and maintain public respect.
4. The degree of the cooperation of the public that can be secured diminishes proportionately the necessity for the use of physical force and the compulsion in achieving police objectives.
5. The police seek and preserve public favor, not by catering to public opinion, but by constantly demonstrating absolutely impartial service to the law, in complete independence of policy, and without regard to the justice or injustice of the substance of individual laws; by ready offering of individual service and friendship to all members of society without regard to their race or social standing, by ready exercise of courtesy and friendly good humor, and by ready offering of individual sacrifice in protecting and preserving life.
6. The police should use physical force to the extent necessary to secure observance of the law or to restore order only when the exercise of persuasion, advice, and warning is found to be insufficient to achieve police objectives; and police should use only the minimum degree of physical force that is necessary on any particular occasion for achieving a police objective.
7. The police at all times should maintain a relationship with the public that gives reality to the historic tradition that the police are the public and the public are the police; the police are only members of the public who are paid to give full-time attention to duties that are incumbent on every citizen in the intent of community welfare.

8. The police should always direct their actions toward their functions and never appear to usurp the powers of the judiciary by avenging individuals or the state, or authoritatively judging guilt or punishing the guilty.
9. The test of police efficiency is the absence of crime and disorder, not the visible evidence of police action in dealing with them.

So the question is, who is correct? None, and all!

I contend that crime prevention can be involved in community policing, such as when the officer is working with a new Neighborhood Watch organization to effect some change in the community. The accepted definition of crime prevention is one that focuses on the actions taken by a trained practitioner, rather than by the community in most cases. "Crime Prevention is the anticipation, recognition and appraisal of a crime risk and the initiation of some action to remove or reduce it" (National Crime Prevention Institute, 1986, p. 2). The most often accepted community policing definition states that it is "a policing philosophy that promotes and supports organizational strategies to address the causes and reduce the fear of crime and social disorder through problem-solving tactics and community policing partnerships." (U.S. Department of Justice, 1997, p.1) In short, crime prevention is usually done to or for someone, whereas true community policing is done cooperatively "with" the community as equal partners. Although the units' duties seem similar, they are very different. Both units, or at least their duties, are equally important if crime is to be reduced. A complementary program that allows each unit to build on the other's work while working toward their mutual goal is most likely to be successful.

■ Lessons Learned

In order to avoid jealousy, incompatibility, and possessive control of certain aspects of the policing function, the job duties of the two units should clearly be defined for each function within an agency. Job descriptions of crime prevention officers generally include the assessment of vulnerabilities and environmental issues, the organizing of community groups, and education. Community policing officers, on the other hand, should have a more hands-on function. Their duties would typically include conducting problem analyses, planning a strategic approach to addressing problems cooperatively with members of the community, conducting door-to-door surveys or interviews, carrying out high-visibility enforcement actions, and being a contact resource to the community organization.

Using this approach, one way that the two units might work together could be that the community officer identifies a neighborhood experiencing specific problems. He and others in his unit may conduct a door-to-door survey to identify the issues and potential community leaders. The potential leaders would then be approached by the crime prevention officer, who would in turn work to organize the community and provide training concerning the specific crimes located in the area. Community officers would attend the meetings to build a rapport with the community and to obtain information as to where to begin high-visibility patrols while other strategies are being developed, and so on. As you can see, each unit has a distinct and separate role, but each action works toward the units' shared goal. Either may work alone, but by working together using a complete approach a positive outcome is likely to come about more quickly.

In the upcoming chapters I will explain in detail how to start both a crime prevention and a community policing unit. The more common specific duties that each unit performs will be discussed and demonstrated as their usefulness is explained. Examples of assessments, surveys, and other tools are included to guide the reader in developing or strengthening his or her particular unit.

■ Chapter Summary

Community policing and crime prevention use the same philosophical approach, that of community-oriented services. Although agencies may have two separate units, their duties should be clearly defined in order to avoid repetition and competition.

■ Review Questions

1. Was the community approach created by Herman Goldstein one of high-visibility or problem-oriented policing?
2. Who was the author of the nine principles thought to be the basis for community policing?
3. At what institute did the definition adopted by most agencies for crime prevention originate?
4. Of the two discussed approaches, crime prevention and community policing, which focuses on working cooperatively with the citizenry?

■ References

Mayhall, Pamela D., Barker, Thomas, and Hunter, Ronald D. 1995. *Police Community Relations and the Administration of Justice* (4th ed.) Englewood Cliffs, NJ: Prentice Hall.

National Crime Prevention Institute. 1986. *Understanding Crime Prevention*. Stoneham, MA: Butterworth–Heinemann.

U.S. Department of Justice, Office of Community Oriented Policing Services. July 29, 1997. *COPS Facts*.

Creating the Community Policing Program

"If the facts don't fit the theory, change the facts."

—Albert Einstein

■ Introduction

The creation of a community policing program is a time-consuming process that requires a complete shift in how an agency undertakes policing in its community. To be successful, the chief executive should be firmly behind the philosophical change and express his or her expectations to other staff. Although it is not necessary for the chief executive or his or her staff to understand all aspects of how community policing is to be accomplished, it is important that they understand the basic principles and goals behind community policing, because any change in philosophy necessitates a change in goals. The executive must understand that reducing an area's fear of crime is as important as the number of arrests made in an area. Any halfhearted attempt at community policing will produce, at best, a minimum success. The transition to community policing is therefore not for the weak.

■ Opposition

Once a department has committed to community policing, it should expect opposition. Opposition will come in many forms. It may come in the form of the dinosaur who refuses to change, or political pressure to return to the more revenue-friendly reactive policing. It may also come in the form of the executive's own staff who secretly try to undermine the effort. Finally, some of the opposition may come from the executive, who is unable to adapt to the changes. In the long run, however, if the executive and the agency stay committed, rewards such as lower crime rates, increased case clearances, improved community relations, and a safer jurisdiction will be worth the struggle. Safer jurisdictions increase officer satisfaction as they see their goals accomplished. A study of the Baltimore, Maryland, Community Oriented Police Enforcement (COPE) Project in 1982 revealed that after 3 years, officers in the COPE unit had a higher level of job satisfaction than their counterparts in the traditional policing units (Roberg and Kuykendall, 1990). In my own jurisdiction, I experienced and still observe that the officers involved in true community policing are much more satisfied, and seem to have a better understanding of the science of policing. Not only will citizens be happier and officers more satisfied, but politicians will also be pleased. When crime decreases and communities are involved in the decrease, citizens are more satisfied with their public officials. The lower crime rate and increased community involvement can be used as a tool for economic growth of the community, which in turn perpetuates the cycle.

■ The Political Culture

The political culture truly guides the direction in which any police agency moves. That same culture interferes with innovative policing by applying political pressure. Few police executives are willing to stand their ground, but stand their ground they must if modern policing is to be successful. Officers are looking to them to lead the organization into success. Thomas Peters and Robert Waterman conclude in their book, *In Search of Excellence* (1982), that the role of the executive is to manage the values of the organization. They further state that excellent companies are marked by very strong cultures. The cultures are so strong, in fact, that employees either conform or vacate their position. Indeed, strong police executives are needed to lead the change.

Smart police executives understand that the train called community policing requires a different style of leadership, and they are getting on board. In a 1991 exercise performed with law enforcement management experts, scholars, and executives regarding future developments in policing, the conclusion was that by 2025 more than 70% of police executives will adopt a "nontraditional" style (Tafoya, 1991). Now that the catalyst of the philosophical change is understood, we must ask, "How does one lead that change?"

Changing the Culture

Organizations share a common set of norms, values, attitudes, and beliefs, commonly referred to as the *organizational culture*. Police agencies are no different. Many officers stay with an organization simply because that organization meets their personal goals and supports their personal perceptions. It is important to understand this fact in order to recognize that any effort to change that culture or organizational philosophy may result in the officer viewing the change as a personal threat to his or her values and beliefs. In view of this fact, a change process must be undertaken that is careful not to attack, but rather to shift the values little by little.

To begin this philosophical change, I suggest the following three-step process offered by Edgar H. Schein in his book, *Organizational Psychology* (1970):

1. Unfreeze, or emphasize the need for change.
2. Identify change agents.
3. Refreeze, or institutionalize the change.

Unfreeze

Schein suggests that the first step is to "unfreeze" or emphasize the need for the change in the organization. One way this might be accomplished in a police agency is by demonstrating a decreasing case clearance, indicative of a lack of citizen involvement, burnout, or other factors. Increasing crime rates indicate that the department is currently employing failing techniques. One might evaluate the average time ranking officers spend on minor decisions and then relaying them back to the officer closest to the problem. An evaluation of officer job satisfaction through a study of employee turnover, use of sick time, and productivity may also be a method of demonstrating the need for change. The smart executive should ensure that officers are surveyed to evaluate feelings concerning officer and supervisory autonomy in decision making and that citizens are surveyed to evaluate their perception of crime, fear of crime, and perceptions of the agency. See **Tables 2.1** and **2.2** for examples of two types of community surveys.

Once the organization has recognized the need to change and the need has been made clear to officers, staff, citizens, and government officials, the second step of the three-step process is to identify a "change agent" to facilitate the change. The executive leading the change should share his or her expectations, avoid coercive tactics, and encourage a team approach with innovative ideas as the foundation.

Table 2.1
Community Survey Derived from a Roanoke, Virginia, COPE Unit Survey

Community Survey	False	Sometimes	True	Very True
1. I often avoid going out during the daytime because I am afraid of crime.				
2. Fear of crime is very high in my neighborhood.				
3. There is a good chance that I will be the victim of a property crime (theft, burglary) in my neighborhood this year.				
4. The police department does the best job it can against crime in my neighborhood.				
5. I believe that there is a drug problem in my neighborhood.				
6. There is a good chance that I will be the victim of a crime against my person in my neighborhood this year.				
7. My fear of crime is very high.				
8. I am more afraid of crime than ever before.				
9. I often avoid going out after dark because of crime.				
10. The police department does the best job it can to make me feel safe in my neighborhood.				

Change Agents

There are three types of potential change agents. The first is the *external agent*, who is hired by the executive from outside the agency to evaluate the needs and to recommend changes. This quite often will be a consultant, but also may be a newly formed position, created by the executive for this very purpose. The external change agent has the advantage of having no preconceived ideas and holding no allegiance to others in the agency, but is often viewed with suspicion and characterized as not understanding the agency. He or she is an outsider and not part of the culture, and so is distrusted. In order to be successful he or she must overcome this obstacle and develop rapport with members of the agency. In view of the problems described, this is the least desirable change agent.

The second type of change agent is the *internal agent*. Although the internal agent has an insider's knowledge of the agency, he or she may not have the necessary knowledge to facilitate the needed changes. The internal agent has little experience in community polic-

Table 2.2

Community Involvement Survey Derived from a Roanoke, Virginia, COPE Unit Survey

1. When you think of neighborhood problems or crime, what are your concerns?

2. How often does this crime or concern occur?

3. What do you feel is the cause of this problem?

4. What could the neighborhood do to correct the problem?

5. What could or should the police do to correct the problem?

6. Is there a community organization established in your neighborhood? Are you an active member?

7. Do you participate in any crime prevention programs?

8. Have you been the victim of a crime in the past year? If yes, what crime?

ing matters, so he or she may require extensive, time-consuming training, and is sometimes viewed as feathering his or her own cap. In fact, the internal agent is likely to have a more difficult time than the external agent in establishing the needed rapport and receiving cooperation.

This brings us to the final type of change agent, the *combination agent*. This is the recommended type of change agent because it draws from the positive of both the other forms while minimizing the negative. Using a combination approach, the external agent brings the necessary knowledge of community policing while the internal agent shares the agency's norms and processes. Working together, the two diagnose and receive input from a committee made up of all affected parties. Once the input is evaluated, the change agents make their recommendations to the executive for action, and once approved, the two train the agency members, each from his or her own perspective, as to how the changes will improve the agency and the community. This change agent activity will take a considerable amount of time because the agents need to ensure that the agency has a full understanding of the philosophy. Specific techniques are part of the training received during this step. The specifics of the training, individual roles, and techniques are discussed in detail later in this chapter.

Refreeze

The final step of the change process, according to Schein, is to "refreeze" or institutionalize the changes. This institutionalizing of the new philosophy is most impacted by the mid-level manager and supervisory-level employee. The role of these key persons cannot be overemphasized. In a 1991 interview concerning the city's move to community policing, New York City Police Commissioner Lee P. Brown said, "You can't expect cops on the beat to be successful if their supervisors and managers don't understand and support the change. So my strategy has been to start with my executive staff, to change its mind set" (Webber, 1991). They will not be coerced; they must be convinced. They must buy into the philosophy in order to sell it to their subordinates. Therefore, they must see the benefit of the change for themselves and the agency. This is begun by openly communicating the reason for the change. This communication should come from the chief executive himself. The executive officer's willingness to share information directly with the supervisor will signal that the change has begun, and its first benefit to the supervisor is open communication. It also communicates the chief executive's commitment to the process.

Once the managers and supervisors have received the information concerning the change, they should be the first to be trained in community policing techniques. By training the supervisors and managers first they begin to change the organizational culture and norms. I have observed a number of agencies in which ranking officials cannot understand why the sergeant or lieutenant does not ensure that officers are "doing community policing." Close examination would reveal the reason—they themselves don't know how and therefore feed their own needs to feel confident by reverting to what they know. This is then relayed to officers who observe their immediate supervisor concentrating his or her efforts only on traditional policing, and before long community policing efforts are nonexistent.

Training is indeed an essential step in this process. It may be developed in house by the consultant or developed by and contracted with outside trainers. Although these are viable training solutions, the better, more cost-effective solution is to use training provided by any of the community policing institutes, crime prevention associations, or police academies. In 1994, the Violent Crime Control Act authorized the use of $8.8 billion specifically for supporting community policing. The U.S. Department of Justice, Office of Community Oriented Policing Services (COPS), funds the community policing institutes for officer training. Thirty such institutes across the United States were funded, and at least one third of them provide training. The local crime prevention associations are mostly nonprofit organizations, with a mission also related to training officers and practitioners. Training provided by these type of agencies was created by experts in the field of community-oriented services and is usually low cost, if not free of charge. Such training can vary, but generally it is better than that offered by contract services. A list of such agencies can be found in the Resources section at the end of this book.

One of the first tangible benefits that should be given to the supervisors and mid-level managers is the autonomy to make more decisions at their level and to be innovative within legal parameters. Although giving the supervisors this autonomy is extremely difficult for many executives, it is absolutely necessary to encourage supervisory buy-in. This demonstration of trust in their ability goes a long way to further their confidence and job satisfaction. Open access to ranking officers should accompany their autonomy, and in most cases the open access will be seen as a reward because they will be perceived as being equally valuable to the organization.

■ The Mid-Level Manager's or Supervisor's New Role

The mid-level manager and supervisor have been trained, given more responsibility, and advised to encourage innovation, but their role must change further to create the necessary environment for their subordinates to succeed. Their role must change from "rule enforcer" to that of "coach." What about the Rules and Regulations Manual? With this question we delve into another area that is quite difficult for executives, governments, and managers, but it is one that needs to be addressed.

In most agencies, the Rules and Regulations Manual governs how officers operate and perform tasks. Eight-inch-thick manuals spell out minute details of officers' duties. These manuals are ineffective and create an unrealistic expectation that officers know and can recall the details written therein. In the traditional model of policing, the manual was used as a tool to punish and to make all members conform to the "one way mentality." In truth, even the supervisor had to consult it to see if a policy had been violated. Under the community policing model, creative thinking is encouraged, not discouraged. Of course there is a need for guidance and some policies, but whenever possible reliance on the manual should be reduced. The supervisors and officers should be the ones to determine how to solve a problem. The supervisor must take on the new role of coach, in which he or she must demonstrate to officers that it is okay to make mistakes within the legal and moral parameters provided. The officers will seize the new freedom to be innovative.

The coaching role involves:

1. Teaching the new techniques
2. Reinforcing the philosophy of the agency
3. Allowing officers the flexibility to do the job

Alan Loy McGinnis has a unique way of stating this "rule" of freedom in his book, *Bringing Out the Best in People—How to Enjoy Helping Others Excel*. He calls this creating an environment where "failure is not fatal" (McGinnis, 1986, p. 71).

■ Obtaining Officer Buy-in

We have discussed the supervisor's role and how to encourage their acceptance of the philosophical change. We've also briefly touched on how to encourage officer acceptance of the change. Now, let's get down to the meat of the matter—how do we motivate officers to embrace the new way of policing?

Officers, like supervisors, want to be confident in what they do, and training on the specific expectations and techniques of community policing will go a long way in helping them to understand and value their new role. Officers gain rewards through transfers, promotions, raises, and a sense of accomplishment. Each of these rewards is tied in some way to one common thread—the infamous performance appraisal. It is no wonder managers often are heard to recite the common mantra, "What gets measured gets done." Another less tangible, but nevertheless important, motivator is job enrichment—job duties that offer the officer a variety of tasks and give him or her a degree of responsibility for decision making. These duties have been proven to give officers greater job satisfaction, and job satisfaction has been proven to be a great personal motivator. Henry Wadsworth Longfellow put it poetically by writing, "We judge ourselves by what we feel capable of doing, while others judge us by what we have already done." These motivators will not work on all the cynics. Some officers are so wary of change that they are like the proverbial cynic who, every time he smelled the sweet aroma of flowers, looked for a coffin. It is, however, my belief that the majority will respond to such incentives.

Once the movement has begun, it will require work to keep it on track. Before we move to the actual techniques employed in problem solving and community policing, consider the most common reasons why efforts in community policing fail:

1. The chief executive is insincere.
2. The organizational structure does not fit the philosophy. (This is discussed below.)
3. Management does not support the effort or subverts the effort.
4. There is a lack of or no communication among the rank and file.
5. Unclear or no expectations are expressed.
6. Officers are not allowed to express creativity.

■ Encouraging Community Policing by Organizational Structure

Moving the responsibility for decision making to the lowest possible point is an important aspect of community policing, so one of the first areas that an executive might wish to address is the organizational structure.

By examining the structure, the agency can be reordered to allow those closest to the problem to make the decisions necessary to facilitate action quickly. Unfortunately, most law enforcement agencies are characterized by an organizational structure that impedes a quick decision-making process. Traditional, or reactive, agencies adhere to a "tall" organizational structure with many levels of rank between the top executive and the line officer. This tall structure is based on the militaristic configuration that many agencies have historically followed. The "flat" structure, with fewer levels of hierarchy, enhances quicker decisions and communication. Many problems, such as roadblocks and filtration, are eliminated or decreased with this type of structure, therefore making it ideal for community policing or proactive policing styles. **Table 2.3** shows a side-by-side comparison of the tall and flat structures, demonstrating the differences. This comparison demonstrates why the flat structure is more conducive to community policing.

As demonstrated in the comparison, the tall structure can become quite taxing on the top executive and upper-management level, whereas the flat structure can be more taxing on the supervisory and middle management level. The adjustment of the structure and decrease in formal policies open the door for supervisors to prepare the line officers for their role of one-on-one involvement and problem solving with the citizenry. In preparing the officers for decision making, the supervisor must gradually develop the officers' skills. There must be a mutual sharing of expectations by the subordinate and supervisor. This sharing develops trust as the supervisor trains and allows the officer to make mistakes without fear of disciplinary retribution. The trust enhances the open communication because officers feel that they can speak without reprisals; the open communication will lead to the supervisor and subordinate participating in the decision making. Once this has

Table 2.3
Tall and Flat Structure Comparison

Tall Structure	Flat Structure
Many levels of rank or hierarchy for decisions to pass through.	Few levels of hierarchy; decisions are made at the lowest level.
Authority for decisions is derived from position.	Authority is derived from knowledge (whomever knows the most about the problem).
Many formal rules and policies.	Fewer "formalized" rules; autonomy and responsibility are encouraged.
Centralized decision making (made by hierarchy).	Decentralized decisions (made by whoever's the most knowledgeable about the situation).
Officers specialize and are efficient in doing one or two things.	Officers are generalists, capable of many tasks.

Adapted from: Stoner, J. A. F., and R. Edward Freeman. *Management*, 5th ed. Englewood Cliffs, NJ: Prentice Hall, pp. 314–316.

been accomplished, the final step, which is perhaps the most difficult for many supervisors, is that the officer must be given the autonomy to make certain decisions at his or her level, that closest to the problem. The officer decides when the problem requires supervisory or intervention at a higher level, and seeks the assistance of those required.

■ Chapter Summary

Successfully creating a community policing program will require a change in the agency's culture, philosophy, and, in many cases, organizational makeup. Each officer at every level will realize a new role and a new paradigm, and many will resist. Once the executive of the agency decides to create the program, his or her commitment and support are essential for success. The executive must choose carefully which change agent he or she wishes to employ based on analysis of the type of resistance expected. Once the choice is made, the executive must express and demonstrate his or her expectations related to the program, and then the training of the practical techniques may begin.

■ Review Questions

1. What is the term associated with a common set of norms, values, attitudes, and beliefs in an organization?
2. Which of the change agents involves an outside consultant working collaboratively with an inside employee to lead the cultural change?
3. In implementing a community policing program, the supervisor's role changes from rule enforcer to what?
4. Tying the newly required duties to which management tool is one of the best ways to encourage officers to buy in to the community policing philosophy?
5. Of the flat organizational structure and the tall organizational structure, which is more conducive to community policing?

■ References

McGinnis, Alan Loy. 1985. *Bringing Out the Best in People—How to Enjoy Helping Others Excel*. Minneapolis, MN: Augsburg.

Peters, Thomas, and Waterman Jr., Robert H. 1982. *In Search of Excellence*. New York: Harper & Row.

Roberg, Roy, and Kuykendall, Jack. 1990. *Police Organization and Management—Behavior, Theory, and Processes*. Belmont, CA: Wadsworth Publishing.

Schein, Edgar H. 1970. *Organizational Psychology* (2nd ed.). Englewood Cliffs, NJ: Prentice Hall.

Stoner, James A. F., and Freeman, R. Edward. 1992. *Management* (5th ed.). Englewood Cliffs, NJ: Prentice Hall.

Tafoya, William L. 1991. The future of law enforcement—a chronology of events. *Criminal Justice International*; May/June edition: p. 4.

Webber, Alan. May 1991. Crime and management: An interview with New York City Police Commissioner Lee P. Brown. *Harvard Business Review*.

Community Policing Techniques

"Most of the important things in the world have been accomplished by people who have kept on trying when there seemed to be no hope at all."
—Dale Carnegie

■ Introduction

The premise of problem solving is essential to any proactive policing strategy because it attacks the underlying causes of the issue at hand, rather than just its effects. It is a strategy of correcting conditions rather than the visible results of the condition. In a 1988 article called *Nothing New Under the Sun*, Chris Braiden, Superintendent of Edmonton Police Services in Canada, illustrated problem solving using the medical field as a comparison. Borrowing from his analogy: problem solving might be described in the following way:

A doctor talks to a patient to identify his symptoms so that she might apply her knowledge to determine a diagnosis. Sometimes the solution to the issue lies with the patient, such as a lifestyle change. In other situations the problem may require a cooperative effort between the patient and doctor, such as a lifestyle change and taking of prescribed medicines. In community policing, the police officer talks to the community to identify and diagnose the problem. Sometimes the solution will be with the community, such as a community member agreeing to board up a house being entered by vagrants and drug users. However, sometimes a cooperative effort is required to address the problem. Such an effort might be the citizen agreeing to board up the property, and the police giving special attention to checking the property and placing criminal charges.

The doctor has certain tools at her disposal to diagnose the problem; likewise, the officer has tools available to him. When making a diagnosis, the officer uses tools such as crime analysis data, statistical information, surveys, and direct observation; just as the doctor might use medicines or physical therapy, the officer might use environmental design or formation of community watches to address a problem. In a minor case, such treatment will be successful, but occasionally the case may be so severe that surgery is needed. Heavy saturation of patrols, use of special task forces, zero tolerance, and use of other agencies to address underlying causes are examples of more drastic steps that might be undertaken by police officers. Once the criminal element has been removed, the community must exercise to become strong. They usually will be on "prescribed" organized community watches for some time afterward to ensure that they stay in "remission." Unfortunately, we sometimes lose a patient to terminal illness, but we still must try to make him or her comfortable. This might mean working with the children to give them a better future or helping to get needed services to the community.

The final point, and perhaps the most important one, is that doctors (police) do not control their patient's health (overall conditions of the community), but they do, to some degree, control sickness (crime). Sickness is better prevented than treated. That is just as true in policing. Doctors try to prevent sickness through diet, inoculations, examining patient family history, and the like. The law enforcement officer tries to prevent crime through target hardening, educational programs, organizing communities, and environmental design. Prevention has a huge effect if the patient follows the advice. If the advice is not followed, the next best thing is early intervention.

Problems may start as a housing issue or a civil dispute, be poverty related, be related to governmental inaction, or be caused by a host of other issues. That is why most problem-solving models look much like a planning process, because in order to address the issue the officer must first get to the originating factor, the problem. I remind you here of Sir Robert Peel's first principle, "the basic mission for which the police exist is to prevent crime and disorder . . ." and his last principle, which said, "the test of police efficiency is the absence of crime and disorder" (Mayhall, pp.297–298). Disorder is the equivalent of what we would call a problem.

■ The SARA Model

A variety of problem-solving models are in use in community policing programs, but the most popular by far is the SARA model. Many of the variations originated with this model, and therefore this is the model that we will examine.

The SARA problem-solving model was created in Newport News, Virginia, in 1983. The name is derived from the four-step process that makes up the model. The steps—scanning, analyzing, response, and assessment—invite creativity and innovation at every level. In other words, people using this model employ no standard methodology. These phases are quite extensive. The model begins with an initial fact-gathering step followed by an analysis of the facts, ideally by all stakeholders, to determine the causative factors related to the problem. The next phase is to develop and initiate a response to address the identified problem. Early on in Newport News, a burglary problem was identified as the greatest concern of residents. Perhaps more telling, though, was the problem that was a close second, the condition of their apartment buildings. This information was invaluable when developing a strategy to address the problems faced by the community. As I said in the opening pages of this book, community policing is something we do *with* the community, not something we do *for* or *to* the community. Without the community's active input, the police would have no doubt concluded that the problem was burglary only.

Once the problem has been identified and a strategy is employed to address the problem, the response should be monitored. Just as a doctor might change a prescription that is not yielding the desired result, so must another kind of problem solver adjust his approach. The final step is to assess the response. This should be part of an ongoing process that begins as soon as the response is initiated and then is adjusted as needed. Once it appears that the response is addressing the problem and adequate time has passed, a closer assessment should be undertaken to measure the effectiveness of the strategy. Basically, this step evaluates the impact of the response. In some cases you may be surprised to find very different results than expected. These different results may still be positive, such as the problem being displaced to an adjoining neighborhood. Obviously this is not good news for the new recipient of the problem, but it is a positive impact nonetheless. The new neighborhood may be better prepared to address the problem; also, we now know what tactics work to some degree, and can begin to improve on them in the new area.

Occasionally the response may have negative results. In some cases this is the result of misidentifying the underlying problem, and a return to the scanning and analysis phases may be in order. In other cases the problem solving begins again to address the new problem. The assessment step is also crucial in identifying what resources will be needed to sustain the new change brought on by the response. No problem-solving projects should be considered a success until steps to sustain the change have been employed and are working. I often have witnessed or been told of wonderful successful responses that reduced crime or disorder in a community, only to have it quickly return. This is another reason why community involvement is essential. Once the police leave, and they will eventually have to leave, the community may be unable or unwilling to sustain the change. The police alone will never produce a sustainable change to a community problem! Therefore, the police may need to work with a number of entities to study and be part of addressing a problem, but it should not be their responsibility to take ownership of the problem. Ideally, those most affected would accept the responsibility of seeing the problem to a successful end and monitoring it thereafter.

As you can see, community problem solving is a time-intensive process, but it is time well spent. Due to the amount of time invested it is imperative that all steps in the process be documented for review and later use.

Although not all problems warrant a full-scale documented SARA project, most will warrant a SARA approach or thinking. Even officers unfamiliar with this process use it every day—they just don't realize it. Recently I was in a firearms requalification class when the instructor began to talk about the safe procedure for a traffic stop: "Be aware of what is going on in the car, your cover, and so on." Sounds like scanning, I thought. "Now ask yourself, what does this driver's action mean?" In other words, analyze the actions. "Then choose an appropriate tactic or approach; if something changes then adjust your tactics accordingly." This certainly sounded like a response in relation to what I had observed and analyzed the situation to be. The final step was the test of whether I acted appropriately to the situation. That was SARA in a nutshell. Problem-solving thinking is, and should be, a part of everyday policing.

In order to start the inexperienced problem solver off using the SARA model, Appendix 3.1 is a simple form that consists of the steps and the minimum information needed for beginning and documenting the process. This format is by no means the only or even best format, but rather an example that may be used as a starting point and later customized to your needs. In order to be sold on the powerful tool of problem solving, one need only try the process.

■ Other Problem-Solving Models

The SARA model I just discussed is by far the most popular problem-solving model in use by law enforcement agencies, but several other models do exist and, in some cases, are preferred to address specific issues or communities. Many of these models are very similar to the process undertaken with SARA, but with some minor changes to address the lack of community involvement, the extreme fear found within the community, and other issues. Because specific instructions are available on these models elsewhere, I will only briefly identify a few of these programs and provide an overview of the processes they follow.

Community Coalitions and Teams

In some jurisdictions a team or coalition made up of representatives from the community and its various factions such as government, schools, clergy, and so on is formed to give input on crime prevention needs in the community as a whole. In Virginia, this coalition or team is a requirement for any community wishing to participate in the state's innovative Certified Crime Prevention Community program. These teams have varying responsibilities depending on the jurisdiction. Most are at least charged with the responsibility of bringing crime issues to the attention of law enforcement representatives. In some jurisdictions the coalition meets regularly with the top law enforcement executive to discuss crime problems. The coalition also may sit in on disciplinary review panels and planning committees, assist the agency as volunteers, and address crime and quality of life issues in numerous other ways. The success of such coalitions lies within the participatory decision-making process, rather than in a hands-on approach to a specific problem.

Weed and Seed

Another initiative that is very popular is the "weed and seed" program, which became very popular after federal grant funding became available in recent years. The weed and seed initiative is a two-part community-based program that, like crime coalitions, involves multiple agencies to address crime. In this initiative, however, the emphasis is on selected neighborhoods rather than crime as a whole. Using methods such as zero tolerance law enforcement, code enforcement, zoning efforts, and other crime prevention techniques, crime is "weeded out." Most of the initial weeding out is accomplished by government intervention rather than by the community residents. Due to the level of crime in the selected neighborhoods, residents often are hesitant to become involved at this stage, although in some communities they have become at least passively involved.

The community usually assumes a stronger role in the second phase of this type of initiative, the "seed" phase. In this phase, the violent criminals and crime have presumably been weeded out and the ground is prepared to sow the "good seed." The seed is anything that would assist in improving the community's quality of life, reducing the fear of crime, and reducing the other crimes remaining such as property or nuisance crimes. The seed phase is designed to build a vibrant, healthy community in which the weed cannot survive. In this phase, the community must take control of its own destiny because, as mentioned previously, the police and government can only help get them to the starting gate; they must run their own race.

Neighborhood Problem-Solving Teams

Often agencies will say that community policing and problem-solving strategies are good for large agencies or those with federal grants to sustain the effort, but we are small and don't have the resources. We can't put five or more officers on a single problem. Of course, the counter-argument is that the smaller agency with fewer resources can benefit more than anyone from community policing. Remember that community policing is a process of addressing crime and problems with community involvement, and is not a police-only proposition.

The process of neighborhood problem-solving teams relies heavily on involvement from all members of the team, thus reducing the number of officers involved and time required by police alone. The team should be made up of representatives from any potential stakeholder, which could include businesses in the neighborhood, churches, maintenance workers at a complex, management of apartments, schools in the area, and so on. The local law enforcement agency holds only one seat on the team. They represent the agency, just as a minister on the team might represent the church in the area. The law enforcement member may have to lead in the formation and guide the process, but has no more accountability than any other team member. This requires the leader to get all members to agree to be held accountable for their role. This team building is perhaps the most difficult aspect of the team process.

You might have sensed that this particular process is my favorite of all I have been engaged in. I initiated this process in a neighborhood several years ago in which all other efforts had failed. The community in question was an apartment complex with 240 units. This small apartment complex was responsible for a large percentage of our violent crime in the city, including about 40% of the homicides that year. We created the problem-solving team with two tenacious residents of the complex. The team ultimately grew to include the two residents, the manager, the maintenance supervisor, the contract security agency owner, the apartment complex owner, and myself. It was during this process that I came to realize that what we as law enforcement see as the problems might be very different from what the residents see as the problems. As a result of a team effort, the violent crime rate decreased by 12% in one year. No homicides occurred that year, and the fear of crime was drastically reduced. The community trust of the police increased and, as a result of the trust and assignment of responsibility, it was determined that one of the major causes of the failure of crime prevention efforts was weak management. A new manager was hired to work with the team, and applied lease regulations properly. The owner created a paid position for one of the residents on the team as tenant liaison. This position oversaw the contract security, among other duties. The changes were sustained for several years until a new manager was hired and many of the changes were undone. Today, the environmental changes are still in place and accomplishing what they were designed to do, but without the other changes that are so important to sustainability, trust in the police and the sense of responsibility will begin to erode and problems will return.

Community Anti-crime Planning Implementation Teams

The model I used above was created by Harold Wright, a Virginia-based security consultant who has done a great deal of work in HUD crime-riddled neighborhoods across the United States. The model is known as Community Anti-crime Planning Implementation Teams (CAPIT). Similar programs may be known by other names such as New York's Community-Based Municipally Organized Anti-crime Teams (COMBAT), but regardless of their name, their efforts depend on the team members accepting responsibility for their role in the process.

At least six steps characterize the CAPIT process:

1. *Formation of the team*—The team should be made up of representatives from any stakeholder group, potential resources group, residents, and the police. If there is a doubt as to the need for inclusion, one should err on the side of caution and include the group in the initial team meeting invitation.
2. *Information gathering/analysis meeting*—During this meeting, the team leader, presumably the law enforcement representative, will overview why all of the members were invited, describe the goals and how they affect each member group, and begin to share data while requesting additional information from the members. For example, the team leader may state that crime in general has grown by a certain percentage and that property crime, including theft, is on the increase as well. The leader may share statistical data such as when the crimes are occurring and in what general area. The members may be able to state conclusively that the reason for the crime in that location is this or that factor, the times correspond to the times that school lets out, and so on. Each of these factors is important to note for the next step in the process.
3. *Problem identification*—In the CAPIT process, all members are asked to use the data given at the analysis meeting to identify three or four underlying problems related to some symptomatic issue and draft a problem statement. For example, a problem statement might read, "There is a sense of community disorder, as evidenced by the number of vacant untended houses in the community being frequented by nonresidents for illegal drug activity." The problem statement gives the symptom, nonresidents hanging out in vacant houses and using drugs, and the underlying problem as well, vacant untended houses creating a sense of disorder. Once the symptom and true problems are identified, the next step is what the SARA process labels "response."
4. *Development of solutions*—Armed with the problem statements, the team members can begin to examine as a team the similarities between statements and begin to hone the statements to an exact description of each problem and its related symptom(s). It is

amazing how each of the statements will point to the same underlying problem. Frequently a different symptom may point to the same underlying problem offered by several members. Once the problems are reconciled and agreed upon, the team begins to determine how they can solve or address them. The team should be instructed that each member should view the problem from the aspect of what their group (the one they represent on the team) can do to address this problem, and also provide suggestions to other members and nonmembers as to what they might do. For example, with the previously identified problem, the zoning official may be asked to board up the properties, the police might be asked to physically check the houses twice per week, the local church might be asked to hold activity during the time the problem generally occurs, and so on. As you can see, the approach needs to be holistic, with no one group doing all the work. Once solutions are developed, it is essential that they be measurable and each member be given a copy of the solution, the measurable response, and identification of the responsible team member for each solution. In the previous example, the zoning official would be given responsibility to get the houses boarded up. If the houses are not boarded, there would be no need for the officers to check the houses twice per week to make sure they remained boarded and have not been re-entered. Each person is held accountable by the team.

5. *Implementation*—Once the responses are planned and responsibility is assigned, the work may be implemented. The committee should establish a time frame in which each step of the implementation should be accomplished. During the implementation phase, the team should meet frequently and require each member to report on the progress of his or her assigned responsibility. During these meetings, adjustments in activities may need to be made. The time frame may be determined to be too short and need extending, or one implemented step may need to be done at a different time for maximum effect, and thus another needs to be implemented earlier. This process, like all problem-solving processes, must be fluid.

6. *Evaluation*—Once all of the team members and outside agencies have handled the steps assigned in the implementation phase, the evaluation can begin. There is no ideal time to begin the evaluation because some problems require more time than others. One thing that can begin immediately is the review of the assigned responsibilities. In other words, did anyone fail to meet his or her promised task? If so, the team should hold that individual accountable and ask him or her why the task was not completed. The evaluation should examine how this affected the outcome; if it was responsible for a negative outcome, the team should examine what, if any, actions they may want to employ. Some actions might be to ask another person to represent that particular group on the team, to draft a letter to the supervisor of the failed party, or to try to find another way to address this person's role. In the case described earlier, the problem was the manager of the complex. The evaluation clearly pointed out that her failure to accept responsibility would have been to the detriment of the entire process, and thus serious action had to be taken by the owner.

Team problem solving truly lends itself to an agency with few resources, to the officers who want to accomplish problem solving in their own area of responsibility, and to the community that has crime problems but is told that the police department does not have the resources to address their issues. I have applied this process in a public housing community in which officers were constantly being required to expend hundreds of hours in specialized patrols, and within 2 months of the implementation the drug-related problems were gone from the community. Consider the man-hours saved by using this approach. In another community, the manager of a low-income apartment complex refused to cooperate to the point of problem identification. That attempt was set up for failure because of the lack of involvement.

I am in favor of using the SARA process on large community-wide projects such as graffiti, gang, and overall crime in a community; however, I advocate using the team process for smaller, selected neighborhood projects. Regardless of the project undertaken or the process used to address it, I believe wholeheartedly in the idea expressed by President Harry Truman, "When we accept tough jobs as a challenge and wade into them with joy and enthusiasm, miracles can happen."

■ Filling the Community Policing Toolbox

A community police officer, like any other skilled professional, needs the proper tools to accomplish his or her job. A multitude of tools are needed to perform community policing successfully. In the next few pages I attempt to break down the tools most often used in community policing into several major categories. As with any job, selection of the right tool is crucial. Applying the wrong tool may accomplish the task, but require more work to do so. Therefore, a description of the most common use for each tool is included.

Public Relations

One of the first tools any community policing program will need is a host of public relations activities. As discussed in a previous chapter, public relations is not community policing by itself, but it is a valuable tool for accomplishing the goals of community policing.

The concept of public relations grew out of the tensions related to the civil rights movement and anti-war protests in the 1960s. In an effort to improve law enforcement's image, public relations units were created. One of the goals of such units was to act as a liaison between the agency and the community and to relay the desires and perceptions of each to the other. These are the units that later grew into what we now call community policing, or in some cases, crime prevention units. The role has changed from one of selling the public a positive image of the agency. Unfortunately, some agencies are still operating under the same public relations role and calling it community policing. Obviously, public relations programs, referred to by some in law enforcement as "feel good" programs, do little to actively involve the community in addressing problems. Having said that, let me state that these programs are not without merit and value. Such programs do a great deal to stimulate citizen support of and interest in crime prevention and problem solving. However, in most of these types of programs citizen involvement is minimal and mostly passive.

The public relations program is generally recognized by its ultimate result, police image enhancement and the distribution of public information. In our modern society, many citizens get their perceptions of the police from television programs or motion pictures, neither of which has been known to provide an accurate depiction of the profession. Because entertainment is their bottom line, police frequently are depicted as untrustworthy, corrupt, or inept. Community policing is a philosophy that encourages open communication and a positive relationship geared toward cooperation, so departments must dispel the image created by the entertainment industry and overcome negative perceptions. This is best accomplished by the public relations function. Good public relations go far in developing the proper environment in which cooperative problem-solving strategies can be accomplished. One major difficulty with public relations programs is that they are not measured by what they are truly designed to accomplish. They must measure the improved public perception they create, the mutual trust they develop, and the amount of accurate information that they relay about both the police and the public. If measured by this, they would be found to be very effective. It is a mistake to try to sell such programs as community policing when they are only a small piece of the puzzle.

Consider the following public relations programs and apply the measure described; I believe you will find that they serve their intended purpose well. I also believe that you will truly see how they prepare the environment for more active community involvement.

Neighborhood Police Stations and Offices

When police survey high-crime neighborhoods, they commonly find that they are viewed as outsiders, neither concerned nor caring about the community. The movement of officers into the community in a neighborhood office or station does much to begin to tear down that perception. The idea of a neighborhood station is not a new concept. In fact, prior to World War II it was the norm. Our need to be more "efficient" came in the 1960s, and the concept of the centralized office was born. The community policing philosophy has more to do with effectiveness than with efficiency. As a result, the move back to the neighborhood is common to an agency with this philosophy. Does this solve problems? No, but it does encourage open communication, trust, and relationship building.

Alternative Patrol Methods

An effective strategy is to remove the physical barrier of the patrol car and create a psychological openness that allows officers to be more often perceived as approachable. Foot patrols, bicycle patrols, horse-mounted patrols, motorcycles, and all-terrain vehicles are among the methods employed to accomplish this task. Of course, many of these methods have added benefits of quick mobility in traffic, stealth approaches, and improved visual vantage points, to name a few. They are not the most cost-efficient patrol method, but they are extremely effective in providing opportunities for conversation, rapport building, and public interaction.

Bicycle Rodeos, Mentoring Programs, Fun Days, Picnics, and Camps

The words of the song "Accentuate the Positive" are applied when officers are involved in fun activities with youth. The gruffest exterior melts away when officers interact in a positive activity with youth and adults alike. The encounter is viewed as being with a neighbor and welcomed acquaintance rather than a confrontation. Stephen Covey, author of *The Seven Habits of Highly Effective People*, describes an "emotional bank account" in which one can either make deposits—good deeds for example—or make withdrawals, such as errors in judgment. He further describes how if you have made enough deposits you are not in any real trouble if you have to make a withdrawal. As an example of this type of bank account, consider the fact that an officer may have to later deal with a person in a confrontational manner. If that officer has made sufficient deposits, such as by playing a game with the youth at a gathering or helping him or her in a mentoring program, this withdrawal will not overdraw the account. These programs demonstrate the human side of officers and create good will. As Covey puts it, "Seek first to understand, then to be understood" (Covey, 1989, p. 235).

Public Demonstrations, Police Agency Tours, Citizen Academies, Intern Programs, and Ride-Along Programs

These programs are public relations programs that require passive participation, but not total involvement in problem solving. They are public relations programs in the truest sense of the term, in that they are disseminating information about the law enforcement agency in an effort to improve the recipient's image of it. One of the most valuable aspects of this tool is the conduit that it provides to demonstrate the openness of the agency. Often, volunteer programs draw from these programs.

Public Service Campaigns, Newsletters, and Media Releases

Such programs are by their nature designed for information dissemination. They can be used to announce problems under review, request information and willing involvement, and put criminals on notice that an effort is underway to eradicate the problem.

Target Group Outreach

Target group outreach programs attempt to reach a certain audience who has a tendency to be victimized. Often the victimization is due to lack of information, cultural issues related to acceptance of the victimization, or fear of reprisals. For example, TRIAD programs attempt to provide information and training to prevent victimization of the elderly. TRIAD is based on three organizations: International Chiefs of Police, the National Sheriff's Association, and the AARP. Law enforcement's involvement leads to a good public image of the police within the senior community. Law enforcement's efforts to work with the poverty stricken, disabled, and refugee/immigrant community are often an overlooked area of concern. Refugees fleeing persecution may feel isolated and be distrustful of police due to corruption in their home country. Their children tend to seek out those with a similar plight, and their perceived isolation may lead to quasi-gang activity. Older immigrants and refugees may be easily victimized due to their lack of understanding of the laws in this country. As you can see, public relations efforts early on can possibly avert a crime problem, simply by sharing information in a way that can be understood.

The public relations tools listed in this section are programs undertaken by the law enforcement agency. These formal programs do not preclude each and every officer from personally engaging in public relations. When an officer stops for a cup of coffee he or she can engage other patrons in friendly conversation. An officer working an assigned beat might stop by a new business and introduce her- or himself and leave a business card with the comment that the business owner can call if he or she has any problems. Finally, the key to successful public relations is for all agency members to adopt the attitude that they will take every opportunity to build a positive relationship with the public. The friendly contact you make today may be the witness you need tomorrow.

Enforcement Actions

Sometimes the best community policing tools available to address a certain problem are old-fashioned enforcement activities. One positive aspect of enforcement activities such as arrests is that the individual causing or contributing to a problem is out of commission while jailed. Unfortunately, that is usually only for a short time. Enforcement actions will rarely bring about any permanent change by themselves on any problem of significant size. Even so, enforcement is a viable tool when used in conjunction with community involvement and the problem-solving techniques discussed earlier.

With the thousands of laws in existence in every jurisdiction, it is surprising how relatively few of them are used in problem solving. Often little-known or -used laws will address a specific problem related to the underlying issue, and in some cases may provide an option of addressing the underlying issue itself. Most problems facing communities fall into the categories of nuisance and quality of life issues. These problems can be positively impacted by building statutes, zoning statutes, fire statutes, and even health statutes. A multidisciplined approach can often net the desired results quickly, whereas one agency working without support may be viewed as of little concern. For example, one of my officers was attempting to influence a motel owner to abate a nuisance on his property. The property was in disrepair, was being used by prostitutes, and was associated with illegal drug use and disorders. The officer was having little luck until he approached the owner with an interagency code enforcement team. This team, made up of fire officials, code enforcement officials, and the officer, was able to document numerous violations against the owner. So many violations, in fact, that the motel was not only shut down, but also sold to a new owner in the community who demolished the motel and created a legitimate business. This problem and solution demonstrate the value of enforcement to address the underlying problem and the truest sense of community policing, in that the community business member did what he could to further eliminate the problem from returning.

The following are a few examples of laws that exist in some form in most states. How to use these statutes to address community problems is limited only by the imagination of the officer. Community policing and crime prevention specialists would do well to take some time to research their state statutes and local ordinances for useful sections. Any potentially useful statutes should be prepared in a resource for frequent reference. As you review the nature of the laws mentioned in the following sections, you should note the importance of not limiting yourselves to criminal statutes. Many solutions lie outside the realm of criminal law. Officers should not neglect the "enabling legislation" that authorizes a locality to adopt the law by ordinance. I have found that other jurisdictions will often have just such an ordinance that you may amend to suit your jurisdiction. To assist in your research, I suggest searching online at MuniciCode. (See the Resources section at the end of the book.) I have drafted several ordinances and submitted them for legal review when I deemed the ordinance to be a needed tool; the practitioner may have to do the same.

Panhandling Laws

One nuisance violation that is frequently cited in business districts is panhandling or begging. This practice discourages patrons from frequenting the area, if not from fear then because of the discomfort in saying no or in being approached. A multitude of laws are on the books to deal with such behaviors. The key is to find one that will work. Many states have panhandling and loitering laws that would not withstand a legal challenge today, but that is certainly no signal to give up and accept this problem as inevitable. My philosophy is a simple one: Where there is a problem, there is a solution. We may have to try many tactics before arriving at the solution, but the solution is there for the persistent practitioner. The most successful panhandling laws address the problem as one that cannot be prohibited, but rather controlled. Therefore, the best laws are those that prohibit panhandling in specific locations, by specific means, or at specific times. We are recognizing the right to panhandle, but we control where, when, and how they do it. How does this help? Consider an ordinance that states panhandling is prohibited within 200 feet of any lending institution, automated teller machine, or crosswalk. Lending institutions and ATMs pose a robbery potential because the person exiting or entering is likely to be carrying cash. Crosswalks pose a safety hazard because pedestrians may rush to avoid such approaches. Now consider the ordinance itself. By regulating the location, the practice is all but totally prohibited in business districts that are likely to be saturated with banks, ATMs, and crosswalks. The ordinance may go further and prohibit any panhandling between certain hours.

The key to understanding a good ordinance in this situation is most likely going to be the justification in prohibiting the location or time. Ordinances that prohibit aggressive panhandling almost always pass the legal test, but are very hard to prove because the individual is not likely to want to testify in court. If these laws are going to be employed and enforced for the first time, a public awareness campaign will strengthen the possibility of their success. One final note regarding exit ramp solicitations—there may already be a tool at your disposal. As I have said before, seek out laws that might normally be considered as dealing with other issues. In this case, seek a traffic law that prohibits a person from stepping into the street, walking on the interstate, or soliciting business without a permit.

Alarm Ordinances

Law enforcement agencies face a dilemma related to alarms. Alarms do provide residents and businesses a sense of security and, as such, must be considered valuable, but false alarms drain time from shrinking patrol forces. In general, the citizen complaints received are related to audible alarms that inevitably shriek in the wee hours of the morning. Silent alarms seem to offer little in the way of prevention; they simply let us know that the crime is occurring, or in more cases, has just occurred. The most problematic of alarms is the vehicular alarm, which has come to receive all of the attention of the boy who cried wolf. These systems may alert the vehicle owner, but are almost totally ignored by others, unless they honk incessantly due to owner inattention. In any event, the question of alarm ordinances is now on the table.

Alarm ordinances that charge fees for false alarms vary as to when to institute the first charge, but are generally supported by the burglary and fire alarm industry. The industry recognizes that most of these alarms are not false alarms, but rather false activations. That is to say, the alarm was working properly—it sensed a change in the environment and alerted. Some outside force, such as weather, wind, animals, or an operator error, usually caused the alert. The alarm industry is striving to ensure technicians are professionally trained and to eliminate the self-trained technician. In many states technicians must now be certified by the state. The alarm industry realizes that if ordinances were in place that required the owners of alarms to pay a fee for false activations, they would be more likely to hire a reputable trained technician.

Law enforcement overwhelmingly supports alarm ordinances, if for no other reason than to encourage the owners to come out and deactivate the audible alarm and to have it checked for malfunctions. The ordinance and fee, more than the officers' pleas, get the attention of the problem business owner. Alarms from vehicles are rarely covered under the ordinances; I believe that is a disservice to the owners of the alarm and car. The ordinance offers one way to control the quality of such alarms and helps to bring peace and tranquility to the community.

Noise Ordinances

As mentioned previously, nuisance calls are a major concern in communities. One such nuisance is the chronic party house. Another is the loud vehicular stereo booming through the neighborhood at three in the morning and activating every dog within hearing range. Thus, the creation of the noise ordinance. Some ordinances allow officers to cite violators, and others allow officers to seize the offending equipment. These ordinances are great tools for the officer attempting to use the law to address a noise issue. One of the most useful noise ordinances is the one that addresses music from vehicles. This is most helpful when the problem crowd is a mobile group that has identified a closed business or vacant lot next to the neighborhood as their second home.

Residential Parking Permit Statute/Ordinance

In some jurisdictions a problem arises from conflicting use, such as a college near a residential area, or a nightclub situated within a residential community. The most common problem noted in these areas is inadequate parking. Complaints of vehicles blocking a homeowner's driveway can be addressed on an individual basis, but when the same event occurs several times a problem exists that needs to be addressed. Likewise, when patrons leave a late night establishment with inadequate parking and are returning to their vehicle early in the morning, they neglect to realize they are in a neighborhood with sleeping residents and children. Complaints of vulgar language, littering, and loud obnoxious behavior are prevalent in such a situation. One solution to these problems is the residential parking permit ordinance. The process for obtaining designation as a parking permit area varies, but the ordinance usually requires a study to determine the most problematic times and the posting of parking by permit only during those times. The permits are usually issued to residents for a nominal fee to cover the cost of producing and processing the permits. The end result is that violators are cited and fined a substantial fee. News of these fines tends to travel rather fast, and the problem is reduced, if not eliminated altogether.

Graffiti Statutes

Graffiti may be just vandalism or it may be symptomatic of a much larger problem, such as tagger groups and even criminal gangs. Studies have consistently shown that graffiti left in place leads to more graffiti. The same studies recommend quick reporting and removal of such graffiti to discourage additional tagging. Unfortunately, this message is not very well received by business owners who choose to leave the graffiti once it is initially painted. Gang experts are aware that graffiti is the newspaper of the street, and that threats and challenges are communicated via this means. Challenges and threats that are removed may lead to a reduction in the potential for gang warfare.

Graffiti hurts the value of properties, discourages shoppers because of the perception of criminal activity in the area, and contributes to a sense of disorder within the community. Graffiti ordinances force the quick removal of such blights. In some cases, the government employs teams to remove the graffiti or paint over it; in others the ordinance forces the property owner to have it removed. The best of all worlds is one in which the residential community or the business area volunteers to maintain their area by removing or painting over graffiti, and the ordinance prohibiting the placement of graffiti assigns an additional penalty for tagging in those areas. The additional fines are then directed to a special fund to be used by that community in their graffiti eradication program. Other successful ordinances have included prohibition of juveniles being allowed to purchase or possess spray paint, and the creation of a registry for those underage patrons purchasing spray paint.

Designated Drug-Free Zones

Drug-free zones are those areas in which people can receive an enhanced punishment for drug distribution/possession. These zones usually include about 1000 feet surrounding schools, parks, and day care centers or areas in which children are frequently present. This tool is vastly underused and vastly underadvertised. The areas with this statute in place should post signs at the fringes of the 1000-foot line and encourage all drug charges to be placed with this enhanced punishment area in mind. A local crime analyst should be able to provide a map designating the zone and marking the zone's entire circumference.

Landlord/Tenant Statutes

Every community policing officer, advocate, or crime prevention practitioner should be familiar with the landlord/tenant laws of their state. These statutes are designed to protect the rights of the landlord, the tenant, and the neighborhoods in which the property is located. There is often reference to the requirement that the tenant agrees to maintain the peace and tranquility of the neighborhood. There is also valuable information as to the condition of the property that the landlord is required to ensure. One of the most important clauses found in such statutes is the portion that deals with both owner and tenant being responsible for providing for the "safety" of others, or some language to that effect. Often these statutes can be used by a community policing advocate to assist the neighborhood in forcing removal of a problem tenant who is endangering the community. The statutes have forced the hand of an unwilling landlord to repair an eyesore property as well. Remember that the landlord is a businessperson and often is driven primarily by the rent that the home produces, so forcing such improvements is to his advantage. When using these statutes, the advocate should be inclined to first provide the violators with notice of the violations rather than to seek legal enforcement. The effort here should be directed at providing a win/win/win situation for the landlord, the tenant, and the neighborhood.

Zoning Laws

Zoning laws may seem like an unusual tool for law enforcement to use in addressing problems; however, underlying problems that lead to criminal activity may be caused by zoning or other issues. The successful problem solver will not limit his or her tools to those normally used by his or her discipline. Remember the old saying, "If you do what you've always done you will get what you've always gotten." A problem solver in community policing uses any and all tools at his or her disposal. Zoning laws are valuable prevention tools that often are overlooked. Recently, in two separate local jurisdictions, a methadone clinic announced its intention to open. Neither of the two areas were zoned to allow such a clinic. Both insisted that the clinic would draw other drug activity and endanger children and residents in the area. The argument spilled over and became well publicized. As with any public issues, the politicians involved themselves, and just a few days prior to this writing, one legislator had proposed a bill to make placement of such a clinic illegal within a certain distance of any school or day care center. In a city environment that would all but force the clinic to be placed on the very outskirts of the jurisdiction.

Zoning laws allow certain types of structures in certain areas where a conflict is not likely to arise. The purpose of zoning laws typically includes a reference to providing for the health or safety of citizens, or both (Code of Virginia, Section 15.1–489). These statutes often include a requirement for property owners to maintain their property in a certain condition. This includes requirements to remove weeds, snow from sidewalks, and trash; how to handle abandoned vehicles; and storage guidelines. This code also generally will have some provision for the locality to remove the above-mentioned nuisances, after providing due notice to the owner, and to bill the owner for the removal of the nuisance (Code of Virginia, Section 15.2–1115 et al.).

How helpful is this tool to community policing officers? A large number of crimes are related to the use of abandoned or dilapidated houses owned by an absentee landlord or homeowner. The absentee homeowner views the property as an investment to be sold later; because they do not live in the neighborhood, they sometimes do not care that the house creates a haven for criminal activity. Anyone who has read the now famous article "Broken Windows," by James Q. Wilson and George L. Kelling, is certainly aware of how such a property encourages even more criminal activity (*The Atlantic Monthly*, 1992). To do nothing about the problem but attempt to deal with the criminal activity that is encouraged by the property is akin to bailing water from a boat with a hole in its hull; you can only keep the boat afloat for so long. Zoning laws allow us to address the problem rather than the symptom. The push here is for compliance in order to make the property less attractive to the criminal element, and thus remove the facilitator of those crimes. Zoning laws provide for the noncompliant as well, and ultimately force them to pay attention or release the property to the government or legitimate owners.

The problem-solving model, described earlier, is designed to identify the underlying problem. For some drug-related problems, the people in the house are the problem; in others, the house itself, the real estate, is the problem that needs to be addressed. The use of zoning and building codes is often the best tactic for real estate problems. Some states have a special enabling legislation that authorizes localities to deal directly with a problem drug house or drug blight. Virginia has such a statute that, once the ordinance is in place, authorizes the locality to force corrective action by a property owner. If none is taken, the jurisdiction can remove the problem, up to and including, if need be, demolishing the property and billing the property owner (Code of Virginia, Section 15.2–907). If the property owner fails to pay the bill, the locality can move to seize the property.

Planning and Building Codes

As mentioned previously, the building inspector can be one of the best friends of the community police officer. Typically, the inspector and his or her counterparts, the code enforcement officials, have limited authority to make arrests and issue citations. They are also frequently not allowed to be armed in any fashion and have no uniform to identify them as government officials. In some cases, the officials are not even given identifying credentials; therefore, they are not apt to be overly aggressive in their duties for fear of attack. This is an opportunity for a true partnership. The community police officer provides the back-up on serious cases that the code official is having problems with, and the code official works closely to cite and remove problems with the officer.

Building codes that are frequently of value in the problem-solving arena are those that require a safe structure, those that require heat and running water, and those that require officers to review building plans. During plan review, a Crime Prevention Through Environmental Design (CPTED) trained officer reviews the plans and makes recommended changes to make the structure safer from a crime prevention standpoint. Some jurisdictions have "sign-off authority" that requires this officer's signature on the plan before the building may begin, but these are few in number. For the most part, recommendation authority is all that can be expected. Other areas in which building codes are helpful are condemning unsafe properties and forcing the owners to bring them up to code.

Building officials and planners are often in a position to impact new ordinances that would create a safer environment, and I strongly suggest that they be given opportunities to attend CPTED training with officers. CPTED will be discussed in more detail in Chapter 12, Crime Prevention Through Environmental Design. The building code official and planner will be more apt to recognize the need for more glazing on a certain building and how one structure in a community relates to the general safety if they are trained in law enforcement rather than just with other code officials or planners. Likewise, given the opportunity, the officer can benefit from attending code officers' training as well.

Fire Code

Crime prevention and other officers might be wondering how the fire code could ever help us in law enforcement. For many years, the two have been on opposite sides of the fence. The fire fighter wants everything open so everyone gets out in a fire, and the police officer wants everything locked up so nobody gets in without difficulty. How in the world do we get those two together? We concentrate on the common goal, public safety.

In my early days as a crime prevention officer, I ran afoul of the fire marshal in an attempt to solve a vagrancy issue. The recommendation I made eliminated the vagrant loitering issue, but unbeknownst to me it violated a fire code. Needless to say, the business owner who had spent a substantial sum to install a fence structure at the rear of his business at my request was not very happy when the fire marshal told him to tear it down or be cited. It was that situation that made me first despise the fire code, and also led me to respect the goal of the fire marshal. Because I was never going to be familiar enough with the fire code, or the other noncriminal codes for that matter, I went to visit the fire marshal with hat in hand. He was gracious enough to work with me to identify a way to meet the needs of the code and the needs that I had to leave the structure in place. It was then that I discovered that the fire code is not created to burn us, pardon the pun. Since that time I have attempted to learn the essential basics of the fire code and established a professional relationship with the fire officials. They have assisted me and other officers in numerous problem-solving projects by using their knowledge of the fire code. Specifically, we have used the code to handle problem clubs and bars (occupancy regulations), drug houses (padlocked inside doors), hotel establishments, and other locations. The fire code is written so that much is left to interpretation and, as such, it is better to have the fire official along than to attempt to interpret the code only to find that he or she interprets it another way.

Other Noncriminal Laws and Regulations

In conjunction with the code enforcement officials, the environmental health office has been extremely beneficial in forcing the removal of items that are eyesores in a community, such as unused tires serving as mosquito beds and breeding grounds. They also have assisted in forcing a cleanup of a dog lot. The animals and the lot were legal in all respects except for the run-off and waste accumulation. Using the rodent infestation aspect of the health code, they were able to have the lot cleaned and thus addressed a quality of life issue in a community.

Another area that has been of value in addressing a problem nightclub was to address the club via the tax code. The business was claiming that it had a certain amount of food business in an effort to obtain an alcoholic beverage control permit. The business operator had had problems in several other locations, and it was obvious that the same issues would be experienced at this site. The local tax assessor came out with the police and estimated the revenue taxes that the business owed. The business was unable to pay the taxes and subsequently closed.

Many regulations are also a viable tool in solving crime and community issues. Although such regulations are not law, some carry the weight of law. For example, the Department of Labor, Occupational Safety and Health Administration (OSHA) "recommends" certain guidelines for late night retail establishments (U.S. Department of Labor, 1998). These recommendations are not law, but consider what happens if the establishment ignores the recommendations and its inaction results in an injury or a death. What liability would be assessed to the business that ignored such a recommendation?

A similar situation is the so-called industry standards. Industries recommend a certain minimal standard of care and, just as in the description above, failure to meet the standard can lead to increased liability. For example, Virginia law requires hotels and motels to exercise due care in installing "suitable "locks (Code of Virginia, Section 35.1–28). The industry standard goes beyond that and requires deadbolt locks, peepholes, and "effective locking devices" on sliding doors.

Numerous regulatory practices and standards can be helpful in at least identifying minimum standards that are set by the industry or regulatory agency.

Crime Prevention Programs

Crime prevention programs facilitate the response to problems and problem solving as related to community policing. As mentioned in Chapter 1, prevention tools can address some problems without having to use other tools. A major difference between crime prevention and community policing is that many crime prevention tools do not require significant involvement of the community to be successful. Some examples are educational programs, production of literature to heighten community awareness about certain crimes, and community and property assessments. Crime prevention is a problem-solving tool and serves a dual function of being a separate discipline in itself. Crime prevention requires its own unique set of special skills; therefore, I have opted to cover this discipline in detail in subsequent chapters.

■ Crime Prevention and Criminal Laws

Who better to understand the legal system than someone who has made his or her living by using it—the law enforcement officer. An officer can recite section after section of the traffic code and understand it inside and out, thanks to repetition and trial and error. The officer may use a section to charge a person only to discover a loophole loses the case. The next time, the officer will not make the same mistake. Use of criminal and other laws in problem solving and crime prevention is no different. We learn from trial and error. I dare say that each state has laws regulating the reporting of crime to the Department of Education. All may not be identical, but they will be similar in what they require. As a result of the similarities, I have opted to list only the Virginia version of the laws here, with a few editorial notes. Officers in other states should be able to use the content to search the code of their own state for something similar.

Virginia Codes

The Code of Virginia provides for the exclusion of certain documents from the Freedom of Information Act. Specifically parties may not be compelled to release documents excluded. The documents usually are excluded by virtue of the potential for physical or other harm to parties or entities included.

22-1–342 Code of Virginia, Neighborhood Watch Member Confidentiality

The following records are excluded from the provision of this chapter [Freedom of Information Act] but may be disclosed by the custodian in his discretion, except when such disclosure is prohibited by law . . . records of local police departments relating to neighborhood watch programs that include names, addresses, and operating schedules of individual participants that are provided to such departments under a promise of confidentiality.

22.1–279 Code of Virginia, School Safety Audit and Crisis Emergency Management Plans Required

This code section mandates that audits be done in every school every 3 years. The audit is defined as "a written assessment of the safety conditions in each public school to (i) identify and, if necessary, develop solutions for physical safety concerns, including building security issues and (ii) identify and evaluate patterns of student safety concerns occurring on school property or at school sponsored events." This code encourages the audit to be completed by a committee made up of "representatives of parents, teachers, local law-enforcement agencies, judicial and public safety personnel, and the community at large." The audit is required to be submitted in writing. These audits, done properly, will allow school administration and the school resource officers (SRO) to identify patterns of problem locations, offenders, and contributing factors that need to be addressed.

22.1–280.1 Crime Prevention Programs in School

This section of Virginia law mandates that schools establish programs to prevent crime, and specifies certain violent crimes that must be reported to the school superintendent. It also mandates that the information be available to the public. The requirement to make available statistics as to violent crime is one that I believe should be emulated across the country. The potential to "skew" the numbers by not reporting them properly, especially when finances are connected with such reports, is too great. Remember, community policing is all about open communication and partnerships. I understand the need to protect identity, but statistical data should be accurate and fully available.

18.2–258 Deeming a Premises a Common Nuisance

Any office, store, shop, restaurant, dance hall, poolroom, clubhouse, storehouse, warehouse, dwelling house, apartment, building of any kind, vehicle, vessel, boat, aircraft, which with the knowledge of the owner, lessor, agent of any lessor, manager, chief executive officer, operator, or tenant thereof, is frequented by persons under the influence of illegally obtained controlled substances or marijuana, as defined . . . or for the purpose of illegally obtaining possession of, manufacturing or distributing controlled substances or marijuana, shall be deemed a common nuisance.

This section goes on to state that any person who knowingly permits, keeps, or maintains such a nuisance is guilty of a Class 1 misdemeanor, and for a second or subsequent offense is guilty of a Class 6 felony. This section also allows the attorney for the state to maintain a suit in equity to enjoin the nuisance. This particular section is of most use when the "people" are the problem in the drug activity. Earlier I discussed how to proceed when the real property was the issue related to the drug activity; using this code is best way to address the problem when it relates to the occupants of the property.

My experience has been to use this section as a follow-up when any drugs are discovered on a property, whether a drug charge is placed or not. Several Virginia localities use this section to follow up on search warrants served by narcotics units, or to respond when narcotics or illegal drugs are discovered in the course of an investigation in a property.

This section applies whether ownership of the illegal drug is established or not. For example, an officer responds to a domestic quarrel and in the process of interviewing the wife observes marijuana on the kitchen table. The property owner or tenant can then be cited with maintaining a common nuisance under this section. If this is a rental property, a letter is then sent to the property owner describing what was found. Why the letter? It is to establish knowledge on the part of the landlord and to encourage him or her to abate the nuisance (i.e., evict the tenant in accordance with their lease guidelines). See Appendix 3.2 for a copy of the letter I used when I was in the community policing unit in the City of Roanoke. If the landlord doesn't abate the nuisance and a subsequent charge is made at that location, the landlord is then also charged with a first offense of maintaining a common nuisance. The City of Virginia Beach went even farther and used information gained from citizen interviews and surveys to establish the nuisance. This section is an excellent tool, and any community problem solver should seek such a section to use for problems associated with drugs.

The Alcohol Control Beverage Act (4.1–317) has a section that reads almost identically to this, except that it deals with the use of alcohol "contrary to law." This section is a great tool for problems involving lots of under-aged drinking. This section also requires knowledge as an element of the crime. I have seen this effectively used in fraternity parties and in unlicensed bars. The letter used is almost identical to the one above, except the terminology is changed to reflect alcohol used contrary to law.

Title 48, Code of Virginia, is a civil action that can be initiated by five or more citizens to complain of a common nuisance. The result of the complaint and petition is to force the circuit court to summon a "special grand jury" to investigate the nuisance and make a presentment against the party, if fault is found. This process is not user-friendly but is one a community organization might choose to pursue. It is particularly useful when a community is fighting a nuisance such as a plant leaking toxins, a business creating a hazard to local children, or other such problems (see Appendix 3.3).

18.2–120, Code of Virginia, Instigating Trespass

All states have the typical common law trespassing statutes at their disposal, but one that is particularly useful in relation to trespass is a statute that allows a tenant to be charged with instigating trespass *if* proof can be shown that the tenant was aware that the subject had been forbidden from coming onto or returning to the property in question. If such a statute is in use in your jurisdiction, the officers should advise the landlords they work with to not only send a letter barring the subject, but also serve a copy of the letter to the tenant and document their receipt of the letter. This will serve as proof of the tenant's knowledge that the subject has been forbidden to come onto the property.

Another anti-trespassing legislation of use is one that authorizes the property owner to designate the local law enforcement agency to act on its behalf for the purpose of forbidding others from going onto or remaining upon their property. The enabling legislation requires a written agreement between the owner and the agency (Code of Virginia, Section 15.2–1717.1). (See Appendix 3.4.) If this agreement is in force, the local officer may bar individuals on the scene. If the officer serves a notice to the individual barring them from the property, he or she should serve a copy to the tenant as well, in case the tenant has a change of heart and invites the problem back onto the property. For a copy of a bar notice used in this type of action, see Appendix 3.5.

Criminal codes of use in dealing with ongoing crime problems and that are useful in preventing crime are located in all state code books. Even codes that simply define a problem can be of use, such as those that deal with criminal gangs—specifically, those that identify the characteristics of criminal gangs are of great use. Their primary usefulness is to open the eyes of those who refuse to recognize the potential for gangs in their jurisdiction. With a clear-cut definition, the template is there to test the groups active in the locality. Once a jurisdiction acknowledges the existence of the street gang, the problem can begin to be addressed. As a final note on using laws as a community policing and prevention tool, any jurisdiction planning to step up its use of new laws should contact its local jurisdiction's prosecutor and, if possible, judges. The contact, even if only by letter, is a common courtesy and will allow the agency to explain what the desired outcome is by using the laws. If a judge or attorney is included, the agency is more apt to see success in the prosecution of such cases.

■ Crime Analysis

One of the most useful yet often underused tools of the community police officer is crime analysis. I have often speculated as to why officers and managers do not take advantage of the vast amount of information available to them from the crime analyst, and have concluded that the word *analysis* sounds so scientific, so mathematical that it frightens them away. After all, who, other than an actuary or accountant, really likes studying numbers and figures? Therefore, I like to consider crime analysis as an information-gathering discipline that supports my work in problem solving. In most cases I am not analyzing crime, but rather using data for problem analysis; that is how it will be discussed as a tool under this heading. Of course, the term *crime analysis* may also encompass investigative, strategic, and intelligence analysis; however, I will concentrate on its usefulness in the problem-solving venue.

A professionally trained crime analyst is a major asset to the problem-solving effort, and many agencies rely on these professionals; however, the absence of a professionally trained analyst does not eliminate an officer's ability to benefit from analysis. Almost all officers have access to some minimal information that can be analyzed using some simple common sense techniques. According to Herman Goldstein (1990, pp. 36–37),

> *analysis requires the acquisition of detailed information about offenders, victims, and others who may be involved in a problem, the time of occurrence, locations, details about the physical environment, the motivations, gains and losses of all involved parties, and the results of current responses.*

This definition points to the nature of crime analysis in problem solving, which is to identify the cause of the problem so that an appropriate response may be undertaken. Even without all of the information, the true problem can often be identified. If all of the information is available, use it; if it is not, don't assume a defeatist attitude. When a trained analyst is available we typically expect them to be able to provide, at a minimum, crime patterns, crime trends, and crime series. The true professional goes even further and provides us with a forecast of future occurrences, researches the M.O., and conducts spatial analysis related to locations and crimes.

Many agencies now have at their disposal access to crime mapping created by geographic information systems (GIS). Such mapping is of great value to the officer, who frequently is more able to recognize the relationship between crimes and problems when information is presented in a graphical context. Using crime maps or hot spot maps offers the practitioner an excellent tool for examining the specific problem as it relates to other factors and to evaluate what crime prevention or other application might best address the problem.

If you have access to an analyst, by all means use him or her and seek him or her out to assist in identification of hot spots and areas that are demonstrating an increase in certain crimes. If you do not have access, then I urge you to attempt to conduct your own analysis. In the following sections, I will attempt to explain some elementary techniques for doing your own analysis. Because I am not a trained crime analyst and do not claim to have an analyst's knowledge of statistical data, I will base my techniques and explanations on my own experience in problem solving and my own analyses.

Conducting Elementary Analysis

Take a deep breath and understand that this will be painless. My type of analysis is not the type limited to a Swiss watchmaker, two actuaries, and a rocket scientist. In keeping with the theme of this book, this analysis is a practical version designed specifically for the novice and inexperienced officer. We will use a common sense approach, drawing on your experience as a law enforcement officer and your knowledge of the criminal mind.

We begin with the first tool that is generally available to all officers, the calls for service data. Calls for service data usually provide, at a minimum, the nature of the call, the date of the call, and the times. This information can be examined to identify repeat locations, patterns in the days of the week, patterns in the times a certain type of call occurs, and other similarities. Other sources of information available to the officer of almost any agency are the arrest reports, community surveys, and anecdotal information obtained through conversations and interviews with other officers, residents, and offenders. Each of these increases the officer's ability to accurately identify problems. For example, when reviewing calls for service data I noticed an increase in certain crimes associated with drug activity surrounding a certain convenience market. Few calls originated from or were related directly to the market, but I had that gut feeling, so important to a career officer, that the market had something to do with the problems. I interviewed the beat officers in the area and some of the residents and my hunch was confirmed. The dealers were using the pay telephone on the fringe of the parking lot for dealing drugs. The solution became easy once I knew that the location was the facilitator of the activity: Get rid of the phone. The removal of the pay telephone addressed the problem by increasing the effort and removing the excuses for the criminal to be at the location. It was the interviews that confirmed the problem identification. Once an officer is able to identify the patterns and trends observed in the data, the officer can apply his or her knowledge of criminal behavior to solving the problem.

The Crime Analysis Triangle

To further understand how to analyze the information, I should explain that many crime analysts apply their own version of what I prefer to call the "crime analysis triangle." Each of this triangle's three sides represents an element required in order for a crime to occur. The three elements are a victim, an offender, and a location.

The analyst examines each support of this triangle by using all of the information available to determine the trend or pattern's relationship to the supporting leg of the triangle. They ask the question: Is this pattern related to the offender, to the location, or to the victim? Another way of stating this is to ask, Are more crimes occurring here because of the environment that is present (location), or because of the suspect's ability to quickly blend into the community (both offender and location)? The data will often point to a particular element that is a major contributing factor in creating the pattern or trend. Once this element is identified, the underlying problem is not far away. This method prevents the officer from wasting time on something that is totally unrelated to the problem, and demonstrates why analysis is often a time-consuming proposition. I have seen the analysis point to social characteristics of a community, environmental issues, and even economic decline as underlying problems. Of course, this is why partnerships are critical in problem solving, because we can do little about these problems alone.

Most crime problems can be identified as related to the victim, the offender, or the location. One study revealed that 10% of the victims are involved in 40% of the crimes (Nelson, 1980). This clearly indicates a relationship between the victim and the crimes committed against them. Briefly put, they are more attractive targets. It is the function of analysis to identify why they are being victimized and to develop a response to address the victimization.

A critical eye in analyzing data will first recognize a pattern, and then further examine the pattern to define the least common denominator. This analysis represents the beginning of the problem-solving process. By way of example, analysis may identify multiple calls to a certain location. Further examination of the data may reveal that there is no common day of the week or common times associated with the calls. The officer without further analysis information takes his or her examination to the next step by physically pulling the reports. The reports reveal no common victim or suspect, and the officer rightly concludes the crime problem is related to the location support of the triangle. Remove the attraction of the location and the crime problem will no longer occur, at least not regularly.

Although the value of a good, professionally trained crime analyst is immeasurable to the community policing efforts of an agency, officers can be successful without one. To measure your ability at this skill, even if you have a crime analyst at your disposal, gather the type of data discussed above and dissect it to see what you identify. If you practice this elementary process and find that you know something more than you did at the start of the analysis, you have achieved success. I am sure that you will be sold on the tool of analysis.

■ Chapter Summary

Community policing techniques are typically those that address problems at their root. The techniques employ strategies that involve information gathering, analysis, actions, and evaluation. Community policing strategies involve a collaborative approach with stakeholders in order to address the problems properly and to ensure maintenance of the solution, once success is achieved. Strategies must continuously be checked and rechecked, using analysis tools and techniques for reoccurrence or newly created issues.

■ Review Questions

1. What does the first A in the SARA problem-solving model acronym represent?
2. Which community policing tool focuses primarily on police image enhancement?
3. When is it recommended to use a team made up of fire officials, police officers, code enforcement officials, and building officials to address a problem?
4. The crime analysis triangle indicates that three elements need be present for a crime to occur; one is an offender. What are the other two?

■ References

Braiden, Chris. 1988. Nothing new under the sun. *Footprints Community Policing Newsletter*; Spring/Summer.

Code of Virginia, Section 15.1–489.

Code of Virginia, Section 15.2–907.

Code of Virginia, Section 15.2–1115 et al.

Code of Virginia, Section 15.2–1717.1.

Code of Virginia, Section 35.1–28.

Covey, Stephen R. 1989. *The Seven Habits of Highly Effective People*. New York: Simon and Schuster.

Goldstein, Herman. 1990. *Problem-Oriented Policing*. Philadelphia: Temple University Press.

Mayhall, Pamela D., Barker, Thomas, and Hunter, Ronald D. 1995. *Police Community Relations and the Administration of Justice* (4th ed.). Englewood Cliffs, NJ: Prentice Hall.

Nelson, James F. 1980. Multiple victimization in American cities: A statistical analysis of rare events. *American Journal of Sociology*; 85(4):870–891.

U.S. Department of Labor, Occupational Safety and Health Administration. 1998. *Recommendations for Workplace Violence Prevention Programs in Late-Night Establishments* (Document # 31531). Washington, DC.

Wilson, James Q., and Kelling, George L. March 1992. Broken windows. *The Atlantic Monthly*.

Crime Prevention in Practice and Theory

"It should be understood, at the outset, that the principal object to be attained is the prevention of crime."

—Sir Robert Peel

■ Introduction

The prevention of crime is, or should be, our ultimate goal in policing. Most states identify this goal in their state code as a principle duty of law enforcement. Indeed, crime prevention is even the primary goal of community policing. I continue to harp on this truth: Community policing and crime prevention are similar in goals and in objectives, but one accomplishes the goal via extensive "active" participation of the community and the other can accomplish some prevention with limited participation of the community. Crime prevention, like its counterpart of community policing, is proactive policing. Both reactive and proactive policing are necessary, but by effectively using proactive policing, the need for reactive policing is reduced. It is cost-effective to spend money on preventing a crime rather than reacting to it. Reactive policing costs untold dollars in investigative hours, lab tests, and court preparation and presentation, not to mention the cost of incarceration. Therefore, it stands to reason that the best course of action, from both a safety and a fiscal standpoint, is prevention. In this and subsequent chapters, I will discuss the theory behind crime prevention and examine the most common techniques that successful crime prevention specialists employ.

■ The Crime Triangle

The definition of crime prevention that is most accepted by practitioners is, "The anticipation, recognition, and appraisal of a crime risk and the initiation of some action to remove or reduce it" (National Crime Prevention Institute, 1986, p. 2). As you can surmise from its definition, crime prevention might involve citizens or may be a law enforcement–only proposition. Like crime analysis, crime prevention utilizes a triangle to demonstrate how the practice of prevention works. Crime prevention practitioners refer to this as the "crime triangle." Unlike the triangle discussed in Chapter 3, the crime triangle presupposes that three elements must be present before a crime can occur. These elements are (1) a person must have a *desire* to commit a crime; (2) that person must possess the *ability* to commit the crime; and (3) the *opportunity* to commit the crime must present itself.

Because the assumption is that all three elements must be present for a crime to occur, it follows that the removal of just one of the elements will prevent the crime from occurring. If an individual makes a $1000 bank deposit daily, and has the ability and opportunity to steal the deposit but does not have a criminal desire, the crime will never be committed. Likewise, if an individual has a criminal desire to steal millions in trade secrets from her company and has access to the computers containing those secrets, but has no computer knowledge, no crime will be committed.

In the history of crime prevention, many have attempted to address the desire leg of the triangle by employing punitive prevention techniques. Punitive techniques that offer enhanced or severe punishments have proven to be ineffective in controlling the career criminal. This type of prevention does have some effect on preventing first-time offenders or those with little in the way of criminal records. Some might say punitive measures do a good job at "keeping the honest people honest." Crime prevention practitioners realize that they can do little to address the desire of the criminal to commit a crime. The ability arm of the triangle also presents a problem in the way of crime control. Short of incarceration, the police can do little to address the criminal's ability. In some cases we actually indirectly contribute to their ability by incarcerating them with "mentoring criminals" who help the individuals develop new ways to carry out their crimes. If we can do little to address their ability and desire, the only option left is the opportunity leg of the triangle. Opportunity reduction is the foundation on which practitioners build their crime prevention strategies and programs. The simple goal to be achieved is *to reduce or remove the opportunity needed to commit specific criminal acts.* This goal is achieved by concentrating on the environment and the actions of the potential victim rather than on the potential criminal. In contrast, punitive and corrective efforts concentrate on controlling the criminal.

In the long history of crime prevention, the many efforts of early crime prevention practitioners have led to modern-day opportunity reduction strategies. Prevention practitioners claim Sir Robert Peel as the driving force behind, and father of, crime prevention because of his principles pointing toward the importance of proactive, specifically preventative, policing. Many pages could be devoted to the rich history leading to the practice and theory of modern-day prevention; however, because this manual is designed to be a practical guide, I have opted to leave the history to the historians. Any reader wishing to know more about this history can consult any of the crime prevention associations listed in the Resources section at the end of this book for assistance in this matter.

■ Opportunity Reduction

As stated previously, opportunity reduction is the foundation of modern prevention programs and processes. In order to see how this opportunity reduction process actually works, it is essential to have a basic understanding of human behavior, specifically criminal behavior. In my opinion, nobody does a better job of addressing opportunity reduction from an understanding of the criminal mindset than Ron V. Clarke in his book, *Situational Crime Prevention* (1997). Dr. Clarke refers to opportunity in the context of a situation and focuses on the "settings for crime." He defines situational crime prevention as, "opportunity-reducing measures that are (1) directed at highly specific forms of crime, (2) involves the management, design or manipulation of the immediate environment and (3) make crime more difficult and risky, or less rewarding and excusable" (Clarke, 1997, p. 4). It is the third part of this definition offered by Clarke that I have experienced to be the most accurate and useful in my creation of crime prevention strategies. Clarke indicates that officers who understand human behavior recognize that criminals rationally choose their victim. He identifies four measures by which this choice is made:

1. The risk involved
2. The effort to be successful

3. The reward to be had
4. The availability of excuses if detected

These measures should be considered by all officers or practitioners when developing any crime prevention strategy or program. Clarke then further categorizes these measures into 16 opportunity-reducing techniques, which he defines by name and description. I chose not to list these here because the point of the list is simply to demonstrate which of his four measures a variety of prevention techniques fall under.

The Four D's

Based on Clarke's four factors, the criminal will typically choose a target that offers less risk, less effort, more reward, and more excuses. The National Crime Prevention Institute (NCPI) teaches a similar theory of accomplishing prevention, which it calls *the four D's* (National Crime Prevention Institute, 1986). The four D's correspond to one or more of Dr. Clarke's categories. The four D's are as follows:

1. Deny the use or access to the criminal.
2. Delay the act.
3. Detect the crime.
4. Deter the attack or crime.

These acts concentrate on making the victim an unattractive target rather than addressing the criminal in a preventative endeavor. The target will be less apt to be chosen if it poses more of a risk of detection or capture to the criminal than other potential targets do. If the criminal views the target as requiring more effort than other potential targets, due to locks that delay their quick entry, they may choose a different target. If the potential reward is substantially less, or rendered useless by some means, the lack of reward/use may deter the criminal from choosing one victim in favor of another. Finally, questioning someone concerning his or her legitimate purpose in certain areas through the use of a badging procedure, signs, or other measures deters the criminal by removing excuses for such uncontested access. Developing prevention with these factors in mind is sure to increase the success rate of your prevention programs. As we go through the following chapters on crime prevention and expound on various techniques, practice asking yourself how this increases the risk, increases the effort, and so on. Get in the habit now of using this thought process and it will soon become second nature. **Table 4.1** demonstrates the relationship between Clarke's situational crime prevention measures and NCPI's prevention measures.

Table 4.1
Clarke's Situational Crime Prevention Versus NCPI's Four D's

Situational Crime Prevention Measures	National Crime Prevention Institute's Four D Measures
Increase the effort.	Deny use/access.
	Detect crime.
	Delay criminal act.
Increase the risk.	Detect crime.
	Delay criminal act.
Reduce the reward.	Deny use/access.
Reduce/remove excuses.	Deter attack/crime.

■ The Crime Prevention Unit

Crime prevention is accomplished by using various approaches. The officer or practitioner choosing the approach must look at the objective being strived for. Crime prevention approaches typically fall under one of three primary categories: educational, physical environment, or community involved. **Table 4.2** gives examples of prevention programs that fall under these three primary categories.

The Educational Approach

A major role of the crime prevention unit in any agency is educating the public on prevention techniques that they may undertake to protect themselves, their families and neighbors, and their property. The crime prevention officer should be the contact person for any requests for presentations about crime and crime prevention that come into the agency. In some cases the crime prevention office is seen as having sole responsibility for the prevention activities and presentations for the agency. This is a serious mistake that law enforcement must overcome. Consider the vast expertise that the agency is allowing to go untapped while the crime prevention officer must attempt to be the proverbial "jack of all trades." The typical crime prevention unit is small, as it should be. The prevention office should coordinate presentations and the efforts of the agency using all members. With the expert giving the advice and making the presentations, the prevention practitioner is free to assist in developing the presentation and materials and to monitor trends and problems. The role of education is one that should be undertaken by those most qualified to educate on the particular subject, facilitated by the crime prevention unit.

The Physical Approach

The physical environment approach is one that crime prevention officers are most likely to be qualified to handle. In this approach, crime prevention officers address crime by offering security assessments and recommendations to residents and businesses based on sound, proven techniques. These assessments, to be discussed in Chapter 8, are a major tool in preventing crime by addressing vulnerabilities. No person should provide such input without adequate training, and therefore the crime prevention practitioner typically will be best equipped to handle this role. In fact, in several states the role of the crime prevention officer is recognized as being so skilled that a certification process for these officers to become a "Certified Crime Prevention Specialist" has been developed. For example, in Virginia, the certification requirements are met by receiving a certain amount of training and having a certain amount of experience; in Ohio, a testing process is used. Having said that, it should be understood that any officer can be trained to offer certain limited advice regarding physical environment protection or even supplied with brochures to present to the public concerning such issues.

Table 4.2
Prevention Program Categories

Educational	Physical Environment	Community Involvement
Drug Abuse Resistance Education (DARE)	Building plan review programs	Neighborhood Watch organizing
Safety fair exhibits	Security assessments	Citizen patrols coordinator
Personal safety seminars	Target hardening	School resource officer program
Robbery prevention seminars	Problem-solving assistance based on Crime Prevention	Citizen police academy
Identity theft seminars	Through Environmental Design	
Brochure dissemination	(CPTED)	

The Community Approach

The final approach for prevention efforts is one of community involvement. Whether passive or active, community involvement is always desired and must be encouraged by prevention units. Some agencies depend on the crime prevention office to be the community liaison in all efforts and consider it their "community policing unit." When the crime prevention officer is engaged in a program involving active participation by the community, he or she is conducting community policing. For example, the community patrols sponsored by many agencies are an active community-policing program, in that they are engaged *with* the agency to address crime and the fear of crime. Often these patrols began as Neighborhood Watch, a crime prevention core program whose natural liaison is the crime prevention unit. (Neighborhood Watch is discussed in more detail in Chapter 5.)

Believing in a proactive philosophy for the entire agency, I advocate that the crime prevention unit should limit its involvement with the community to the roles of facilitator and organizer. It is wise for the unit to assist the community in getting organized and trained in operating an organization. Once organized, the officers working the area should be the contacts for neighborhood problems and issues. I have seen a wide variety of structures and assignments shared by crime prevention units. Those agencies in which the unit is always the contact for a neighborhood have had problems, because the officers who need to establish a neighborhood connection for problem solving are unable to do so. The beat officer who has not developed a rapport previously with the community is not trusted, and problem-solving efforts are hindered. Instead, when a problem arises, the crime prevention officer is apt to get the call and be unable to give the issue due attention because of his additional responsibilities, which in turn hurts his relationship with the neighborhood.

■ Chapter Summary

Crime prevention theory is based upon the premise that for a crime to be completed, the criminal must have the ability and desire, coupled with opportunity. Opportunity is the element that prevention techniques successfully address. The opportunity reduction techniques discussed in this chapter stress removing the object of the crime or making the crime less opportune by increasing the potential hazard of capture and the required effort for a successful crime.

■ Review Questions

1. The foundation upon which crime prevention practitioners build their prevention strategies is the reduction of which element of the crime triangle?
2. Dr. Ron Clarke's opportunity-reducing measures indicate that criminals choose their victims through what means?
3. What words are represented by the National Crime Prevention Institute's four D theory?
4. There are three approaches, or categories, of crime prevention techniques; the first is educational, what are the other two?

■ References

Clarke, Ron V. 1997. *Situational Crime Prevention—Successful Case Studies* (2nd ed.). Guilderland, NY: Harrow and Heston.

National Crime Prevention Institute. 1986. *Understanding Crime Prevention*. Stoneham, MA: Butterworth–Heinemann.

Crime Prevention Community Programs

"It should be understood, at the outset, that the principal object to be attained is the prevention of crime."

—Sir Robert Peel

■ Introduction

Hundreds of excellent crime prevention programs and techniques are available to be adopted and used. The agency must choose which are best suited to its needs. In this chapter, our discussion will be directed at programs that are facilitated by crime prevention units with substantial community involvement. These programs are designed to encourage the smaller unit of community, such as an apartment complex, neighborhood, or campus, to become passively or actively involved in accomplishing crime prevention in its small area. The crime prevention practitioner's role in these programs should be one of leadership in the beginning, but later should become more of a liaison and advisor. Such community programs are extremely valuable.

When settlers first began to arrive and colonize North America, there were no police forces. The colonists depended on their neighbors for survival, and each took a turn at patrolling and watching. The sense of community was strong because one's own survival was contingent on the strength of the whole community. Today, neighborhood groups have a major stake in their neighborhood's survival as well. Criminals seek out the weak communities in which to commit their crimes. High crime rates further deteriorate the neighborhood, and before long, the neighborhood becomes dilapidated, dangerous, and uncared for. Government loses the tax base that residential units bring in, housing stock and quality of life deteriorate, and industries seek other communities with a ready work force to build in. In short, all are affected. Additionally, government budgets continue to shrink, and it is impossible for law enforcement to place an officer on every block to address all the crime issues. Neighborhood-based prevention programs represent a means for police to continue to be effective at addressing crime in most neighborhoods while not taxing already strained budgets.

■ Neighborhood/Block Watch

In the early to mid-20th century, homes were built in traditional ways. Houses were built on open lots, and the front porch was often a social gathering place for neighbors to visit in the cool of the evening. Beginning in the 1960s, a transition was made to homes constructed with enclosed back yards, back decks, and air conditioning, which discouraged the practice of community interaction. With more women working as well, the community lost many of the "natural guardians" who had been present prior to this time. This resulted in fewer people at home during the workday and a lack of community cohesiveness. The lack of natural guardians and the closed society that we had become have frequently been blamed for the increases in community crime during that time. In 1971, the National Sheriff's Association initiated the Neighborhood Watch program. Since that time, almost all communities have some form of the program in place. The program was designed to replace that which was lost.

The Premise

The premise of the Neighborhood Watch program consists of three main goals:

1. Establish a sense of community cohesiveness or family.
2. Encourage the practice of neighbors watching.
3. Develop a rapport with local law enforcement and neighborhood services.

Crime Prevention Application

By establishing a sense of community, the resident is likely to know his or her neighbor and think of them more as a friend or even a family member. A person observing suspicious activity that may be harmful to a friend or even an acquaintance is much more likely to be concerned enough to call the police than if the would-be victim is a stranger. When residents know their neighbors they are more likely to extend their sense of ownership, or concern, to include their neighbor's home, and therefore will react to suspicious noises or sights. Plus, the rapport this program builds with the law enforcement agency decreases the hesitancy that the neighbor may otherwise experience in calling.

Having said this, let's now apply what we know to the four D's and Dr. Clarke's (1997) categories offered for prevention. With more eyes and ears watching and listening, the risk of capture and detection is increased. The effort required to commit a crime also is increased due to the watching and the lack of hesitancy in calling the police. By some estimates, only 33% of crime is reported to the police, and the police discover only some 2.5% of the crimes themselves. If we can encourage more community members to report suspicious activities, the rates of reported crime and consequently solved crime will increase substantially.

You may wonder about the actual effect that neighbors watching the area have on criminal activity. While assigned as the supervisor of crime prevention services, I was fortunate enough to have detectives who understood the value of prevention. In one case we had a rash of burglaries, and the detectives called upon us to organize a watch group. Within 3 months the burglars had been caught because of calls, and the community experienced no additional burglaries for some time. In another incidence of cooperation, a detective had arrested a well-known burglar. Once he completed his interview concerning the numerous cases that the burglar had been involved in, the detective turned his questions to methods, and received some of the most valuable information I had experienced in prevention. The burglar stated that he and his associates chose target houses by several techniques. First, they sought a house with few people around watching. They would be dropped off in the neighborhood and simply knock on doors. If a person answered, they would ask for a fictitious person; if they were watched by the person, they would wait for their pick-up driver and leave. If the person seemed uninterested, they would go on to another house until they found one with no answer, and then go to the side or back and force entry. (The physical security information we will be discussing later in Chapters 11 and 12 would eliminate their method of entry.) As you can see, if there were even a passive Neighborhood Watch, the crime would be averted.

The Process

Neighborhood/Block Watch programs are by design geographically small. A small area is more likely to be successful due to the close-knit relationships developed and is easily maintained. Watch groups can be made up of neighborhoods of three or four streets, individual streets, blocks, apartment buildings, dorms, mobile home parks, and so on. Most watch programs are started by an individual approaching the law enforcement coordinator or by the agency itself recognizing a need and approaching the neighborhood. Unfortunately, many agencies feel that it is the responsibility of the neighborhood or block representative to approach them. In some cases, efforts are made to educate the public of the availability of the program, but little else is done to approach them. This is an area in which the community policing specialist or officer should intervene to identify the need and assist in developing the contact to initiate a watch program in problem neighborhoods, where they are most useful.

The process for forming a recognized watch group varies from jurisdiction to jurisdiction. Some require one meeting for the group to be identified as a recognized watch; others require several meetings to be eligible, and still others require some training. Some jurisdictions will not even meet with the community until a certain number of households are guaranteed to attend. I do not advocate any minimum number of attendees, because even one extra person watching and assisting the prevention effort is worth my time. If the job is done properly, the attendance will grow to include more of the represented neighborhood.

The Multiple Meeting Approach

Because the success of Neighborhood Watch programs is based on the community's cohesiveness, and because people need to know how to do what they are being asked to do, I support a multiple meeting/training approach prior to identifying any group as a Neighborhood Watch. The following are the steps that I have found to be successful in this type of approach.

Step 1: Identify a Starting Point. Once an area has been targeted for a watch, the crime prevention practitioner should seek to identify an existing organization that might be a jumping off point for the organization of a watch. Frequently, existing tenant organizations, homeowners associations, or other groups exist and, even if too large, may be amenable to you speaking to their group about organizing a watch. I have actually spoken to large groups and formed several neighborhood watches from the one larger group. If no existing organization is available, then the neighborhood contact person should be asked to identify two or three people in the neighborhood who could assist them in getting the word out and encouraging attendance at an organizational meeting. Often the contact may know of a meeting location; however, if one is not known, the first job of the crime prevention officer is to identify a location. Meeting in homes is not out of the question, but becomes a burden later on. Most community churches, schools, and recreational facilities are open to allowing this type of meeting without cost. The officer may also have to assist the contact and the initial team in producing flyers to disseminate information about the meeting. Most police agencies understand that this is a necessity and don't balk at the cost of a few copied flyers.

Step 2: Hold the Initial Meeting. At the organizational meeting, the crime prevention officer typically asks the contact person or one of the initial team members to welcome their neighbors; ask them to sign in with their name, address, and telephone number; and then briefly describe the purpose of the meeting: to determine the need and desire to form a Neighborhood Watch. After the initial comments by the contact person, the officer should be introduced and allowed to overview the neighborhood statistical data and Neighborhood Watch. First, I ask that everybody speak to someone who they did not know before and find out where they live and something else about them before they leave. This serves as a kick-off to tearing down the natural uneasiness that humans share when among strangers. It never fails to amaze me how so many people live in the same area and do not know their neighbors. Second, I have the crime analyst prepare general calls for service data for the area, and I share this with the group. (See Chapter 3 for more information about crime data analysis.) I also hand out a simple questionnaire concerning their perceptions about crime in the neighborhood. (You may wish to use one of the surveys included in Chapter 2 as your survey. The survey will be a valuable guide for training if the meeting is successful in creating a new watch group.) I summarize the premise and purpose of Neighborhood Watch, as discussed earlier, and explain to the group the value of the Neighborhood Watch sign. Many people tend to think that they should attend the one meeting and then the signs be put up. Certainly the signs are a deterrent, and quite often are the only reason a group wants to form a watch. It should be understood that the criminal element is aware of jurisdictions where the signs are active and is just as aware of those areas where the signs mean absolutely nothing. The sign is just one part of the overall program, and if not controlled loses its effect. Although I have never found a jurisdiction that controls the signs in this manner, I believe the signs should be leased to the community for a nominal fee. If the signs are part of a lease agreement that specifies that the group must meet a certain number of times per year or receive a certain amount of training, then the group is held accountable if they want to remain an active watch. The signs in that situation will certainly mean something to the criminal. In any event, the specific guidelines for obtaining the signs should be clearly defined.

After the overview, I typically ask for a vote as to whether the people attending wish to form a watch. If they choose not to form a watch, I have identified myself as a police department contact, obtained some very valuable information about their perceptions from the survey, ensured that they know one other person in their community, and heightened their awareness about crimes in their neighborhood. If they choose to start a watch, I advise them of the number of meetings that they are required to have prior to the watch being certified and receiving the signs. I also advise the attendees that each of them will be notified concerning the next meeting, which is to identify leadership and the boundaries of their territory, establish their meeting schedule, and provide their first training.

Step 3: Determine Leadership. The leadership of a fledgling watch group is of utmost importance. Without an excited, driven leader the group will soon fall apart. During this second meeting, the importance of leadership and of the roles of each participant is emphasized. I encourage term limits to avoid problems, but remember that the watch belongs to the neighborhood and should be governed by them. The prevention officer's role at this point is to teach and organize. The minimum recommended leadership positions and their related duties typically found in watch groups are as follows:

- *President/chairperson*—Conducts the meetings in an orderly manner using an agenda prepared ahead of time. This person introduces the trainers or other speakers and shares information or news regarding the Neighborhood Watch. This person is the primary contact with the police concerning neighborhood problems, and as such will be familiar with all issues that are brought to the police.
- *Vice president/vice chairperson*—Fills in for the president in his or her absence. The vice president arranges for any needed training programs and keeps committees, if any exist, organized and on task.
- *Block, building, or street captain*—The contact person for all residents on the block or in the building; in the case of an apartment watch. This person is responsible for passing out newsletters or notices from the watch. He or she should retain an updated street or building directory and establish emergency communications within his or her area of responsibility. Typically, communication in the passive watch group is by way of the telephone tree. (See **Figure 5.1.**) The telephone tree

lists each member of a watch group along with their address and phone number, and identifies who each person must call in the event of an emergency alert or an alert to look out for a suspicious person or activity. In some jurisdictions, this information is gathered by the police and put into an automated dialing system that plays a prerecorded message from the police when the phone is answered.

It is the responsibility and role of all members to act as eyes and ears to detect and report any suspicious activity. Each also holds the responsibility of reviewing any material delivered to them by other members concerning crimes, prevention tips, and watch announcements. They are encouraged to check on the elderly and young and to practice prevention techniques learned during the training sessions. Each member should have a block map (similar to the one shown in **Figure 5.2**) to assist them in identifying house addresses when calling activity in. Often the caller may know the resident or the person living next door to the location, but be unfamiliar with the address. This map is of great assistance at those times.

Territorial boundaries for the watch should not be chosen arbitrarily. Instead, maps should be consulted to choose a manageable sized area not separated by barriers such as major roadways, waterways, rail crossings, parks, and the like. If an agency has the capability, a map of the area with crimes overlaid on it may be useful in determining a territory. Allow the members to suggest boundaries after advising them that the area should not be very large or separated by natural or man-made barriers.

Training Sessions

The focus of the first training session should be on teaching the attendees how to identify suspicious activity and what information to prepare to report when they call the police. I suggest having hand-out material to accompany the training and peppering the training with examples or stories of actual situations in which watches called the police. Stories reinforce the idea of success in preventing crime to the watches. The following list identifies the activities that members are requested to report:

1. Unknown persons entering vacant houses or removing boards from windows
2. Someone looking into windows and parked vehicles
3. Vehicles driving slowly through the neighborhood or without lights

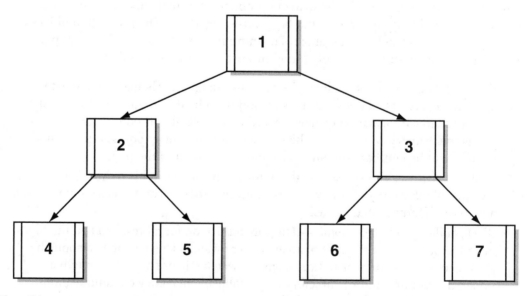

Figure 5.1
Block captain (No. 1) calls No. 2 and No. 3; No. 2 calls 4 and 5; No. 3 calls 6 and 7; and so on.

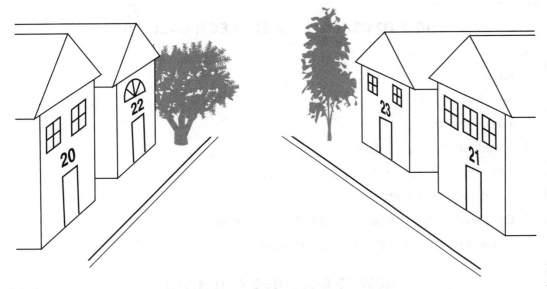

Figure 5.2
Block map.

4. Unknown persons removing parts from cars or siphoning gasoline
5. Out of the ordinary sounds/noises such as screams, breaking glass, and alarms
6. Unknown persons going to the rear of neighbors' homes
7. Strange vehicles left parked unoccupied in the neighborhood
8. Property being removed from homes where the resident is not home
9. Persons running carrying valuable items
10. Persons removing window air conditioning units or entering windows
11. Persons screaming for help
12. Strangers in vehicles stopping to talk to children
13. Strange occupied vehicles parked in the neighborhood at unusual hours
14. Any force being used to gain entry to a house, vehicle, or outbuilding
15. Frequent vehicular business transactions at a specific address

Another handout that is of use is a card or sticker that members can keep near their telephone. In **Figure 5.3** you can see the kind of information included on these cards and the type of information that is to be requested when a call about a suspicious person or vehicle is received at the communication center.

There should be one or two additional training sessions—one on home security, and the remaining session dictated by the information provided in the surveys collected at the organizational meeting and/or the calls for service data.

Common Problems

Although Neighborhood Watches often experience great success initially, they tend to become complacent once the targeted crime problems are under control. Many program coordinators have expressed their dismay at the death of their successful watches, and none has the perfect panacea for me to share. It appears the common thread is to find something that the neighborhood cares equally about and can work on together. This common thread often shifts from crime-related topics to neighborhood improvements. I have actually encouraged this transition in order to keep the watch alive. Some benefits are that the members get a better understanding of government and may be asked to sit on building or zoning commissions that affect their community. They may qualify for grants and funding to plan and, in some cases, lead in improving the infrastructure of their

HOW TO DESCRIBE A SUSPECT: CALL 911.

1. Name
2. Race
3. Sex
4. Age (approximate)
5. Height (short, medium, tall)
6. Weight OR skinny, thin, medium, stocky, heavy
7. Hair color/style/length
8. Complexion: –Tan –Fair/light –Red/ruddy –Acne/rough
9. Clothing from head to shoes (color and style)

HOW TO DESCRIBE A VEHICLE

1. Color
2. Make (Ford, Nissan, etc.)
3. Model or description (F150 pickup truck or medium-sized pickup truck)
4. License plate number, state, or color of letters/background
5. Other descriptors (damage, bumper sticker, etc.)

Figure 5.3
Information that will be requested by the communication center.

neighborhood. Jurisdictional crime prevention awards programs offer an incentive to members to continue their original prevention focus.

Other tips offered by practitioners to keep the watch alive are to encourage regular meetings with time built in for socializing. Some have suggested that meetings too often discourage active participation. It appears that meeting no more than once per month or less than once per quarter is accepted as a proper meeting schedule. Some final tips for keeping the watch alive:

- Involve the members in volunteerism within the law enforcement agency.
- Expand the focus from passive watching to active patrolling.
- Create a court watch to ensure judges mete out justice properly.
- Involve select members in providing training for new watch groups and publishing a newsletter of activities.

■ Neighborhood Patrols

Since the earliest days that the Europeans came to settle in North America, citizens have voluntarily patrolled their community to protect the village. Their role was essential because no organized militias or police forces existed. They were to patrol and observe, and to call for assistance when a problem was found; all who heard would come to their assistance. Citizen patrols today are organized around a volunteer group of patrollers who patrol specified areas and also call for assistance when problems are found. The early settlers were more concerned about safety from attack by the indigenous peoples than about crime, but otherwise little has changed. Both are based on civic duty to ensure safety, and both do only what it is every citizen's duty to do—observe and report any problems they see.

Modern neighborhood patrols, when organized and properly controlled by specific guidelines, are of great assistance to the police and the community in which they serve. These patrols not only provide a service to their own neighborhood, but also often augment sworn law enforcement at events that may drain police resources. Citizen patrols are used in varying degrees to patrol or assist in holiday shopping mall patrols, at festivals and large events, and in areas experiencing a rash of crimes, and to man barricades during road closures or natural disasters. In the following sections, I will attempt to describe a basic neighborhood/citizen patrol program. This program can, and should, be customized to meet the needs of the individual community.

The Premise and the Crime Prevention Application

The neighborhood/citizen patrol program is a means of extending the passive observations role of a Neighborhood Watch to a role of actively patrolling an area with the purpose of identifying and reporting crime-related activities.

With more eyes and ears actively moving in an area, the risk of detection is substantially increased for the criminal. Signage notifying persons that the community is actively patrolled by a citizen watch group puts would-be criminals on notice, thereby causing them to see every person as a potential patroller, which increases their effort and deters their criminal behavior.

The Process

In order to ensure uniformity of purpose and to discourage vigilantism, a jurisdictional sponsored neighborhood/citizen patrol program is the desired approach. Such a program should be developed and guidelines for participation created by a committee made up of the law enforcement coordinator and citizens. Guidelines should include, at a minimum, the following:

- *Background checks pertaining to who may participate*—A typical design specifies that no person with a felony conviction may participate. Additionally, misdemeanor convictions are frequently addressed by the type of misdemeanor or in some cases by the time expired since the last misdemeanor conviction. In order to protect privacy rights while still ensuring that honest citizens staff the program, the application should include a waiver that allows the law enforcement coordinator to conduct a background check, but to reveal to the committee only the status of qualified or not qualified. The coordinator should never reveal the nature of the results of the background check to anyone other than the applicant. Once an applicant has cleared the initial screening by the coordinator, the committee should review the applicant for additional information, which may be known, and vote to approve or disapprove the applicant. It should be specified in the application as to whether a rejected applicant will have the right to learn what information led to their rejection and whether any appeal process is available.

- *Attendance at a training course or seminar*—Training of participants is essential to avoid injury and costly litigation. The training usually includes such topics as how to use any equipment available to patrollers, recognizing and reporting suspicious activity, rules or procedures for patrolling, and safety techniques to avoid confrontation. The nature of the patrols should be predetermined by the committee. A written copy of any rules should be issued to all members. Patrols should always be acting in the capacity of an observer/reporter only; safety is of the utmost importance.

- *No patrolling alone*—In most cases, a person patrolling alone is not only a potential liability to the program, but also a danger to themselves. It is recommended that only teams of two or more be authorized to "officially" patrol as part of the organized program. The person patrolling alone is much more apt to be accused of harassment, prowling, and a host of other complaints without a witnessing partner. A team will ensure that each person adheres to the proper patrol guidelines and rules, and will avoid accusations that may tarnish the program's reputation.

- *No team patrolling without some form of emergency communication*—This mandate should be addressed by the sponsoring agency by providing two-way radios or cellular/digital telephones for use by the patrols. Due to the advent of the Citizens On Patrol (COP) program a number of years ago, cellular and digital telephone companies are making emergency telephones available to jurisdictions for this very purpose. There are very few guidelines for the use of these phones, and most major companies dealing in such telephones participate with local law enforcement upon request.

The following are some suggested rules for maintaining a safe and successful neighborhood/citizen patrol team:

1. No person may patrol alone as a representative of the neighborhood/citizen patrol.
2. The issued communications device must be carried and used by the team when patrolling. The device must be checked prior to beginning the patrol shift.
3. No team, or team member, may patrol more than the maximum time limit of 8 hours without a break of 8 hours before resuming patrol duties.
4. No person may sell, solicit, or engage in any political, religious, or business activity while acting as an official patrol.
5. Police dispatchers will be notified by teams prior to teams beginning their patrol. The team shall advise police dispatchers of their names, their vehicle description, the location/area to be patrolled, and the duration of the patrol.
6. Patrols shall not confront persons/suspects, but rather shall observe from a safe location, and report and monitor the persons, giving frequent updates to the police dispatchers.
7. Patrols shall not approach police on a scene that they have called police to, but rather shall wait until the police advise the dispatcher to have the caller come to them or the officers come to the caller's location.
8. Patrolling members shall have in their possession their patrol team member identification card (if one is issued) or some other form of photo identification.
9. The nature of the patrol will dictate whether members shall wear any issued patrol identifying clothing (vests, jackets, caps, t-shirts). Typically, such clothing will not be worn when requested to assist in surveillance of an area or when on patrol in potentially dangerous situations. The clothing will typically be worn when assisting in street barricades, festival events, or other preventative patrol situations.
10. Absolutely no firearms or weapons are permitted to be in the possession of members while on patrol.

Common Problems

As with Neighborhood Watch programs, retaining the interest of the patrols becomes difficult once the newness of the program begins to wane. I have found that the best way to truly motivate members of an active group is to ask them to participate in a meaningful way. Such active groups want to make a difference, and to have them patrol a quiet secluded neighborhood with absolutely no crime problems will kill the program. On the other hand, asking them to patrol in an area that has experienced a rash of car break-ins or asking them to work a special event where they can see the fruits of their volunteer labor makes them feel important.

Another problem that some citizen patrols experience is one of vigilantism. I alluded to this earlier, and stated that this is one very important reason for having the jurisdiction sponsor the program. With jurisdiction sponsorship, the internal operation of the program and any problems are known.

Few localities with a law enforcement coordinator have such problems as mentioned above, and those that have experienced them were quickly made aware of them and able to address the issues. Written guidelines and rules that specify that a member can be expelled from the program as a consequence of violation also contribute to avoiding misconduct by members.

■ Court Watch Program

Alluded to earlier in the discussion of Neighborhood Watch, the court watch program is one that is totally unnecessary in most localities; however, where it is needed, it is considered essential. Such a program is not truly a crime prevention program, but it is listed here because it generally is an activity adopted by Neighborhood Watches or other community-based crime prevention groups.

Premise
Court watch is a political action in which members, identified by some common clothing such as a vest or t-shirt, attend the offending judge's court in an effort to pressure a more appropriate finding and sentencing of cases.

Crime Prevention Application
In jurisdictions that have a judge who is known for leniency to the detriment of the community, this process may be a useful tool. As mentioned before, this program is not truly a prevention program, but does relate to prevention in several ways. A judge with lenient tendencies becomes known in the area and results in criminals making the rational choice of committing the crime in the more lenient judge's jurisdiction rather than an adjoining jurisdiction in which the punitive sanctions are apt to be more severe. It is common sense—even a child knows to go to the more lenient parent for punishment. The crime prevention application is to remove that reputation of jurisdictional leniency to at least deter criminal activity based on the choice made by the potential findings and punishment.

The Process
Rarely is this program one that will be initiated by, or even openly supported by, local law enforcement. The political ramifications are such that a citizen or citizens group must start this program. Many of these programs are described in detail and encouraged by crime prevention practitioners surreptitiously when the need exists.

The program operation and process are simple. Members of this group identify the offending judge and determine his or her schedule. Once the schedule is known, the group will usually send a letter to the judge stating their intention to be in the courtroom during his or her scheduled court dates to observe and document his or her actions related to cases. The wording and content depend on how strongly the group wants to express their resolve to deal with the judge's lenient policies. Some letters have included specific actions that the group will take, such as contacting the appropriate overseeing court official.

The next step of the watch process is to ensure that one or more members wearing some type of identifying clothing attends the scheduled dates and locates him- or herself conspicuously in the courtroom so as to be seen by the judge. The attending members are to listen to the cases and findings and document the names, charges, findings, and sentences handed out by the judge. After several days of obtaining such information, a second letter is usually drafted to the judge demonstrating his or her record for leniency and expressing a strong concern. This letter often includes a statistical breakdown of convictions and sentences as compared with other local judges, if the information is known. It may also be compared to national statistics, generally available on the Internet. The letter closes with a plea for the judge to reconsider his or her practices and a reminder that the group will continue to document his or her courtroom.

In subsequent visits, the judge may appear to be improving, but usually, if this is the case, it is short lived. Several methods are practiced at this point. Some groups continue to monitor the court, but without wearing identifying clothing. This may reveal that the judge goes back to his or her old ways rather quickly. Another method is to send the judge a letter of thanks and advise him or her that his or her courtroom will no longer be regularly monitored by identified monitors, but rather will be visited periodically by unidentified members.

If all of these techniques fail to bring about the desired change, the final step is to publicize the judge's record. Although this seems like a drastic step, remember the harm being done to the community. The record may be publicized with little commentary or with much commentary, but the emphasis should remain on the record of the judge and not be a soapbox to air opinions. Most publications begin initially as a flyer and may be distributed by mail or by individual members handing them out at public venues. One caution: Before a group hands out flyers, they should be sure of their local ordinances concerning passing out handbills. Some fortunate jurisdictions are able to find an existing neighborhood newspaper or publication that allows them to post the information in it for free. If the crimes being discounted by the judge are related to identity theft or scams, senior-oriented newspapers may be willing to include the information; if they are related to drugs in the public housing community; you may find a willing partner there. The most important point in publicizing the rulings of the judge is accuracy. A copy of the publication is generally sent to the judge, the judge's superior(s), political representatives, and prosecutors. Initially some publicity may be gained from the mainstream press, but this usually is not sustained beyond the first story and perhaps one follow-up story.

The effort is never wasted in these situations. At worst, some limited success may be gained by forcing the judges to take a hard look at themselves; at best, the effort may lead to the offending judge changing his or her methods and adhering to proper sentencing guidelines.

Common Problems

The most common problem associated with this program is political pressure being applied on the local law enforcement representative who works with community groups. The pressure will, as they say, flow downhill until the representative is asked to intervene. In most cases the officer involved is fully aware of what the effort is all about and, as stated earlier, may have assisted in starting it in some way, so he or she should already be prepared to deal with this pressure. Occasionally the judge will attempt to put pressure directly on the court watch group, but this is rare because it would obviously backfire and create the publicity that he or she wishes to avoid. More often than not, the problem will be one of a team that is motivated at first but quickly loses heart. As with any political action, the members must understand at the outset that this process is likely to be a slow one. Just a few dedicated people with some time can make a huge difference in this type of program.

■ Crime Stopper Programs

When one thinks of the crime stopper programs, it is easy to discount them as not being prevention but rather an investigative tool. I used to agree. Crime stopper programs are primarily used to solve rather than prevent crime, but the law enforcement coordinator is frequently chosen from crime prevention officers rather than investigators. Until recently I would have argued extensively against crime stopper programs having any significance in preventing crime—that is, until I started to look at programs by applying the four D's and the "rational choice" test (Clarke, 1997, p. 10).

The Premise
The premise of the crime stopper programs is to use an anonymous tip line to receive tips about crimes that occurred or are going to occur, and to encourage such tips by offering financial incentives.

Crime Prevention Application
By applying the rational choice test mentioned above, it is clear that such programs not only offer the potential to identify the crime and prevent it before it occurs, but also offer additional value in prevention. A functioning crime stopper program serves as a deterrent by putting criminals on notice that even their friends may be encouraged to reveal their involvement in crimes because of the financial incentive offered. This certainly increases the risk that their participation in a crime may be discovered. The highly publicized crime might also affect their ability to use the fruits of their crimes. Of course, this decreases their reward and denies them the use of the stolen articles. When examined against the guidelines for identifying crime prevention programs, one can see that crime stopper programs truly do qualify as a prevention program as well as an investigative tool.

The Process
Crime stopper programs differ very little from one jurisdiction to another. The program includes three partners, each with a distinct role:

- *Board of directors*—The board is made up of citizens and businesspeople without any law enforcement officers as voting members. The role of the board is usually to conduct fundraisers and oversee the funds and awards paid out for tips.
- *Law enforcement coordinator*—The role of the coordinator is to provide the board and media with crimes to be profiled for awards and to provide the board with information as to tips that were received and the usefulness of the information. The board can then evaluate this information to make an award, if one is due.
- *Media*—Like the coordinator, the media representatives have no vote. The role of the media is to publicize the crimes to be profiled and to give notice, in some cases, that an award is due for certain information. This is usually done by publicizing that the caller identified by a certain number should call the coordinator to collect a cash award. The media may also offer to assist in advertising fundraisers for the program, which usually is a nonprofit organization and designated as such.

The program operates by use of a secure telephone line, Internet site, or both, which is staffed by volunteers or paid employees, 24 hours a day. A system of receiving calls and asking pertinent information needs to be adopted. Typically, the caller is assigned an identifying code number or name, which they can use to collect a reward if any of their information leads to an arrest associated with a crime. Methods of payment vary and may be through a volunteer citizen, through a bank teller who is notified of a password and then pays the person using the password, by a drop method, and or by another means. Most awards are determined by an award schedule developed by the board of directors to avoid arguments opinions of the crime that was solved. For example, a burglary might receive two points and a stolen firearm three points. If the crime solved was a burglary in which a firearm was stolen, the point value would go up. The points are then compared to a payment schedule. Naturally, as the points rise, the award rises, right up to the maximum allowed by the Internal Revenue Service for such anonymous programs: $1000.

Many schools are creating specialized school crime stopper programs, which operate in essentially the same way. Generally the cash awards are less and the crimes are related to issues in or around the school. Some type of active participation by a student board is recommended. This involvement is often limited to selecting the crimes to profile, maintaining a crime stopper bulletin board on which crimes are posted along with notification to callers of due awards, and conducting "crime stopper awareness" activities. Many states regulate how the school program must be initiated and operated, so you should consult your state code prior to beginning such a program.

Common Problems

The success of crime stopper programs hinges primarily on their promise of anonymity. Anything that threatens the anonymity of a caller is a major problem. Should a caller's identity be revealed for any reason, it is assumed by those involved in these programs that the program's value is essentially dead. Therefore, protecting the anonymity of any caller must be a top priority. In cases where the caller is identified, it is often due to the zeal of an investigator who fails to see the forest for the trees. The investigator will see the one serious crime as needing to be solved at all costs, without recognizing the number of serious crimes that will not be solved due to the distrust caused by revealing the name of the caller. This anonymity is so important that when coordinating our local program, I mandated to our call takers that even if the caller states his or her name, it should not be documented anywhere. The information should be taken and forwarded, but no names of any caller could be included.

Another related problem that must be addressed is a problem referred to as "filtering." Filtering is the act of investigators receiving information from their confidential informants and having them call the information in to the crime stopper line in order to get cash payment. This not only violates the anonymity so important to the program, but also drains the funds set aside for such information.

One final problem that is encountered is when the caller calls back and an investigator needs additional information. Some investigators have requested that we have the person contact them directly. This is a recipe for disaster for your program. I recommend instead to have the investigator draft any additional questions that he or she needs answered and then have the caller's number advertised to call the tip line for an update on their tip. When they call, the call taker should document the caller code number on the questions and forward the answers to the investigator. Care must always be taken not to inadvertently point to the identity of the caller. For example, if an investigator's question was whether the caller was present during the crime and it is known that only two people were present, this question should be excluded.

■ Security Escort Program

Security escort programs have taken off in recent years. These escorts are just what they sound like: They are escorts provided to people walking from parking lots to their building or their building to a car.

The Premise

Security escorts are provided primarily in areas where personal safety is an issue. Most often security escort programs are found on college campuses, retirement communities, or other locations where activity requires arrivals and departures to and from large isolated parking areas after dark. A security escort might also be beneficial at an amusement park, an airport, or a stadium.

Crime Prevention Application

The security escort program concentrates almost exclusively on removing the opportunity for personal attack against the client or citizen. Many sexual assaults, robberies, and purse snatches occur in isolated parking areas, and it is common knowledge that such attackers prefer no witnesses, which is why they target such areas. By providing an escort, the risk and effort for the attacker is increased to the degree that the probability of such an attack is all but eliminated. The reward or motivation driving the activity (access to the victim) is denied, and by adding a witness to the mix, the crime is certainly deterred.

The Process

The escort program may be started by a Neighborhood Watch, a tenant association, a facility's manager, or any number of other entities. Paid or volunteer staff may staff the program, but regardless of how it is staffed, some scheduling and management of the program is necessary. All volunteer or paid staff should submit to a screening process to ensure the integrity of the escorts. Escorts must be identified by some type of clothing or markings clearly recognizable from a distance to prevent the attacker from posing as an escort to accomplish his or her criminal act. It is also customary for escorts' pick-up/drop-off locations to be placed in a safe location and clearly identified. In some apartment complexes, identified persons volunteer to meet other residents and escort them on foot to their building. The most often used transportation, when transportation is needed, is a golf cart, or in large facilities a shuttle bus.

Common Problems

The most common problems associated with this type of program are the lack of volunteers and the uncertainty of the availability of escorts. As a result of the lack of staff, escorts are often sporadic and therefore eventually disregarded by the targeted users. This program can lead to a false sense of security by targeted users who park in the isolated area expecting an escort who doesn't arrive, leaving them vulnerable. Signage placed at the entrance to the lot may identify when an escort is on duty, but this is problematic because it also identifies to the attackers when no escorts are on duty. To address this, in many cases the users of the escorts are advised to always assume that no escort is available and the service will be provided as scheduling permits. Some programs have addressed this problem by providing a telephone number to call for information regarding an escort.

■ Other Community-Based Programs—An Overview

Community Safe House/Safe Havens

The community safe house is a home in which the occupant has volunteered to receive and assist distressed youth, and in some cases adults, in their home for a short time until police or parents can be contacted to assist them. They go by many names, the best known of which is the McGruff House program. The volunteers in these types of programs must generally undergo some type of a criminal background check and be cleared prior to being allowed to be designated as a safe house. The homes that are approved and designated as safe houses are then issued a sign or insignia that is displayed on the property. The jurisdiction in which the program operates publicizes the program, and the specific insignia that the distressed youth should seek in the event of a problem is described. An awareness campaign in the school usually accompanies the initiation of such a program. Children who are lost, have missed the bus, are being stalked, or find themselves in a host of other distressful situations should seek refuge in the safe house. As part of the program, the resident volunteer agrees to be trained and to adhere to guidelines set forth by the program in handling specific situations. This program is ideal for stay-at-home moms or dads, retired people, and anyone who is frequently at home. The program offers children an opportunity to quickly find a safe haven, and substantially increases the effort of any would-be attacker to accost a child, denies access to the child, and increases the risk that the attacker will be detected as the child runs into the safe haven, where a trained person is apt to witness the attacker and quickly disseminate information to the police concerning the attacker.

Good Neighbor Check-Up

Originally created as a check-up to ensure that senior citizens who lived alone had not fallen or otherwise become incapacitated, this program has since expanded and taken on other forms. The program, usually part of a Neighborhood Watch, involves training individual volunteers to check on the elderly, not only to ensure that they are physically okay, but also to ensure that scam artists are not targeting them. Senior citizens are prime targets for such criminal endeavors, and the victims are often ashamed to report the crime or are unable to break free of the grip that the scam has on them.

This program trains citizens in what specifically to look for and listen for, and how to deal with the senior when they are being victimized. Certain indicators such as large amounts of junk mail, junk trinkets about the home, calls from telemarketers when the volunteer is visiting, and how the senior handles the calls are but a few ways that the citizen may notice the victimization. More tips related to fraud and scams will be addressed in detail in Chapter 9.

The check-up program is often a great service to neighbors. Latchkey children can be called and checked on when their parents are not able to be there when the child arrives home. More and more seniors are residing in the homes of their adult children, and often parents suffering from dementia, Alzheimer's disease, or other incapacities must be left home alone while the adult child works. Seniors suffering from these types of problems may wander away and become confused, and therefore be unable to help others return them home. Good neighbors–type programs give the working child piece of mind, knowing that someone is there to check on their parent. Along the same lines, Project Lifesaver, a relatively new program that helps to quickly recover missing participants, is becoming widely used. This program uses modern global positioning satellites (GPS) to pinpoint the location of a missing participant. The participant wears a transceiver bracelet device that is unique, and the participating agency can use a receiver to find the person. Project Lifesaver is part of an effort by the National Alzheimer's Association to improve the quality of life of patients and their families. The devices have also been used for Down syndrome patients and others with limited mental capacity to prevent them from falling prey to the criminal element.

Citizen Volunteerism

One final community-based approach that really is a part of all of the others is community volunteers. Specifically, I am referring to the volunteer in police service who frees sworn officers to return to the street, not auxiliary or reserve officers, although both of these are of great service. Over the last few years, police chiefs have come to realize that there is a vast resource called citizen volunteers that they are not using. In the past, when the idea was to keep the doors of the police department closed and maintain secrecy at all cost, volunteers never would have been considered. Administrators have finally come to realize that citizens have a right and a desire to be of service in preventing crime. Because of national and state accrediting agency guidelines, many cannot meet the stringent time requirements to become a reserve officer, but they can volunteer a few hours each week. Volunteers can be trained for many tasks. In agencies today, volunteers are serving in the following capacities:

- Staffing information switchboards
- Taking informational reports via telephone

- Filing nonsensitive documents
- Assisting victims in forms completion
- Assisting with victim witness benefits
- Staffing court information booths
- Conducting police department and other tours
- Conducting residential security surveys
- Conducting telephone satisfaction surveys
- Coordinating volunteer/Neighborhood Watch programs
- Serving on citizen advisory boards
- Staffing citizen disciplinary review boards
- Distributing brochures and crime prevention materials
- Conducting crime prevention training seminars

The volunteers are a valuable crime prevention tool in that they free the sworn officer to patrol the streets. Preventative patrol increases the risk that the criminals will be detected and arrested and increases the effort that they must make to accomplish their goal. More officers on the street means more visibility, and thereby crime is deterred. The trained volunteer becomes more acquainted with the internal operations of the agency and is apt to call suspicious activities in to the agency with greater accuracy. The more involved citizens are in the agency, the better the rapport they have with the officers in the agency. Volunteers are much more willing to be active in efforts when they are treated as equals and with the respect due them. A clear indication of that trust is increasing the variety of tasks available to them.

■ Chapter Summary

There is always safety in numbers, and more eyes and ears available to witness events represent an increased potential to detect criminal acts. Community programs that encourage citizen involvement create a sense of caring for neighbors and protection of neighborhood property. These programs emphasize building community cohesiveness and encourage the idea of being "thy brother's keeper" through watching for friends and neighbors. Once the criminal is aware that the community cares, the perceived opportunity decreases and crime is prevented.

■ Review Questions

1. Which of the National Crime Prevention Institute's four D's is increased through the existence of an active Neighborhood Watch?
2. Which crime prevention program extends the passive role of a Neighborhood Watch to an active one?
3. What program might be recommended to address a judge who is overly lenient in the sentencing of serious crimes?
4. What are the three major partners (roles) in a crime stopper program?

■ References

Clarke, Ronald V. 1997. *Situational Crime Prevention—Successful Case Studies* (2nd ed.). Guilderland, NY: Harrow and Heston.

Crime Prevention Campaigns

"Forewarned, forearmed; to be prepared is half the victory."

—Miguel de Cervantes

■ Introduction

Perhaps the most famous crime prevention awareness campaign is that associated with McGruff the Crime Dog. The National Crime Prevention Council (NCPC) works with a number of partners, including the U.S. Department of Justice, the Advertising Council, and the Crime Prevention Coalition. Using McGruff as its symbol, the NCPC's crime prevention campaign is that crime prevention is everyone's business, and it is more than just a matter of security. It emphasizes that crime prevention truly requires a central position in law enforcement and that community collaboration is a must. Awareness campaigns concentrate on public education and tailoring their programs to the served locality. Awareness campaigns may be short lived or, as is the case with the National Citizen's Crime Prevention Campaign, may be ongoing.

The common thread among all crime prevention awareness campaigns is that they are designed to provoke thought and to draw attention to crime and its prevention methods. Such campaigns attempt to plant the seed that crime is a problem that does not discriminate. It is a problem that can happen to anyone. Once the seed is planted, the campaign's effort is geared toward educating people in methods to prevent crime. It is believed that with such heightened awareness, the citizen will be more careful and will implement the strategies of prevention that have been provided. In the case of these campaigns, knowledge truly is power. In 1993, this fact was proven when an evaluation of the advertising efforts of the National Citizen's Crime Prevention Campaign revealed that four out of five adults were familiar with the campaign's public service announcements and nearly one third of these said that they learned from them. Additionally, more than half said that they became more concerned about crime after viewing the advertisements.

■ Targeted Crime Prevention Campaigns

Some campaigns target a specific crime or criminal activity in a locale or specific neighborhood. These targeted campaigns are, as the name implies, not widespread, but are geared at educating a certain area related to a crime problem.

Their Premise and Crime Prevention Application

The rationale behind the targeted campaigns is to saturate a specific area that is suffering from a rash of crime or experiencing an increase in criminal activity in general with information concerning the crime(s) being perpetrated. The saturation thereby increases residents' awareness of these crimes, resulting in their being more attentive to issues related to them.

By saturating only the area experiencing the increase in crime, resources are used much more efficiently. The information can be disseminated quickly to the residents of the area and, because the information is targeted, they are more likely to heed the message as being important to them in particular. Alerting the area to the increased number of crimes and providing descriptions of any known suspects will increase the risk that the suspects will be captured or detected, increase the effort needed for them to continue to carry out their crimes due to prevention efforts, and, due to the attention given the crimes, deny them access to their favored targets.

The Process

Directed or targeted campaigns usually are the result of a crime prevention specialist, community policing officer, investigator, or crime analyst recognizing a trend or pattern of crime in an area. The pattern to be addressed by this type campaign is usually geographic in nature; that is, the criminal activity observed is linked to an isolated geographic area such as a neighborhood, residential district, city quadrant, or the like.

The crime analyst then takes the next step, mapping the area where the criminal activity takes place. Once the target area is clearly identified, the campaign methodology must be decided upon. The steps will vary depending on the method chosen. The following sections detail a few commonly employed methods.

Mass Mailings/Written Information Distribution

If a mass distribution of written information such as brochures or letters is the chosen method, then the practitioner must decide whether to use existing brochures or to develop new ones. He or she must identify how many brochures or letters will be needed and find the resources to print the material. Once the materials issue is settled, the decision on delivery comes into play. If the target area is small, volunteers may distribute the material door to door and emphasize the importance of the residents doing "their part" in preventing the crimes. If a larger area is targeted, the mail may be the best alternative. Often mailing can be timed to coincide with other existing mailings such as water bills or property taxes, and the information may be allowed to be inserted in that mailing. This eliminates the need to identify postage resources and greatly limits the work of the practitioner, but is not likely to be viewed with any urgency by the recipient.

Billboards and Flyers

Some practitioners have taken advantage of relationships with owners of billboards, store marquees, and store bulletin boards to post crime awareness information. This is not as successful as some of the other methods, but when used in conjunction with these other methods, it really drives the message home.

Fax Machine and E-mail Alerts

If the target area is a business district, a fax machine or e-mail alert system is a quick and easy way to distribute information to participating businesses. This is an excellent tool for any number of alerts related to business. This network needs to be established prior to the need because it is a violation of law to send unsolicited facsimiles. Technological advances have made it possible to create a fax or e-mail listserv so that the sender can target a specific group to receive the message. The sender sends the message once to all recipients on the authorized list.

Telephone

The telephone is still a valuable tool for getting the message out. Of course, a lone crime prevention practitioner is not likely to accomplish much by calling each house in the target area. This is an ideal time to use the telephone tree of the Neighborhood Watch (discussed in Chapter 5). Telephone trees are not the only method in which the telephone is used, however. An auto-dialer system that accesses a prepared database of phone numbers and calls them to play a prerecorded message is very helpful in this situation. The most commonly known system of this type is the "Reverse 911" system. If this type of system is used, the practitioner need only prepare the message, isolate the area on the 911 grid, and activate the calling sequence.

Common Problems
Targeted campaigns may displace the criminals to another area, but more often they will choose to change their method or even their crime of choice. Often the changes will be what will ultimately lead to their capture because their abilities are not as developed or as well suited for the new crime. One problem that law enforcement agencies might wish to be prepared for when implementing a targeted campaign is the backlash of community outrage; the targeted area may feel the need to point the finger of blame at the agency for having provided inadequate services to their neighborhood. The agency should always have a response planned in case this occurs.

■ Crime Prevention Media Campaigns
Media campaigns are awareness campaigns that are geared toward heightening the awareness of certain types of crimes or crime in general rather than targeting a certain isolated geographic location. They are by nature broad-based, and are the most efficient way to reach a large audience. Media campaigns are generally divided into two categories: electronic media and printed media. Electronic media include television, radio, videos, and interactive software. Printed media include newspapers, newsletters, advertisements, static Web pages, magazines, and billboards.

Their Premise and the Crime Prevention Application
Through a partnership with electronic or printed media channels or both, crime prevention media campaigns disseminate crime and crime prevention information to their respective audiences.

Considering the law of averages, it is believed that a substantial number of those receiving the message will apply at least some of the information. Some people may become more alert, some may take extra precautions, some may discuss the information with others, and some may apply the prevention tips given. If even a small percentage of those reached apply the tips given and crime is deterred, the program is successful. The potential for large-scale success is enhanced when the message is in the form of a public service announcement (PSA) that is repeated frequently or supported by other media avenues. These programs alert not only the community, but also the criminals that more people are aware of the crime and will be watching. This translates to risk for the criminals and results in their seeing the effort and risk required becoming greater than they can afford to chance. The criminals' choice of crime or target is likely to be influenced by their knowledge of this factor, and thus the crime is averted.

The Process
The first step in the process of a media campaign is to select a crime or crimes to be addressed. This can be an arbitrary selection, but preferably will be based on an identified need. The need may be due to an increase in a particular type of crime or an anticipated increase in criminal activity, such as during a special event or holiday. Once the crime is selected, a media partner or partners must be identified and agree to produce or publish the requested information, PSA, or article.

Electronic Media Partners

If an electronic media partner is being used, they will usually give a time frame for the message, such as a 3-minute or 30-second spot. They will usually agree to assist in the editing and production phases. The crime prevention practitioner must make sure that the message he or she wants to get out is the focal point of the production. If the decision is made to use several different media partners, the practitioner should remember that what plays well on television does not necessarily play well on radio. In other words, it might be better to produce one story for the radio and yet another for television. A public access media partner will likely have more time available to the practitioner; of course, the trade-off is that there is a much smaller audience for a public access station than a network station. After a PSA is completed, the electronic media will most likely use it as filler and play it several times per day, helping to drive home the message.

Printed Media Partners

When using the printed media as a partner, a topic is usually allotted one article, and often that article will be associated with crimes of the type being targeted. In other words, there may be a news article about a purse snatching in a local mall parking lot, and your article may be used for information in that article or it may be a secondary article near the main article. I have found that newspapers in large urban areas with a large general circulation are much less agreeable to partnering with a crime prevention officer than are newspapers in smaller communities, unless one can link the information to a "news" story or a national campaign. See Appendix 6.1 for a list of these national campaigns.

Officers have had to become quite creative to get their message out. My preference is to partner with community newspapers, such as free periodicals that target seniors or parents, and with weekly newspapers. These papers are generally understaffed, and therefore they ask the people submitting the article to draft it themselves. They generally proofread and edit it only as related to grammar and spelling. Most articles I have submitted were published in their entirety. Drafting an article is not as difficult as it might seem. Using a few local crime statistics and tips taken from sources such as this book, one can usually draft a relatively decent article without much effort. A crime prevention officer can often draft one story and use it in a number of publications to get the information out to the community. Some consider submissions to these community newspapers to be a waste of time, but I have found that the readers of these papers are often the people we want to reach. Readers of such papers are often the elderly, the disadvantaged, and young people. Also, some smaller community newspapers have given me the opportunity to produce a series of articles, whereas the large circulation daily papers will generally only publish one article, and then it is edited down to fit the space allocated. The more articles published, the better the possibility of getting the attention of the target audience.

Other Methods of Distribution

Another method of getting crime prevention information to the public is to produce your own newsletter or contribute articles to other newsletters. A newsletter does not have to be long or of a certain format to be effective.

A one-page newsletter inserted into another mailed item, a Web site that is accessed through links from the local government's site, and an e-mail list are inexpensive ways to make crime prevention information available to those seeking it. Another method to get out general information is to place brochures and posters in the buildings that are the site of specific types of crimes. For example, child safety materials might be placed in schools, financial crime information in banks, and vehicle theft information in automobile dealerships. Officers may also distribute information while on related calls to assist in heightening residents' attention to crime.

Common Problems

In that the information in this type of program is broad-based, it may be ignored by many as information not resulting from a crime problem. Another problem experienced is a lack of cooperation by the media, as already discussed. A final complaint among practitioners is that many of the awareness programs overlap with national programs, and as such the local emphasis is lost.

■ Chapter Summary

Awareness campaigns are organized efforts that draw attention to crime and its prevention methods. These campaigns accomplish their prevention goals through education, information sharing, or large-scale media usage. Awareness campaigns may be short term or ongoing. The National Crime Prevention Council works with their partners in an ongoing campaign that asserts that crime prevention requires a central position in law enforcement and that community involvement is essential. Awareness campaigns concentrate on public education and community-tailored service.

■ Review Questions

1. Which type of awareness campaign saturates a specific area that may be suffering from a rash of crime?
2. Of mass mailings or fax machine alert methods, which is most likely to be successful in reaching a business target audience?
3. What is the primary reason for linking a local media campaign to a national campaign or event?

■ References

National Crime Prevention Council. 1993. *Uniting Communities Through Crime Prevention.* Washington, DC.

Preventing Property Crime

*"I have six locks on my door, all in a row, and when I go out I only lock
every other one. Cause I figure no matter how long somebody stands there
and picks the locks, they're always locking three."*

—Elayne Boosler, Comedian

■ Introduction

Property crime makes up about three quarters of all crime in the United States.
Urban households have historically been and continue to be the most vulnerable to property crime, burglary, and motor vehicle theft in the United States.

Based upon statistical data from the year 2004, property crime, regardless
of the type, is more often perpetrated against those living in rental property
(National Crime Victimization Survey, 2004). Just because these crimes are
perpetrated more often on the resident living in rental property does not mean
that the crimes do not have a negative effect on the rest of the populace. The
cost in insurance premium increases and other resources makes this an important issue for everyone, and the prevention of property crime is no less important than the prevention of any other.

In this chapter, property crime prevention will be related to programs that
address the crimes of burglary, larceny, and auto theft. This chapter does not
address the physical "target hardening" per se, but will overview the programs
available for preventing the most common of these property crimes.

The following property crime statistics are from the National Crime Victimization Survey (2004):

- In 2004, households in rented property experienced 201 overall property crimes per 1000 households, whereas those that were owned experienced 143.
- Between 1973 and 2003, rented households were burglarized at rates 56% higher than owned households.
- Households living in rented property had more than twice the rate of motor vehicle theft than those in owned property.
- The western portion of the United States experiences the highest rates of property crime in the nation.

■ Extended Absence Property Check

Often the criminal is seeking an easy mark—one that they know will offer no
resistance and that they feel will ensure that they are undetected by the resident. Any delay in reporting is a positive step toward their success. As such,
experienced criminals know what indicators to seek in choosing their target.

This program is designed to eliminate, or at least reduce, those indicators. This program is actually a service provided by local law enforcement agencies to their citizen constituents to prevent such indicators from being present, and therefore making an absentee resident obvious. A second goal of this program is to educate the citizen about preventative measures to take during future absences.

The Premise

The premise of this service is that if a citizen plans to be absent from his or her property for an extended period of time, he or she notifies the law enforcement agency, which then assigns personnel to spot check the property during the resident's absence. The agency personnel checking the residence endeavor to identify any indicators of absence and remove them as soon as detected. The checks and problems are logged, and the resident is notified of them by some means upon his or her return.

Crime Prevention Application

Advertising this service is the first leg in the application of preventative measures. If the program is well known, the criminal may actually be deterred from choosing targets based on the common indicators. Second, the property checks being conducted by trained individuals should result in the indicators being removed or corrected, thereby making it more difficult for criminals to identify the residence as a potential target (increased effort). With nonroutine spot checks being done by trained personnel, the risk of detection is increased as well. This program also offers a very tangible, efficient use of resources by enabling the agency to direct resources to where they are most needed. Finally, after the resident returns he or she is educated as to indicators found during his or her absence and given recommendations for future absences. Information from the Police Executive Research Forum (1996) and Mawby (2001) indicated that a home that has been burglarized is much more likely to be reburglarized than one that has not been entered. This program allows for quick detection, even in the absence of the resident, and includes measures that can be taken to prevent re-entry.

The Process

This program, like so many others, depends on citizen awareness and use. The first step in the process is to make citizens aware of the availability of the program at no cost to them. This first step may be accomplished as part of a prevention awareness program. The length of time when a property may be checked, and under what conditions, vary with each jurisdiction. Most departments will not check properties during an absence of less than a week, and will not check vacated properties placed on the open market for sale. Some agencies in a resort area may wish to check vacation homes, and others may want to set a maximum property check time period, such as no more than 3 months.

Once the details of the program are settled, a central location for citizens to register for the program should be identified and the telephone number or e-mail address included in all advertisements concerning the program. An ideal contact number is the local law enforcement agency's published public information telephone number. It is important that any person responsible for registering participants understands what each block on the registration form means and to whom the form should be routed. Registration forms can include a variety of information, depending on the needs of each program's coordinator. All forms should include, at a minimum, a contact name and means of contact, length of absence, and the address to be checked. Ideally, one person will receive, log, and assign all property checks. For an example of a property check registration form, see Appendix 7.1.

Trained individuals should complete all assigned property checks. The individuals in some agencies are sworn officers, in others they are civilian employees, and in yet others they are volunteers. The coordinator will be responsible for ensuring that all checks are accounted for and recalled when expired, that any problems are noted, and that the residents are informed of any problems upon return. In order to accomplish this educational piece of the program, some programs have used a duplicate copy of a check form. When using this form, the person checking the residence indicates the date, time, and any problems found. One copy is slipped under the door or placed in a prearranged inconspicuous location while the other is returned to the coordinator for filing and reference. Other programs call for the person who is checking to turn in the checklist at the end of the absence time frame and, upon the individual's return, send the resident a letter with relevant information. Regardless of the chosen means, the educational aspect is an important part of this program. It not only educates, but also confirms that the agency is indeed checking the property.

Common Problems

The most common problem experienced in property check programs is that the properties are not checked properly. In some cases the property is checked in passing and indicated as being thoroughly checked. Unfortunately, this lack of precision is most often discovered when a resident comes home early to find their home burglarized or vandalized and the law enforcement agency has indicated that it was checked after the date of return with no problems. The program can stand few publicized failures such as this.

Another related problem that has been reported occurs when the resident returns home early without notifying the agency, and people are discovered in a home that is supposed to be empty. Embarrassment is the least of the problems in these situations. To avoid this potentially serious problem, the agency should emphasize to the homeowners during registration that they need to notify the agency immediately upon return. This information should also be included on any checked property forms left at the residence.

■ Operation Identification

Operation Identification is a simplistic approach to theft reduction that attempts to make items less attractive to thieves by marking them, which also can assist officers in recovery of the property.

The Premise

Many thieves are motivated by the easy disposal of stolen property. Fencing operations can quickly move stolen property in a variety of ways. Items that cannot be easily identified or traced are top sellers because of this fact. Operation Identification helps to take the profit out of burglaries and other thefts by making the stolen property easier to identify by officers and harder to sell. The property decreases in value to the fence because of the risk it creates for them. If the criminal knows your property is marked, he or she will most likely look elsewhere. It is not worth the trouble and risk.

Crime Prevention Application

This program is one of the few that emphasizes the reduction of reward and denying access to the criminal as the major focus. Items that are marked can be traced to a legitimate owner, so the "honest" citizen, who might otherwise convince him- or herself that everything is legitimate when a super deal on an item comes along, will not even consider purchasing a marked item. Why? Because it can be traced and more easily prosecuted. In other words, the risk is simply too great. This translates to a lack of market for the item, thereby increasing the effort needed to sell the item and decreasing the potential profit. The increase in effort and decrease in profit is so great that the criminal ultimately just leaves the item behind.

The Process

Agencies purchase and make available etching pens or engravers and brochures detailing how to mark the property, and decals to identify would-be thieves that the property is marked. Some law enforcement agencies have etching pens that they give away, others loan electric engravers from the station, and still others offer the engravers on loan through local libraries or other venues. Once the engravers are made available, the citizens are directed to engrave an identification number in a prominent location on the item; some agencies even encourage engraving the number in a second, less obvious place. The desired number to be engraved varies. Some jurisdictions specify that a driver's license number be used; others recommend the person's date of birth and state initials. Regardless of what's chosen, it should be a unique number that the owner can easily remember. The number should be engraved on a nonremovable part of the property if possible. Because the property is marked, it should be entered on an inventory list. Such a detailed list will aid the owner, the owner's insurance company, and the police department in the event of a theft.

Valuable property that may be marked includes guns, radios, cameras, CD players, DVD players, kitchen appliances, tools, lawn mowers, and stereos, to name a few. Items that don't lend themselves to marking, such as antiques, heirlooms, artwork, and jewelry, are treated differently. Some officers recommend photographing and recording such items in the inventory list as an alternative to marking them. Within the past 10 years, however, a new, high-tech alternative has emerged that is safe for these items, and will not mar the property. Identification Technologies has produced a product called DataDots, a microdot embedded with a unique alphanumeric code. DataDots are applied with a brush, and once applied cannot be removed. The microdots are only the size of a grain of sand, and can be read by law enforcement with a special reader. The unique code is entered into a special database that is included in the kit and can serve as your own property list file as well. This product has been used in the United Kingdom for some years and has experienced great success in deterring theft. It is heat resistant, so it has been a great deterrent in reducing motorcycle thefts in which parts were removed and sold separately. Identification Technologies boasts that in communities in which the product is introduced, theft reduction rates of up to 90% have been realized within 6 months (personal communication with Kyle Claringbold, Identification Technologies).

Common Problems

The most commonly experienced problems with Operation Identification are the lack of education concerning the program, the difficulty in making marking tools and decals available, and ultimately the lack of follow-through by property owners to actually mark and record their items. It becomes one of those things people had planned to do but never did. Most jurisdictions provide information concerning the program via brochures in information kiosks or by request, but really fail to make an impact by not educating groups and publicizing the program.

Police departments sometimes offer engravers for loan, but this also limits the success of the program because there is a limited number of engravers so they are not as easily available as they could be. To resolve this issue, agencies have purchased numerous engravers and placed them, along with engraving information, in libraries to be loaned to anyone with a library card. Others have taken them to Neighborhood Watch meetings and, after providing an informational presentation about the program, made them available for loan for a 2-week or more period of time. I am also aware of some insurance agencies making etching pens available free for distribution in such a program. I personally worked with the Allstate Foundation to make such pens available as part of a larger educational program. To combat the lack of follow-through, volunteers or agency personnel sometimes mark the property for residents.

Another method of following up is to provide storage of property records for the participants in Operation Identification. This ensures that at least some information is documented if an item is stolen, and encourages the owner to follow through and mark the property.

■ Bicycle/Moped Registration Programs

This program is quite similar to Operation Identification, except that in this case the items are registered using the serial number and description and, in some cases, the owners are provided a registration form to prove ownership and a license plate for display. Why a special program just for these items? Approximately 1.5 million bicycles are stolen annually, and less than 3% of those are returned (www.nationalbikeregistry.com). The use of mopeds is a growing trend and, as such, similar theft issues are being seen. Many of my colleagues in the security field are also anticipating the rising gasoline prices to result in more use of bicycles and mopeds and thus increased theft potential.

The Premise

The rationale behind this program is to address the inability of owners to identify their property when recovered and to make the items less desirable for theft. In areas where theft is prevalent, a quick paint job could easily render a bicycle or moped usable by a thief. The registration program creates an opportunity to heighten awareness of the theft issue. The program also enhances the possibility of recovery and return of the item to the rightful owner, thereby reducing the motivation for theft of such items.

Crime Prevention Application

This program is successful primarily because it denies the thief the ability to use the item and reduces his or her reward by making it more difficult to use or sell the property as legitimate. When a local ordinance requires that mopeds or bicycles display a license plate issued by the locality, the risk of theft detection increases. With a license plate requirement, the thief may be forced to bring along another plate to replace the one on the stolen item. This creates an additional effort and represents a delay that just may result in the capture of the criminal.

The Process

Bicycles are registered in a number of different ways. There is a National Bike Registry program in which a bicycle owner may register his or her bike for $1 per year in a national database. Go to the National Bike Registry Web site for more information.

In order to require registration for bicycles or mopeds, a local ordinance requiring the display must be passed. Once the ordinance is implemented, officers may use the absence of the registration decal or plate as probable cause to stop the vehicle for further inquiry. The typical local bike/moped registration program uses the following steps:

1. The owner must bring his or her bicycle/moped to a location or event to have it registered.
2. The bicycle/moped description, including brand, size, color, serial number, and other identifying markings, is entered into a computerized database (local or networked).
3. The name, address, and contact telephone number of the owner is entered into the database along with the above descriptors, and the registration number is assigned. In some cases a metal license plate is issued; in others a durable rip-resistant decal is applied. This decal should be of a quality that makes it difficult to remove, and if removed, removes some of the paint or at least leaves a heavy residue. When issued, the plate or decal must be displayed in the same way on all bikes or mopeds. This allows officers to quickly look for the marking; therefore, the location should be

clearly visible without requiring the officer to manipulate the bike/moped in any way to view the number.

4. In some cases, a digital photograph of the bicycle/moped is taken and inserted into the database.

5. A copy of the recorded information is often printed and given to the owner to serve as the registration form. It also provides the owner all of the information needed for a report and entry into the National Crime Information Center computer if the bicycle/moped is stolen.

Common Problems

Officer apathy in checking the untagged bicycles or mopeds presents the most problematic issue in seeing success with such a registration program. Usually once officers realize that this program is yet another tool leading them to additional criminal activity they tend to warm up to the use of the program. I have heard officers state that they had stopped a person for riding an unregistered moped and found that the person was wanted for other crimes.

Another problem experienced in this program is obtaining compliance. This program is especially successful in campus settings, primarily because of the school's strict enforcement of the requirement to register. Other agencies would most likely overcome their compliance issue as well if they took a similar stance.

Maintenance and accessibility of the database information by officers in the field is sometimes a problem. Our agency used the in-house computer network to allow all authorized persons to read the information but not edit it. Police dispatchers can check the information and relay it to the field if a synchronized field computer system is not in place to allow officers to access the information from the field on a laptop computer.

■ Automobile Theft Prevention

Professional thieves have the ability to steal the average car with little trouble. To protect their car, citizens must take extra steps to make theft more difficult and to reduce the opportunity for such thefts. The level of auto theft in your area may depend on where you reside in the country. In 2002, those living in western regions of the United States experienced more property crime, including auto theft, than other regions. Urban environments accounted for more of the crimes than did suburban areas, and those people living in rental properties had more than twice the rate of auto theft as those residing in owned properties. Of the vehicle thefts attempted, about 77% were completed (U.S. Department of Justice, Bureau of Justice Statistics, 2004). Motor vehicle theft is the costliest of all property crimes in the United States. More than 1.2 million vehicles are stolen annually, and it is estimated that an automobile thief strikes every 25 seconds.

The Premise

The majority of auto thefts are not perpetrated by professional car thieves, but rather by opportunists. In fact, joy riders account for a large percentage of vehicle thefts. Therefore, auto theft prevention programs are directed at removing the opportunity and hardening the target.

Crime Prevention Application

Target hardening techniques included in this program are designed to increase the effort required by the thief. The detection and tracking of stolen vehicles using technology certainly is apt to increase the risk that the criminal will be caught and therefore deter the theft. Use of certain devices deny access, delay the theft, and remove the reward of the use of the vehicle.

The Process

Most of these programs concentrate on three areas:

1. Educating owners to use common sense techniques
2. Making the target difficult to successfully steal through use of security devices
3. Ensuring quick recovery

There are numerous auto theft prevention programs, so they will be listed and discussed separately in this section.

Education

Opportunist criminals often seek the easiest target, not necessarily the most desirable. Most educational programs concentrate on teaching citizens about the opportunities that criminals look for. Brochures and presentations are often built around the following:

- Take your keys with you, even when just running into the store to "pick up one item."
- Don't leave your car running unattended to "warm up," using a popular device that's now available called a remote starter. A locked door poses little difficulty to most thieves.
- Do not hide a second set of keys in or on your car.
- Park in well-lighted areas.
- Park in attended lots, when possible.
- Leave only an unmarked ignition key with valet or parking attendants.
- Lock your car even when it's parked in your garage, and lock the garage door.
- Park with your wheels turned toward the curb when you must park on the street.
- Avoid leaving your car unattended in public parking lots for extended periods of time.
- If your car has electronic coded keys, use them.
- Just as you ask to have your home watched when out of town, include information about watching your vehicle(s).
- Secure motorcycles and ATVs to a fixed object with a heavy chain and padlock.

Some jurisdictions drive home their point of removing the opportunity by assessing sanctions against vehicle owners who fail to comply. For example, South Carolina law prohibits motorists from leaving cars running unattended, punishable by a fine. The city of Charleston, South Carolina, went even farther by increasing the fine to get the attention of motorists. Some of the attention received was not favorable, but the educational value cannot be argued. See the following article from *The Charleston Post and Courier* (Smith, 2003):

> ### Deter Auto Theft, but Fairly
>
> *Charleston law-enforcement authorities understandably want car owners to take sensible precautions against auto theft. But that doesn't justify draconian fines against those who leave their cars unattended and unlocked with the engine running.*
>
> *Though the police should be able to enforce the law against that risky practice, their primary target in stemming the rising tide of car thefts in the city of Charleston should be the thieves, not the victims. Though a small fine is in order for those who foolishly boost local stolen-auto statistics by making the criminal act all too easy, severe financial punishment seems unreasonable.*
>
> *The state law prohibiting motorists from leaving cars unattended with the engine running carries a fine of $93. A Charleston municipal ordinance prohibiting motorists from*

*leaving cars stopped and running for more than five minutes unless blocked by traffic carries
a fine of $240.*

*Surely there's a fairer way to encourage car owners to better block auto theft. What's
next? Heavy fines for leaving your house door unlocked or your house windows open?*

*Sgt. David Fair, an auto theft investigator with the City of Charleston Police Depart-
ment, told* The Post and Courier's *Glenn Smith that the fines for leaving cars running were
necessary because "some people don't learn unless they learn the hard way."*

*Clearly, motorists who don't use common sense to protect their property against car
thieves give the police a harder job. Police estimate that a quarter of the auto thefts in
Charleston last year were facilitated by motorists leaving the keys in the cars. As Sgt. Fair
explained, "These are crimes of opportunity, and if you decrease the opportunity, thieves are
not going to have much chance to steal a car in that fashion."*

*Certainly the opportunity for easy auto theft should be decreased, bringing with it a
decrease in the workload for police investigating that crime and a decrease in the dangers
associated with it, including the potential of high-speed chases. The 3,000 fliers distributed
by police, warning that it is "negligent, dangerous and illegal" to leave cars running, should
help spread an important message.*

*Still, there should be a more prudent limit on the legal penalty paid by those who risk
what is, after all, their own property.*

Reproduced by permission of The Charleston Post and Courier, *from an article originally
published Friday, January 31, 2003*

Auto Theft Security Devices

Security devices can be divided into two categories, those that are observable or detectable
by thieves and those that are less obvious but in effect disable the vehicle's ignition.
Devices in the first category include the following:

- *Audible alarms*—Anti-theft alarm systems can be installed on a vehicle and can be
  wired to go off if any door, hood, or trunk is opened and to detect any movement of
  the car. Their deterrent effect has been largely compromised because they are usually ignored as just another false alarm.

- *Steering wheel locks*—These devices can be installed quickly and are quite effective.
  An added plus is that they prevent the theft of the air bag, which is becoming a popular theft item.

- *Steering collar locks*—These are a shield that locks around the steering columns to
  prevent access to the switch, and therefore deters "hot wiring."

- *Brake locks*—These locks add another level of locking protection that must be overcome to move the vehicle easily.

- *Wheel locks*—These are similar to a "police boot" used to immobilize vehicles. Due
  to their cumbersomeness, use of these devices generally is limited to extended
  parking.

- *Window etching*—In this process, all glass on the vehicle is etched with the car's
  vehicle identification number (VIN), targeting those who would remove or replace
  the VIN plate.

- *Laminated glass*—This type of glass is much more difficult to break to enter a vehicle, and may be used as another level of preventative protection.

Disabling devices are generally found only on the most expensive vehicles, primarily
because of the related cost to install and use such products. Some devices that disable the
vehicle are as follows:

- *Smart keys*—These keys are equipped with a microchip built into the head of the
  key that must be recognized before the lock will activate.

- *High security locks and keys*—These are great tools, but as mentioned earlier the biggest problem is the lack of use.
- *Starter, ignition, and fuel disablement switches*—These are generally hidden, and cut power to the starter, ignition, or fuel pump when activated.

Auto Retrieval/Recovery

Although retrieval programs/systems may seem more like an investigative tool than a proactive or preventative one, consider what effect the knowledge that an area or vehicle is served by some type of retrieval system will have on a criminal's choice of targets. When an area is served by a program that pays for tips concerning stolen autos, chop shops, or crime rings, the risk is indeed perceived to be greater. These programs, such as Help Eliminate Auto Theft (HEAT) and Combat Auto Theft (CAT), not only assist in the recovery of stolen vehicles, but also contribute indirectly to preventing future similar crimes. Their success is proven by the fact that they are often supported by the insurance industry, which finds it much more beneficial to pay for tips and advertisements than to pay for stolen cars. Using global positioning systems (GPS), stolen vehicles are quickly located and recovered. Vehicles with decals advertising this program affixed to them are less attractive targets.

Common Problems

I agree with the Charleston Police Department that the most common of all problems is that individuals rarely recognize the harm done to the entire community by not securing their own vehicles. Use of any of the listed programs will reduce the opportunity for auto theft to occur; consider the effect that several of the techniques will have overall on auto theft in your area. The number of auto thefts can be drastically reduced if crime prevention practitioners can convince their community of the need to take some level of action to remove the opportunity.

■ Graffiti Vandalism

Graffiti is more than just a spray-painted wall; it is an act of vandalism that costs hundreds of thousands of dollars to remove or cover every year. If not quickly removed, graffiti could lead to additional crimes and even acts of violence. Accumulated graffiti sends a message that the businesses or residents are not in control and care little about the activities in the community. This message translates to criminals that the area is ripe for their illegitimate use. It has been properly stated that graffiti begets graffiti. Not only does one unattended piece of graffiti result in more, it often also brings with it littering, loitering, and other more serious crimes. Property values are reduced in areas where graffiti is prevalent.

Graffiti done without the owner's permission is a crime, and needs to be dealt with quickly. Unfortunately, like many forms of vandalism, it often goes unreported and untreated.

The Premise

Graffiti prevention/intervention programs presuppose that the graffiti vandal is motivated by a reward of notoriety. One form of notoriety is personal notoriety, as in the case of a tagger whose primary goal is to gain prestige by display of his or her artwork. A second form of notoriety is territorial or challenge notoriety, as in that of a street gang. Yet another form is idealistic notoriety, which is gained by a person espousing his or her brand of ideals, such as a hate group might involve themselves in. Regardless of the motivation, most graffiti vandals seek notoriety; therefore, the best prevention method is one that robs them of that which they seek. This is usually accomplished through programs that force the removal of the graffiti, remove the instruments of the crime from those most often responsible, remove the opportunity to revisit the most popular targets, and redirect the individuals to legitimate sources of notoriety.

Crime Prevention Application

The primary focus of graffiti prevention programs is to remove the reward (notoriety) sought by the vandal. Prevention programs also concentrate on making the property less attractive by improving the surveillance in the area, thereby increasing the risk of detection. Some programs take the opposite road, and by addressing the environment make it difficult to get to the desired property (wall), thereby denying the vandal access and increasing the effort.

The Process

In order to remove the rewards sought by the vandal, many jurisdictions have adopted a graffiti ordinance that compels owners of vandalized property to report the graffiti to the police. In fact, this is the most successful means of addressing graffiti vandalism. In some cases, the jurisdiction takes responsibility for removing the graffiti; in others, the owner is held responsible for the removal. A typical time frame for removal in such ordinances is 24 to 48 hours. Another means employed to ensure that notoriety is not gained is by having police or volunteer monitors frequently check favored areas for graffiti, report it, and have it removed, often within hours of the application. This quick removal of graffiti has seen more success than other programs. Painting over the graffiti is the most common method of removal; however, other forms of removal exist, including cleaning with chemicals, sandblasting, and pressure washing. In order to ensure the proper treatment is used, victims are usually referred to a painting professional or provided with a list of items that may be tried.

Some properties lend themselves to targeting by graffiti vandals more than others because of the environment. Prevention programs often encourage such locations to address the environmental issues to reduce the opportunity that they might be targeted. Some environmental recommendations may include the following:

- Keep the property clean and well maintained.
- If others can see the property, increase the lighting around the property.
- If people do not use the area regularly, install motion detector lights where possible.
- Plant clinging vegetation near the surface and encourage the vines to climb.
- Have a painting professional apply a sacrificial or protective coating to the surface. Such a coating is a silicon-based product that allows paint applied to the surface to be removed without removing the entire coating.

The following list identifies various methods for removing graffiti applied to different surfaces. Some of the products may be toxic and require special protective equipment when using. Consult a painting professional before using any of the following products:

- *Wood siding*—Apply a stain-killing primer to seal the graffiti and prevent it from showing through the new paint. Repaint the surface with a matching color.
- *Brick, cement, or concrete*—Use extra-strength paint remover or graffiti remover. Apply with a wire brush and allow it to dry, then pressure wash the surface.
- *Stucco*—Use paint remover and wash off with a high-pressure water hose.
- *Metal, aluminum siding, or fiberglass*—Use carburetor cleaner. Then use paint thinner and rinse.

Another prevention method that has seen some success is controlling the instrumentation of the crime, or the paint. Since 1980, Chicago has had a ban on the sale of spray paint to minors. In other states it is illegal for a minor to possess such items that may be used in graffiti vandalism. Although this method may increase the effort for the vandal to carry out his or her crime, it is best used as part of a larger prevention effort. Curfew enforcement programs also may contribute to the success of a graffiti prevention program. Sanctions that either require graffiti vandals to pay fines that are used to clean up graffiti or assign them to community service to force them to physically clean the graffiti are another method used in some jurisdictions. Such graffiti abatement projects may be more successful when using volunteer youths who have not offended in such a manner. I experienced a positive result as part of a "clean-up day" that addressed a number of vandalized properties with the use of volunteer youths. The youths involved expressed pride in what they had accomplished, and some stated that they would turn anyone in who painted graffiti on their work. Other jurisdictions have used their Crime Stoppers program to provide a means for anonymous tipsters to give information on such crimes.

Common Problems

Obtaining support to enact an ordinance for the removal of graffiti, for prohibiting minors from obtaining spray paint and markers, and for other graffiti-related crimes is problematic because many legislators do not understand the seriousness of the crime. The practitioner pushing for an ordinance should do his or her research, have the crime analyst map the occurrences of the crime, and share the economic impact as well as the criminal impact when seeking support for an ordinance. The practitioner should use the information to target repeat sites for an environmental assessment. A holistic approach that includes both education and active environmental assessments is needed to begin to address this type of crime problem.

■ Arson Prevention

Arson is unlawful intentional fire setting without permission of the owner of a property. This may seem like a crime that should be addressed by the fire marshal and fire prevention unit of a local fire department, but in some cases no such units exist. Therefore, I have provided this brief section to address fire prevention from an educational standpoint.

The Premise

The premise behind arson prevention, like other prevention programs, is to address the opportunity to commit the crime. As with crime, three elements must be present for a fire to be ignited—oxygen, heat or a source of ignition, and fuel. Combine the elements required to generate fire with those required for a crime, and it becomes clear that in order to prevent the crime of arson one must remove the opportunity for the fire setter to bring together the three elements needed to generate fire, while also addressing the environment sought by such a criminal to carry out the crime.

Crime Prevention Application

The crime prevention application in this crime is no different than for others. The efforts are focused on increasing the perceived risk of capture or detection of the arsonist; removing the reward, which often is done by using quick fire suppression techniques; and delaying the crime by increasing the effort needed for the arsonist to be successful.

The Process

Arsonists can be divided into several categories. Some are considered delinquent or mischievous, some are categorized as seeking attention, and still others are considered pathological arsonists. Very few arsonists fall under the latter category; the majority fall under the first two, so most prevention is focused at preventing their crimes.

Fire prevention practitioners often emphasize the safety aspect first. Their programs educate citizens on safe practices such as having an escape plan, staying low when moving through a smoky room, and so on. One program that is safety related but also addresses the motivation of the arsonist is the fire and smoke detector giveaway program that some agencies have in place. Using such a device quickly alerts residents to a fire and thus results in quicker suppression of the fire, thereby removing the reward sought by the arsonist.

One program that addresses opportunity arsonists involves educating the public about securing the elements that would be needed for a fire. Statistically, most fires are set using matches, lighters, and fuel found near or around the home or target. Removing or securing such items increases the effort, and the arsonist is forced to bring his or her own fuel. Chemicals such as gasoline and paint thinner are often used because of their quick ignition and easy access. Prevention programs emphasize that the property owner can do his or her part to prevent arson by doing the following:

- Secure flammable material safely.
- Dispose of garbage, leaves, lumber, and other flammable items properly.
- Report any smoke or fires.
- Consider installing an audible fire/smoke alarm system.
- Install smoke detectors and change the batteries once a year.
- Keep matches and lighters out of reach of young children.
- Develop and practice a home fire escape plan.
- Keep emergency numbers handy.
- Do not allow any exit to become blocked with clutter.
- If there is a fire in your area, report any suspicious persons or activities that you may have observed.

Arsonists, like other criminals, typically prefer to start fires in locations that are secluded or hidden. Prevention programs often suggest improving the surveillance in these areas by lighting the area, removing visual obstructions to natural observation, and moving the targets, if the targets are movable, such as dumpsters. The risk is often too great to the arsonist to start a fire in a more visible location, and such a location is also more apt to be quickly detected and suppressed.

Practitioners also emphasize the need for preventative education by parents and other responsible adults, because the majority of arson fires are started by one of the youth categories mentioned earlier. Parents are encouraged to teach children about fire safety and the dangers of using matches, lighters, and candles.

Common Problems

The most prevalent problem in arson prevention programs is the lack of staff to conduct educational programs. Often fire departments are staffed mainly by volunteers, and therefore the information is not carried to the community by the staff. Some departments have found success in distributing printed materials to Boy and Girl Scout leaders, teachers, and crime prevention partners so that they can present the information to youth and community groups.

■ Burglary Prevention

Burglary is often considered one of the most serious of the property crimes because of the privacy invasion that generally occurs. As stated previously, urban households are the most vulnerable to property crime in general. Between 1973 and 2003, those residing in rental properties experienced a 56% higher burglary rate than owner-occupied homes (U.S. Department of Justice, Bureau of Justice Statistics, 2004). What do those statistics mean to a city? Consider that all cities are by their nature an urban environment, and therefore more susceptible to property crime; add to that the fact that many urban areas are made up of substantially rental units, and one quickly sees the need for a viable burglary prevention program. This fact was driven home when I was given a socioeconomic trend breakdown of the Roanoke Valley in which I work. Of the two counties, one town, and two cities in the valley, only the City of Roanoke had any public housing units, and it is believed that only Roanoke had any Habitat for Humanity units. As of the 2000 Census, the City of Roanoke had 44% of residents in the city who were renters. That translates to 44% of the residents of the city being potential burglary victims. Based on the national statistical data related to burglary in 2004, property stolen was valued at $1642 per offense (on average), 62% of the residential burglaries occurred between 6:00 a.m. and 6:00 p.m., and about 32% of the entries were gained without the use of force (U.S. Department of Justice, Bureau of Justice Statistics, 2004).

The Premise

Armed with the above information and local statistics, one can recognize that any burglary prevention program will address the location, the times, and the victims through education and target hardening. Because hardening the target, which in essence is the primary crime prevention program related to burglary, will be discussed in detail later in the book, in this section I concentrate on providing detailed information concerning the selection of targets by burglars. This section emphasizes the education approach in an effort to change the mindset and behaviors of the victim.

Crime Prevention Application

As with any other educational prevention program, this one depends on the target audience heeding the warning. A reduction in the crime's opportunity requires a change in behaviors of the would-be victim. Opportunity reduction can be addressed using many of the techniques listed throughout this text. Effort will be increased by the citizen's adoption of the behaviors taught; the behaviors will result in delays by the criminal in gaining entry; perceived risk should be increased by enhancing the detection possibilities; property owners' use of existing security devices aid in denying access to the rewards sought; and therefore, the crime for this property is deterred. This may seem like a lot to be accomplished simply by modifying the behavior of a property owner, but when one considers that in 41% of the burglaries entry was gained without force, it is easy to see how just a few behavioral modifications may reduce the potential for being burglarized.

The Process

This program can be initiated by anyone—civilian employee, crime prevention practitioner, volunteer, or street officer. It is a simple three-step process:

1. Obtain burglary prevention tips from a knowledgeable source in prevention. This is easily done by using information offered in this section or contacting one of the state crime prevention associations, the National Crime Prevention Council, or another agency that specializes in the prevention of crime, many of which are listed in the Resources section of this book.
2. Identify a venue for presenting the information. Suggest that local Neighborhood Watch meetings, tenant council meetings, media campaigns, or written tips in a brochure format are viable options.
3. Fully educate yourself as to local and national statistics to drive home the point, and make the presentations. National statistics are available from the Bureau of Justice Statistics and other Web sites, and local data may be available from your crime analyst.

As mentioned previously, this program concentrates on the educational aspect of preventing burglaries, with the goal being to modify behaviors. A more holistic approach would include the option of having a physical security survey or a security assessment conducted of the home or business. Such programs are discussed in chapter 13 in the context of using target hardening and environmental changes as a foundation for creating a target that is well beyond the acceptable risk and effort levels of the average criminal.

Much research has been conducted to identify the favored signs that a burglar seeks when selecting a target. You should not limit yourself to other people's research. I have found that once a career burglar is finally caught with substantial offenses, local prosecutors are not apt to want to spend the additional time and effort in adding punishment that is a moot point because of the existing charges. This provides the resourceful detective or officer an opportunity to give the burglar a "free ride" on the remaining burglaries that he or she confesses to if he or she provided details as to (1) how they committed the crime, and (2) where any of the stolen articles may be recovered. I have gained a great deal of insight of our local burglars through just such an effort.

When providing tips to prevent burglary, or any other type of crime for that matter, it is helpful to identify a shortened version of the tips that overviews what you will present in detail and to reinforce the presentation through a brief written handout. This will help ensure the retention of the information.

An example of the short overview might be: "Burglary can be prevented by using a three-L strategy: (1) Look out for suspicious activity and report it; (2) Lock up your house and outbuildings; and (3) Light up the perimeter of your home to improve surveillance by neighbors." Some general burglary prevention tips taken from research and based on victim behaviors are as follows:

- Use the existing locks on windows and doors. Most burglars are looking for an easy mark—don't give it to them. Pay special attention to the back and sides of the property that are less visible to passersby and are often preferred entry points.
- Change the locks on new residences and newly constructed houses. Prior residents may have loaned keys to others, and most construction crews use a standardized lockset that they can easily obtain a key for, if they don't already have a copy. In commercial applications, the contractor generally uses one lock during construction and changes all lock cores prior to turning the completed building over to the new owner.
- Secure your outbuildings, tools, and garage when absent, and encourage your neighbors to do so also. Most opportunistic burglars find the instruments they need to facilitate the entry at or near the victim's property.
- Start or join Neighborhood Watch.
- Report suspicious activity any time, day or night; almost half the burglaries reported occur during the daytime hours.
- Pay attention to suspicious activities by people who may reside in the area as well. Burglars like convenience, and often commit their crimes near their own residence.
- If you have been burglarized, promptly address any entry points or vulnerable areas identified to you by the police and alert your neighbors. Previously burglarized houses are four times more likely to be burglarized again, potentially within 6 weeks of the first burglary.
- Participate in Operation Identification or other similar programs and mark your valuables.
- Store valuable items away from the "usual locations." Most burglars spend only a few minutes in the home and the first stop is the master bedroom, where they know most people store their cash, jewelry, firearms, and other desired items.
- When absent, ensure your house looks occupied. If your jurisdiction offers an extended absence property check program, take advantage of it during any extended absence. Otherwise, have your newspaper and mail delivery stopped, or

ask a friend to pick up the mail. You can also use a timer to give the impression that lights are being turned on and off.

- When possible, vary your routine. As stated previously, many burglars reside in your neighborhood and can easily monitor you for routine extended absences, work hours, and routes home.

Common Problems

As one might imagine, the prevailing factor affecting the success of this type of program is the willingness, or lack thereof, of citizens to implement the recommended behavioral changes. It is incumbent upon the person initiating the program to demonstrate success through use of such practices and to sell the community on the idea of their responsibility to assist in preventing burglaries by undertaking the changes put forth.

■ Larceny Prevention

Larceny is generally defined as the taking of one person's property by another with the intention to permanently deprive the owner of the property or its use. Depending upon the value of the property, it is classified as either a felony or a misdemeanor. Of the 14 million property thefts in 2004, 4.1 million involved the taking of items valued at less than $50 (U.S. Department of Justice, Federal Bureau of Investigation, 2004). Typically, larceny does not involve breaking into a building, although in some jurisdictions some outbuildings or sheds may be included under the title of larceny. In this section we will concentrate on the crime of larceny that includes larceny from individuals, cars, workplaces, and certain other locations where someone might enter and commit theft without forcing entry. Shoplifting and other such types of theft specifically related to business will be covered under business crime in Chapter 8. Although not all specific locations will be covered, many of the techniques discussed apply to a multitude of environments. As with the burglary discussion, this section will also concentrate on the educational aspect of removing the opportunity rather than the environmental or physical security aspect.

Premise

Of all the crimes, larceny is perhaps the most opportunity-driven one. Larceny is the result of a person with both the desire and the ability to steal being provided with an opportunity that is much too tempting to resist. Yes, the victim is a large contributor to many of these crimes. Larceny prevention programs rely heavily on educating the public and obtaining their cooperation in reducing the opportunity. Based upon honesty survey data, it has been estimated that as many as 80% to 85% of people would steal if presented the right circumstances and given the opportunity. This clearly indicates the need to remove the opportunity from even the relatively honest people in society. Larceny prevention aims to do that by teaching others what presents an opportunity to steal, and then giving tips on how to avoid presenting such opportunities.

Crime Prevention Application

The overwhelming motivating factor for this opportunity thief is the rewards that he or she seeks. Therefore, the larceny prevention program naturally focuses on removing the rewards and denying the thief access to this reward. This thief is generally an opportunist who is apt to be discouraged from his or her crime by increased risk and effort factors. Anything that might result in the possibility of detection is apt to prevent this crime.

The Process

Crime prevention practitioners find that gaining compliance with their suggestions about larceny is very difficult. They prepare and distribute brochures with tips on how to avoid theft, present seminars, and even build awareness campaigns around the idea of larceny prevention, but still are often ignored until the crime has occurred. Once victimized, the victim seems to practice the techniques suggested earlier. One successful technique that some practitioners have employed is what I refer to as "compelled prevention." This is a program in which the practitioner approaches businesses, schools, and other locations with statistical analyses of thefts that occurred at their location and demonstrates to them how carelessness led to most of these occurrences. If it can be determined, the practitioner may even identify company-owned property that was stolen because of the opportunities presented. For example, in recent years, company laptops have been targeted frequently because of their portability and high demand. After providing the statistical information, the practitioner can encourage the company to provide lockable desks, lockers, or cabinets to the employees and compel them to use them by drafting a security policy. A selling point for this program is that the increased security can often lead to insurance premium reductions. In some cases, a law enforcement agency may even provide a model policy for use by the company or school. Included in the policy should be the following security-related tips:

- All company property used by individuals should be inventoried and marked, and any theft resulting from the employee's carelessness charged to the employee for replacement.
- Only authorized employees or persons with written, signed authorization may remove property from the business.
- Lockers will be provided to all employees and must be used to secure all personal valuables such as purses, jewelry, or other items when not directly in the possession of the employee. If it is not locked up, it will be considered unattended. Such items left unattended will result in the employee receiving censure in the form of a reprimand. More than one reprimand may result in disciplinary action.
- No repairperson not regularly assigned to a work area shall be permitted to work unattended in that area. All employees shall be responsible for reporting unattended persons to management or security or for approaching them to inquire as to their business and accompany them to their business location.
- Any property found on the premises shall immediately be turned in to a location designated by the business, and the property logged in on a document to identify when it was found, where it was found, and by whom it was found, as well as witnesses and the name of the party completing the log.
- Any canteen operating on the honor system will provide a secured payment container that will be emptied regularly, no less than daily.
- In order to keep costs down, office supplies should be inventoried and assigned out as needed to employees by request. This provides an audit of any person using more supplies than obviously needed, and reduces pilferage.

Larceny from residents is generally related to items taken while the person is out in public, or those taken from inside the home by acquaintances of the victim. Larceny prevention techniques outside of the business or organizational arena are much more difficult to influence. We must once again rely upon good common sense, which is often not so common anymore. Presentations and brochures are most often used to encourage citizens to employ the tips given to prevent theft. Some success has been seen by encouraging the Neighborhood Watch to remind residents when they observe larceny opportunities, but in the end it is the citizens themselves who must decide to use the techniques. Tips to include in brochures or presentations include the following:

- When in restaurants or public places, never leave purses, cellular phones, or other valuables unattended or out of your sight.

- Close your purse or bag if your wallet or other valuable items are within view inside.
- If you check your coat in a public place, do not leave any valuables in it. Although this sounds like an obvious tip, many people actually leave their cellular phones or jewelry in the pockets of checked items to avoid having to keep watch over the items.
- Park your vehicle in a well-lighted area, remove or conceal all valuables from view, and lock the vehicle. I conducted an experiment with a television news crew once in a mall parking lot and discovered numerous vehicles with valuables in clear view and left unlocked or with the windows down. One vehicle had a checkbook, cash, and a cellular phone left in plain view on the console. Such carelessness is far too tempting for a criminal to pass up.
- Secure all bicycles with at least a cable lock; a steel "U-lock" is preferred. When using a cable lock, ensure the cable passes through both wheels and around the frame and is secured to a fixed object when not in use in public. Remember to register bicycles. (See the section on bicycle registration earlier in the chapter.)
- Secure all outbuildings, garages, sheds, and tools when not in use. Power tools are easily resold on the street and may not be discovered missing for some time. In order to assist in their return, mark them as described in the section of this chapter discussing Operation Identification.
- When at home, don't share information about valuables that you may have in the home, display them, or tell their locations to persons whom you do not know well or trust.

Common Problems

As alluded to earlier, the major factor that leads to the lack of success in larceny prevention programs is the apathy of the would-be victims. Stringent education and compelling compliance with prevention techniques are the only ways to address this problem. The larcenies mentioned in this section are some very common types of larcenies. Others, such as thefts from construction sites and transport trailers, pose further issues that must be examined as part of the business crime prevention setting (see Chapter 8).

■ Chapter Summary

Property crimes make up the majority of all crimes in the United States. Urban households are the most vulnerable to property crime, burglary, and motor vehicle theft. The methods used to prevent theft or damage caused by a property criminal must address the desired outcome of the criminal. Once the motive of the criminal is identified, the appropriate technique of prevention may logically be chosen.

■ Review Questions

1. What property crime prevention program endeavors to reduce the criminal's use of or ability to sell stolen property by marking it and making it more traceable?
2. What type of criminal commits the majority of the auto thefts in the United States?
3. Why are disabling devices generally found on the most expensive vehicles?
4. What is the maximum number of hours that are recommended for graffiti to be left on property before being removed?
5. Do rental properties or owner-occupied homes experience more burglaries?

■ References

Chmura Economic & Analytics. 2000. *Vital Signs of the New Century Region*. 5th Planning District Regional Alliance and U.S. Bureau of Census, Roanoke, VA.

Mawby, R. 2001. *Burglary*. Cullompton, England: Willan Publishing.

Police Executive Research Forum (PERF). 1996. *Reducing Repeat Victimization of Residential Burglary: A Measure of Police Impact in Three Cities*. Report, Police Executive Research Forum, Washington, DC.

Smith, Glenn. Jan. 31, 2003. "Deter auto theft, but fairly." *Charleston Post and Courier*, p. A18.

The U.S. Department of Justice, Bureau of Justice Statistics. *National Crime Victimization Survey*. 2004.

U.S. Department of Justice, Federal Bureau of Investigation, Criminal Justice Information Services Division. *Crime in the United States*. 2004. Clarksburg, WV.

Business Crime Prevention

"Thieves respect property. They merely wish the property to become their property that they may more perfectly respect it."

—Gilbert K. Chesterton

■ Introduction

Business crimes take on many forms. Internal and external theft, fraud, and trademark infringement are merely the beginning. Because this book is purposely written with the law enforcement community policing and crime prevention staff in mind, I will concentrate on the areas in which they are usually called upon for advice.

For business-related crimes, law enforcement is apt to spend its time where the need is the greatest. Unfortunately, businesses have been known to apply their economic hammer to receive special treatment, and the department's limited resources are often allocated to the company with the loudest voice or the biggest purse, not necessarily the largest need. Such erroneous allocation of resources often is influenced by political factors; now the crime prevention practitioner also must deal with the economic factor, which frequently is routed through political entities. I mention this solely so the practitioner can be on the watch for highly publicized problems, even if they are only a figment of someone's imagination, and be prepared for the "acute political emergency" (APE) attack.

Crime prevention professionals will spend a substantial amount of their time addressing crimes against businesses, so it behooves the practitioner to be familiar with techniques that address the most common business crimes. In this chapter we will examine these common crimes as well as the programs that have been developed to prevent the opportunity for them to occur. Because most of these crimes involve the same basic premise and crime prevention applications, these will not be listed separately under every category. To simplify the organization of these programs, the chapter has been divided into four main headings, each with subheadings for varying programs. The first category is *business watch*, a program that may be the catalyst for delivering the remaining three programs, which fall under the categories of *external crimes*, *internal crimes*, and *business fraud*.

■ The Premise and Crime Prevention Application

The law enforcement community's prevention programming in the business arena can be related to one single motivation, financial gain. I also include property that will be used by the thief in this category. With the exception of the terrorist attack and the disgruntled employee, financial motivation is generally behind a crime. Therefore, this entire chapter will concentrate on targeting techniques criminals use frequently to commit crimes against businesses, and then will identify activities or programs that create barriers to those techniques or opportunities.

If financial reward is the motivating factor behind most business crimes, it stands to reason that prevention programs should concentrate on the technique of limiting the rewards and denying the criminal access to that which is their motivation, financial gain. Although other techniques are employed, such as delaying the criminal, which translates to increasing their effort and consequently their perceived risk, addressing the reward is the leading technique in business-related crime prevention.

■ Business Watch

Small businesses are the target of many criminals seeking to take advantage of the limited resources available to the small business. Large retail chains have resources such as trained loss prevention staff, an expense that the small business simply cannot afford; therefore, the criminal sees them as a much easier mark. Business watch programs seek to create a means for the small business to access the same expertise available to the larger chains. By creating a cooperative crime prevention organization, small businesses can pool limited resources to obtain information, provide policy guidance, and frequently improve insurance rates. The cooperative unit also may take advantage of its size to obtain additional benefits such as discounts on similarly purchased items. Although the precipitating factor leading to the start of a business watch has little to do with such benefits, the watch often evolves to include an emphasis on taking advantage of them.

Interestingly, it is rare to find two business watch programs that are totally alike. Although they may not be identical, most business watch programs do focus on providing the business community some sort of crime prevention service. A crime prevention practitioner within the local law enforcement agency facilitates most business watch programs, at least in the beginning. Some business watch programs evolve into a self-sustaining program operated by its members, with the crime prevention officer serving in an advisory capacity. Business watches offer crime prevention services to their members for free. Some services provided in business watch programs are information sharing, training, policy development, and model policies available to businesses for reference. Also provided are security assessments and evaluations. Methods of delivering these services include business watch newsletters, e-mail and facsimile alerts, and crime prevention seminars. There is also crime prevention policy development and review assistance, which provides the business with a resource for model policies other businesses currently have in place to address certain crime-related activity. Crime-specific or business security assessments also can be provided by a trained crime prevention practitioner who identifies crime-related vulnerabilities and provides recommendations to reduce them.

Business watch members usually are provided with an identifying membership emblem, such as a decal, certificate, or plaque, but only after the business has met a minimum standard of prevention. For example, the emblem may not be provided until a security assessment has been completed at the business or the manager has attended a short orientation. These minimum standards, if publicly known, may lead to the emblem or designation as a member of the business watch program having some prevention value in and of itself.

One of the major problems experienced with these programs is the belief that the program, and designation of membership, should prevent crime. Businesses in these watch programs neglect to understand the primary value of the program, which is not the existence of the program itself but rather the services it provides by acting as a centralized location for the dissemination of information and other programs. Membership in such a program should not be a requirement for the provision of crime prevention training, security assessments, and the like; however, membership strengthens the standardization of crime prevention techniques and provides a much more efficient way for the practitioner to deliver services.

■ External Crimes

External crimes are perpetrated by subjects not actually working for or within the business. These crimes against businesses are often considered the most problematic by business managers, and therefore receive most of the attention. Although problematic, external theft represents a smaller percentage of the total losses than does internal theft. Nevertheless, a loss that is preventable demands attention; a number of programs exist that address the potential losses and theft by external sources.

General Retail Robbery Prevention

Robbery is defined generally as involving the taking of one's property by another, without the owner's permission, through threats or the use of force or intimidation. When robbery involves weapon usage it is usually referred to as armed robbery; when no weapon is used it may be referred to as simply robbery, strong-arm robbery, robbery by force, or some other similar phrase. In 2004, a weapon was used in 46% of the robbery cases (2002 National Crime Victimization Survey). Historically, on average a firearm is used in weapon-related robberies about half of the time. Recently, punishment for use of a firearm has increased; this may have contributed to a decrease in the use of firearms, but the jury is still out on the total effect of enhanced punishment programs.

The Premise, Application, and Process

Statistically, businesses are much more likely to be robbed than are individuals. This is no doubt related to the reward motivation; there is a potential for a larger reward from robbing a business than from robbing an individual, even though the latter may be an easier target. Of course, there are cases when an individual makes her- or himself a better target by flashing large sums of money or jewelry, and simply promoting the perception of having such wealth available. All of this background information points out the preferred method of developing robbery prevention programs: Reduce the perceived reward. Reducing the reward and denying the criminal access to his or her target is most likely to be the most effective prevention strategy for combating the criminal's choice of targets. As with all crime prevention, anything that one can do to increase the perception of risk and effort will go a long way toward increasing the criminal's lack of opportunity to victimize the business and will discourage him or her from choosing that business to victimize.

Most business robbery prevention programs include several methods of attacking the problem. One or all may be implemented, depending on the specific need. The methods include environmental or store design changes, policy enhancement or implementation, and employee training. Each of the methods attempts to address one of the situations sought by the criminal when choosing a target for this crime.

Store Design Changes

This topic will become much clearer after reading and understanding the chapter discussing environmental design (Chapter 12), but at this juncture should be understood to aid in the prevention of robbery. Simple design changes to increase the perceived risk of detection and increase the difficulty in successfully completing a robbery have been proven to prevent robbery. In brief, design changes generally include the following:

- Remove tinting, posters, and displays that block visual surveillance into the business (referred to as creating the "fishbowl effect").
- Use proper lighting for visibility into and out of the business.
- Install and record closed circuit television cameras, focused on the register and surrounding area.
- Install hold-up alarms.
- In a high-risk community, require transactions to take place through secured ballistic windows.

Policy Enhancements or Implementation

The use, and value, of policies to prevent robberies should not be overlooked. All too often in my years as an officer and investigator it was determined that prior to a robbery, policies were violated. As related to robbery, the following are the most frequently recommended prevention policies:

- At least two employees should be present during the key hours of opening and closing.
- Two employees should be on duty late at night at convenience retail establishments.
- Frequent deposits, till pick-ups, and deposits to drop safes should be made to minimize the amount of cash on hand at any given time.
- Regular bank deposits should occur, at varied times.
- Do not open the business door to anyone before regular opening times or after regular closing times.
- Create a list of actions to take after a robbery has occurred; all employees should be trained on the procedures.
- For applicable retail establishments, minimize the number of viable entrances and exits after dark.
- Employees in retail establishments should be prohibited from carrying weapons. (Armed employees are much more likely to be harmed in a robbery.)
- Clearly state that employees are not to resist during a robbery, but rather should comply and concentrate on descriptions.
- Post signs that indicate only a small amount of cash is available to the employees on duty, and follow through with that policy.

Employee Training

The first responsibility and desire of both the police and business is to protect the employees of the business from harm. If this is considered priority one, then priority two is to assist the police in the investigation and solving of the robbery. Most police agencies will provide free training to businesses on what actions to take during and immediately after the robbery. In fact, training most often is either translated into, or supported by, the store policy, which reiterates the same basic principles. Some key robbery prevention and robbery safety tips to be included in policies and to be provided during training are as follows:

- Do not linger at or near the register when not ringing up sales. Create some distance, requiring extra effort on the part of the robber.
- Make eye contact and greet customers as they enter the store. (This helps you to later identify a suspect and psychologically removes the criminal's anonymity.)
- During a robbery, stay calm and do what the robber demands as quickly as possible. (The quicker the robber gets what he or she wants, the quicker he or she leaves and you are safe.)
- Tell the robber of any potential surprises, such as the presence of other employees in the store. (Surprises create panic and may cause a violent reaction.)
- During the robbery, concentrate on making mental notes of physical descriptions, words, actions, and anything the robber touched.
- Immediately after the robber leaves, lock the door, call the police, ask any witnesses to stay or ask for their names and phone numbers, and do not open the door to anyone until the police arrive.
- Do not touch anything the robber handled until the police have arrived and instructed you regarding what to do.

Public Transportation Robbery Prevention

Many of the same techniques taught as part of general retail robbery prevention apply to prevention of robbery in general. As with retail robbery prevention, the focus is on denying the criminals access to the rewards they seek, in this case almost always cash.

Bus Driver Robberies

For many years, robbing a bus driver was a relatively simple and profitable proposition. The criminal simply rode the bus to the end of the line and through a ruse or other means waited until the other passengers were off-loaded. The robbery produced the cash required to make change during the route as well as the cash gained from the day's fares, and allowed the robber to direct the driver to stop at an appropriate location where he or she could easily escape into a crowd or safe location. Recognizing the motivation and opportunity aspects of this crime, crime prevention practitioners applied techniques to remove or reduce the rewards. Programs that require tickets or tokens to ride, rather than accepting cash, have all but completely eliminated this crime of opportunity. In addition, some jurisdictions have installed change safes equipped with readers that are inaccessible to drivers, and some have implemented a policy of frequent collections of the change, limiting still more the rewards.

Taxi Driver Robbery

Unlike the bus driver, the taxi driver, by the nature of the job, must carry cash for change, and therefore presents him- or herself as a target to the would-be robber. Consider the fact that in this case, the robber can have his or her victim, the driver, transport him or her willingly to a place suitable for committing the crime, and the difficulty of the situation becomes obvious. Programs that address taxi robbery are likely to emphasize minimizing the amount of cash retained in the taxi. If this is not possible, the driver should keep a small amount of cash for making change separate from the remaining cash kept elsewhere in the taxi, such as locked in a safe secured to the vehicle in the trunk. Some other tips for preventing taxi robberies are as follows:

- Post signage in the taxi, visible to patrons, that states the policy of limiting the amount of cash allowed to be retained in the taxi at any given time.

- If the driver is asked if he can cash a large bill, the driver should respond that he will stop at a location on the way where the passenger can make change.

- Drivers should never leave the taxi to get payment or make change for the customer. The driver should be prepared to drive away while waiting for the fare, in case the claim for needing change was a ruse for robbers to move in on the driver.

- If the passenger gets out and leaves the door open, the driver should not exit the vehicle, but rather drive forward to force the door to close and then drive to a safe location to get out and better secure the door.

- Never drive to an undetermined destination. Require a specific destination be given before moving the taxi. Refuse passengers who ask to "just drive around" or "just take us out in the country."

- Radio your departure location and destination in to the dispatcher.

- Turn and look all passengers in the eye as you speak to them and prior to accepting the fare. If they appear suspicious to you and you do not wish to chance it, advise them you are off and call for another taxi to pick them up at the location.

- Work out code words with your dispatcher and other drivers for a suspicious acting passenger and a robbery in progress. A procedure for handling each should be known in advance.

Taxi drivers, like other employees, should be trained regarding the actions they should take during and immediately after any robbery. Safety is of the utmost concern, and this should be expressed to them. Weapons in taxis are a recipe for disaster and are not recommended. The after robbery tips listed previously apply to all types of robbery and should be included in the training of taxi drivers as well.

Food Delivery Driver Robbery Prevention

Although modern convenience is great for a busy society, it offers new opportunities for the enterprising criminal. Food delivery drivers provide robbers an easy mark. Experience has shown that the majority of food delivery robberies occur under the cover of darkness in poorly or unlighted areas. To reduce opportunities for this type of crime, we need to take control back from the criminals, or at least limit their control of the situation. The best way to do this is through the implementation of and consistent compliance with policies and procedures for honoring delivery orders. The following are some policies and procedures that attempt to limit the opportunity for such robberies to be successful:

- Require the call-taker to place the caller's first and last name on all orders and require a call-back to verify orders. Ask callers to turn their porch light on to expedite delivery.
- During the taking of the order determine the payment method—cash, check, or credit card.
- Equip the telephone with caller ID and document caller ID information on the order form.
- Use carbonless copy orders to retain a copy of all orders.
- Orders originating from pay telephones are especially suspicious, and extra precaution should be taken.
- Flag problem areas on a map posted near the order telephone. Retain a printed list of corresponding call-back numbers, names, and bad check locations.
- Specify in policy the maximum amount of cash that delivery staff are permitted to carry, and require that any cash in excess of that amount be deposited or stored at a secured location in the business. (This will also aid in deterring employee theft and false reporting of robberies.)
- In all business advertisements and on vehicle signage and delivery food containers, include a printed line that states "Delivery personnel are not permitted to carry more than $XX of cash at any time."
- Provide delivery staff with some form of two-way communication such as a radio or digital telephone.

Delivery staff may be of assistance in reducing robberies based on how they handle their deliveries. Some tips for making deliveries are:

- Park in lighted areas.
- Keep a working flashlight with you and use it when approaching a house after dark.
- Keep your doors locked until you exit to make the delivery.
- Be alert to suspicious people loitering nearby when making deliveries. If the person seems very suspicious, arrange a call-back to have the customer come onto the porch to meet you and ask them to wait until you leave once delivery is made.
- If the address given is dark and/or appears vacant, do not exit. Drive around the block and have the customer called back to verify the address. If the address is verified, ask them to turn the porch light on and wait for the driver.
- Don't carry cash or valuables of your own when delivering. Lock them in the business or leave them at home.

As with the other types of businesses discussed in this section, employees should be trained to cooperate during a robbery, and told what actions they should take during and immediately after the robbery.

Business Larceny Prevention

Thefts, or larceny, in the business setting by external entities (nonemployees) usually involve shoplifting, product delivery drivers, or storage site theft. It would be unwise, if not impossible, to discuss crime prevention for each of these crimes as one general topic of larceny. Each presupposes a different environment and method. Therefore, they will be considered separately with the assumption that financial gain is their ultimate goal.

Depending on the type of larceny being addressed, the crime prevention techniques may vary. Preventing larceny from a storage trailer may involve either target hardening and policy implementation or change to reduce the opportunity. A situation involving theft by dishonest delivery drivers may require an entirely different approach. Therefore, I have separated several of the most frequently addressed business larcenies into subcategories.

Larceny from Offices

One environment that is often overlooked by police in their prevention efforts is the office. Many businesses operate solely or partly from an office, and theft can be an easy crime in these areas. The blame for lack of attention does not fall on law enforcement alone; in many cases the business is not concerned until after a rash of thefts or a large theft is discovered. Businesses are frequently unaware of the thefts that are occurring for some time. A recent trend has demonstrated that electronics, specifically notebook or lap-top computers, have caused office-based businesses to take a closer look at their theft potential and probability (as discussed in Chapter 7). The result has been that more and more office-based businesses are implementing design changes and procedural guidelines to alleviate the more obvious opportunities for thefts. These design changes are concentrating on placement of employees to ensure that access and egress points are monitored, thus making it difficult for the nonemployee to enter and move freely about the business. Controls are implemented in varying degrees. The high-risk business will require greater controls than a low-risk office; however, all offices should have minimal controls that limit access by nonemployees who are not conducting business with them. Some controls that can be implemented to reduce theft opportunities are as follows:

- Require all visitors to sign in and out with the receptionist and display a visitor pass at all times in the facility.
- Require any subcontracted maintenance staff to identify themselves with company identification, be verified by a business contact person requesting the work (facility manager), and be signed in.
- The receptionist should verify that the visitor is expected by calling the party being visited.
- Offices should be clearly marked to remove any excuse for someone being in an unauthorized area.
- Lockable space should be provided to employees, who should be required by policy to use it.
- Mandate that all stolen or lost keys be reported immediately; if they are not immediately reported, require the negligent employee to share the cost of rekeying the office.
- Limit the number of master keys to as few as possible (one is best).
- Train, and require, employees to speak to and "offer to assist" any nonemployee observed in the building.
- Train all employees to escort any visitor not displaying an appropriate visitor badge to the reception desk to obtain a visitor's badge.

- If a vault or safe is used, change the combination frequently; always change the combination when an employee possessing the combination quits, retires, or is terminated.
- Mark all expensive office equipment with the company name and an owner-applied number (OAN) to make theft less desirable and more difficult, and the item more traceable.
- Keep sensitive business documents secured in a locked location. When sensitive items need to be destroyed, destroy them by shredding or burning and crushing.
- Even in an office environment, "lock-in theft" is possible. To prevent this, ensure that a closing procedure is in place to verify that the building is vacated and that all access and egress points are secure.

Although I recommend that reception and counter staff be the first line of defense in an office environment, it behooves the practitioner to understand that such people are frequently the victims of hostile behavior, so you will need to recommend some ways to provide for their protection. Many of the following recommendations are based on designing the area to limit access to the staff and to provide a comfortable setting that is likely to calm the aggressor. In addition, training the staff in crisis intervention and how to deal with difficult customers is essential to prevent escalation of the problem.

- The area should be well-lighted rather than dim. Also, research has determined that subdued, soft colors, rather than reds and other "hot" colors, have a calming effect and should be considered for use in the waiting or lobby area.
- The reception area should be raised to present a psychological advantage to the staff and to make it difficult for someone to assault the employee. The desktop or countertop should also be of sufficient width to make it difficult for a hostile person to perpetrate an attack.
- Install a duress alarm button.
- Establish a duress code word that the counter staff can use surreptitiously if needed.
- Develop policies and procedures related to the most common situations that may be encountered, and train the reception staff about what kind of behavior the criminal may exhibit in such situations.

Storage Trailer Larcenies

Construction and retail businesses use trailers to store equipment and products. Although a large percentage of thefts from these trailers result from internal theft, thefts by outside entities pose a significant concern as well. Trailer larcenies can be deterred by hardening the target within a secured terminal storage lot or by hardening the trailer itself. Because Target Hardening (Chapter 11) and Crime Prevention Through Environmental Design (Chapter 12) will address those topics in detail, I will provide only brief information here that is pertinent to this issue outside those areas.

First, understand that trailer cargo is at risk during use, loading, unloading, and storage. Seals and shipping documents, when used properly, provide effective controls during transport, but it is what happens before and after transport that law enforcement is generally called upon to investigate. It is in this time frame that the crime prevention practitioners should be prepared to assist. When items are stored in trailers or in open storage, access must be a primary concern. The storage site should not present an easy opportunity to remove the items from the location. In addition to target hardening the storage areas and trailers, the following important controls are frequently recommended:

- Restrict access to the storage site with appropriate fencing and signage.
- When not actually loading, unloading, or in actual use, secure the trailer doors with suitable locks.

- Place storage trailers within view of a staffed office or other location and position them so that the doors are visible.

- Prohibit off-duty employees and employees not assigned to work in the area from being near the processing, receiving, and storage areas.

- Require visual inspection to ensure that the receiving/shipping documents match the actual items (inspect each crate) and that seals remain intact and numbers match until opened in your presence. (Documentation is one of the best controls against this type of shipping or in-transit theft.)

- When a container must be opened (seals or bands broken), do not store the remaining loose items in the trailer.

- Do not allow personnel to carry personal packages, bags, or containers into or out of the receiving/shipping storage area.

- Policy should dictate that all trailers must be inspected for loose product and locked by a manager at the close of each workday.

- To ensure manager integrity, shipping, receiving, and storage should not be managed by one manager, but be the responsibility of separate managers, each of whom controls his or her individual function through systematic documentation.

Construction trailer theft is often best addressed through target hardening—using heavy, high security padlocks; adequately lighting the surrounding area; and even installing an alarm in the trailer in some cases. One of the most common causes of losses in this environment is lack of control over equipment. Equipment is often left unsecured on the site, making it an easy target for thieves, or it is taken by crewmembers themselves. Add to this situation the fact that the equipment often is not marked or documented, and it becomes easy to see how this crime can easily cost a business large losses. A few recommendations that will reduce the opportunity for this type of crimes are:

- Prior to moving a work trailer to a site, the site foreman should complete and document an inventory.

- All company equipment should be inventoried annually, complete with the type of equipment, brand, serial number, purchase date, and price along with the site foreman or other responsible party's name and signature verifying the inventory as being correct.

- All company equipment should be marked with the company name, telephone number, and any inventory number used to track the item.

- Equipment should be signed out from the equipment trailer by crew supervisors, and it should be their responsibility to ensure that the equipment is returned and signed in by the end of the workday.

- At the end of each workday, the equipment sign-out/sign-in log should be picked up by or delivered to the site foreman. All equipment should be accounted for on the log.

Shoplifting

In his 17th Annual Retail Theft Survey of 27 U.S. retail companies, Jack Hayes found that for the fourth straight year shoplifting apprehensions have increased (2004). Shoplifting is also suspected of being one of the most underreported crimes in retail, partly because businesses often have a policy of not prosecuting shoplifters who steal merchandise less than a certain value and partly because businesses do not understand their rights under the law. Some stores that I have worked with actually had no shoplifting policy at all to guide managers and employees. A policy should always exist to give some direction to the employee of what is expected. I have provided a sample policy in the Resources section of this book.

Even though shoplifting arrests represent a high percentage of those stealing from a business, shoplifting itself is responsible for only a small percentage of the losses that a business experiences annually. Nevertheless, shoplifting does pose a loss threat, and a unique one at that. Consider that the very people whom your survival depends on also may be stealing from you, and you can see the delicacy of dealing with shoplifting prevention. When handling other crimes, you can simply remove the access to the products; with shoplifting you must make the product available to potential criminals while at the same time reducing or removing their opportunity to steal it. The approach to shoplifting prevention must be driven by increasing the perceived risk that the shoplifters will be detected, increasing the effort required for them to succeed, and ensuring that shoplifters receive little or no reward from the stolen article. In this unique environment, much of the prevention effort must be undertaken by store design, policy, and psychological innuendo. The recommended approach is to begin with a store design that discourages shoplifting, followed by instituting effective policies and then training staff in these policies and local laws, as well as pointing out indicators of a potential shoplifter. Following are some common recommendations for securing a business from shoplifters:

- Control the fitting rooms in a clothing retail establishment.
- Constant "fronting" of merchandise and straightening of items on shelves or racks will enable the employees working that area to quickly determine if an item is missing.
- Mark stockroom and other authorized use only areas with appropriate signage to remove unauthorized people's excuse for being in such areas.
- Display items with shoplifting in mind. Display more expensive items behind glass cases, secured by cables, or in a constantly monitored area. In some cases it may be prudent to require the items to be paid for in such an area.
- Design the store to funnel all customers to and through the main exits. Arrange aisles so that concealment locations are limited and that open visibility is encouraged.
- Train and encourage staff to approach every customer who enters the store area and look them in the eye while asking if they need assistance.
- Employees working in areas such as cameras or jewelry should be instructed to give their complete attention to one customer at a time when items are out of the case being examined. Items should be limited to one or two out of the case at any given time, and this amount should be specified by policy.

If a potential shoplifter is identified, the employee must act within store policy. I encourage preventing the crime by being overly courteous, engaging the person in conversation, remaining in the area to work, offering to assist them, and if they become agitated, kindly offering to call a manager. If a shoplifter is caught, one of the best prevention tools available is prosecution. The following tips regarding potential "cues" are not foolproof, but can be indicators of a potential shoplifter:

- Customers who appear to be loading a cart with clothing without looking at sizes or price tags.
- Customers who drape clothing over the edges all around the cart may be creating an area of concealment within the cart.
- Large containers or bags that appear almost empty (as the customer enters staff should be cognizant of this).
- Customers who appear to be looking around at people rather than at merchandise.
- Several customers entering together who part ways immediately (as though planned) without discussion of where they will meet later.

- Customers with used or crumpled shopping bags.
- Customers dressed inappropriately for the weather.

Delivery Person Larceny

Sometimes the thief gives while he or she takes. Such is often the case of the delivery driver who steals from his or her clients. Businesses depend on timely receipt of their goods, and often establish a trusting relationship with their regular delivery person. In most cases this is fine, but when the driver is dishonest it can be disastrous for the merchant. Some delivery people have stolen for years from their clients without ever being discovered. They most likely steal only from those who provide them the easiest mark. As crime prevention practitioners, we are very likely to find it quite difficult to convince a merchant that a long-time delivery driver may be stealing from their store. After all, the driver may have developed a friendly relationship with employees by giving them extra incentives or some leftover product, and the merchant may insist that the driver has never taken anything from the business. The smart crime prevention practitioner should not argue with the merchant, but encourage some changes in policy "just in case" it may happen in the future.

The delivery person may steal in numerous ways—too numerous to mention all of them here. For example, he or she may deliver at times when the store employee(s) are too busy to properly check the delivery and/or credits. While the store is busy, the delivery person might stack product on the outer edges to give the illusion that there is much more there than really is. The hollow inside represents losses to the store. The same hollow may be created when removing expired products or credits and may conceal other store merchandise on the way out. Another method associated with this technique is that the delivery person may "front" the shelf with fresh product while leaving the old in the back of the fresh and taking much of the same fresh product out (as a credit) that was brought in. There are indicators to tell whether this type of theft, generally prevalent at the small business level, is occurring. Just as with the shoplifter, as the indicators mount up, the possibility of this type of theft increases. Some of the indicators are:

- The delivery person is generous and gives lots of free samples.
- The delivery person parks the delivery truck away from the clerk or staff's view and unloads from the opposite side of the truck.
- The driver brings in the fresh or replacement product before checking or removing the old credited items.
- The driver "assists" the receiver by holding the invoice and reading it while they check what is being delivered.
- The driver carries out his or her own "empty" cases or containers for disposal.

Now that the business owner knows some theft techniques, he or she can make some simple policy and procedural changes to greatly increase the effort required for such thefts to be successful. Recommendations that address this type of theft include:

- The merchant should specify the allowed delivery times. Set the range of delivery times to when the store is typically slow, and refuse all deliveries during especially busy times such as rush hours.
- Receiving staff should be trained to visually check and count each item delivered. This may involve opening cases and checking the delivery against the packing slip or invoice.
- Require that credits be checked first and removed prior to new product being brought in to replace the outdated.
- Vendors delivering through the front door (e.g., at convenience markets) should be required to stop at the front entrance and be checked when making deliveries.

- The store should adopt and make known to delivery drivers that two deliveries will not be checked in or made simultaneously. To avoid confusion and collusion by drivers, one delivery transaction should be completed prior to the next being started.
- No containers, empty boxes, or shipping crates should be removed until they are examined by an employee to ensure that they are empty.

Other Commonly Observed Larcenies

Certain larceny offenses are especially problematic for the law enforcement agency. They are problematic because they account for thefts that are frequently minor, and the business plans in advance to "write off" the resulting losses. Police reports are usually required to satisfy the insurance needs of the business or to aid in the collection of payments, resulting in law enforcement assuming the role of collection agency. These crimes obviously result in lots of small losses that can add up. Even though frequently compensated for by insurance or other means these larcenies still result in higher insurance premiums and ineffective use of law enforcement to draft useless reports and collect debts. These crimes should be prosecuted but can be prevented as well, frequently through environmental changes within the retail setting or through law enforcement policy changes. These types of crimes generally fall under the heading of "defrauding a business." Such crimes, which are all too frequently reported, include failing to pay a taxi fare, failing to pay for a meal, and most frequently, gasoline drive-off theft. Following are some suggestions of ways to aid in preventing these types of crimes.

The "Ride and Slide"—Failure to Pay Taxi Fare.
As with most crime prevention, the more approaches undertaken simultaneously, the more likely the effort will achieve the desired result. Even if only one method is used, the crime rate is likely to be impacted. One method to address this type of crime is to make the punishment outweigh the crime. This may be done by working with local judges to ensure the maximum penalties allowed are imposed with convictions. This approach will work in all of the so-called defraud cases, but it is rare indeed to find a court system that is willing to cooperate to this extent with law enforcement on punishing fare evaders. Another method that may be employed is to increase the risk of detection and arrest by installing taped closed circuit television (CCTV) in the vehicles and to adopt a zero tolerance for violators; that is, all fare evaders will be prosecuted. If this policy is in place, it should be posted in the taxi to increase the perception of risk. Other methods for addressing this crime include those discussed previously under the robbery section of this chapter, including the use of auto-lock rear doors where permitted.

The "Dine and Dash"—Failure to Pay the Meal Tab.
One of the best methods of addressing this type of crime is good customer service. Customers who are greeted and given a lot of attention are less apt to think that they cannot be recognized or that they can slip out unnoticed. Again, a strict prosecution policy is helpful, and posting of the policy enhances its effect. In this situation, one often-overlooked crime prevention tool is the restaurant's design. Effective design changes may make this crime much more difficult by increasing the escape effort and the potential for detection. For example, in some establishments, the staffed point of payment at the exit door and narrowing the corridor to funnel all patrons close to the register area will make it difficult for any such criminal to escape without detection. Conversely, payment at the table makes such a crime much easier and affords the would-be dasher an opportunity for excuse if confronted. If payment at the table is a must, the ratio of wait staff to patrons should be increased to ensure closer attention to the customer.

The "Gas and Go"—Gasoline Drive-Off Offenses.   One of the most preventable defraud offenses, and the most irritating for law enforcement officers, is the gasoline drive-off. This crime could practically be eliminated if businesses required payment before permitting pumping of gas. Many businesses have found this to be the best way to prevent losses and have implemented such a policy; unfortunately, our society's demand for convenience has forced many others to succumb to the demand and to allow payment after the fact. Crime prevention practitioners have long fought the battle of cash over convenience, and thus far have been unable to sway the majority. Police chiefs have taken the step of adopting a policy of refusing to take a report on these cases if there is to be no prosecution by the business. Prosecution is a very real prevention tool, especially when it is mandated. Businesses cite the reason for not wishing to prosecute as being a financial one. Specifically, they say that customers wanting convenience will choose to go to another retailer that does not require pre-payment. They also believe that they lose money due to the customer's tendency to underestimate gas purchases in order to have to return to the store for change and this results in less in-store shopping. (Virginia Crime Prevention Association, 2005). By requiring gas stations to prosecute, we may effectively force businesses to look realistically at the value of pay before you pump policies to overcome what to them is a lose–lose situation.

One other very effective prevention tool is the design of the store lot, specifically the pumps. Retrofitting a small "gas shack" that sells the essentials typically desired by patrons such as cigarettes, soft drinks, and the like may help discourage drive-offs. Another possible prevention method is the installation of CCTV to afford the view that should have been provided by the original design. Newly constructed gasoline stations are installing machines at the pumps that work like soft drink vending machines and accept cash at the pump.

It is the hope of law enforcement that some of these methods will be employed to at least reduce the losses to businesses. If businesses refuse to implement the recommendations made by crime prevention practitioners, we can at least assure our employers and others to whom we are responsible that we have attempted to assist the unwilling. It might help to recall the words of Thomas Jefferson to George Hammond in 1792: "It is reasonable that everyone who asks justice should do justice."

■ Internal Crimes

Although internal theft is responsible for 70–80% of business losses, preventing such crimes is given much less attention than preventing their external counterpart. According to a 2004 survey by ADT Security Services (2004), retailers lost approximately 14.6 billion dollars to employee theft.

Some employee thieves steal small amounts over an extended period of time; others steal only on occasion; and still others are responsible for large amounts of losses. Employee thieves often justify their actions through a self-convincing sense of entitlement. They consider it as a benefit, "for all I do," or because they were denied a well-deserved raise or promotion. In some cases an employee simply views the taking of certain items as a benefit for working for the company. When caught and interviewed by authorities, many, if not most, contend that they did nothing wrong. This is why education and written policy play such a crucial role in preventing internal theft. In this section I will discuss some of the more common internal thefts that a local law enforcement crime prevention practitioner might encounter. I will attempt to present techniques that, if employed, will greatly reduce the opportunity for such internal thefts to be successful.

The Premise and Crime Prevention Application

Stealing from an environment with which one is intimately acquainted is a simple task if no safeguards are in place to remove excuses and encourage accountability. Planning a theft in such an environment offers almost no hurdles to overcome. Internal thieves are acquainted with the policies, the procedures, the schedules, and the locations of the valuable items, so the majority of their work is already complete. They have access to the locations of more valuable items, so their rewards are enhanced. They are employees, so they are viewed with little or no suspicion and therefore risk is rarely a factor that they even consider. All they have to do is to put their plan into action. The premise behind preventing internal theft is simple: If you must have the fox in the henhouse then some added protection for the hens is needed. Employee thieves seize every opportunity given, and lack of management controls enhance such opportunities. Although employees require a certain amount of trust, guidelines and controls can aid in removing temptations form those employees prone to steal.

The crime prevention practitioner must realize that if caught, the internal thief will frequently rely on his or her knowledge of policy to find an excuse and a way out. The rationale behind all internal theft prevention programs is to tip the scales against the employee thief by implementing inventory controls, employee monitoring, punitive measures, and rule setting. Inventory controls and monitoring increase the risk of detection, while rule setting (policies) removes possible excuses. Punitive measures, such as termination and prosecution, are intended to tip the scales when the criminal is weighing potential gains versus losses. It is this tipping of the scales that seems to be the most successful means of preventing employee theft.

There are a number of types of employee theft that must be discussed separately, because the techniques vary. Each of the types discussed in the following sections are based, for the most part, on prevention.

Embezzlement

Embezzlement is generally defined as taking, or converting to one's own use, another's property as a result of a relationship of trust with the owner. The most important words in this definition are *trust* and *relationship*. The taking or converting must be intentional for a crime to have occurred. The crime of embezzlement often is not reported and even more frequently is not prosecuted. Reasons for this lack of reporting and prosecution are many, but most often stem from the company's fear of appearing vulnerable or not in control. The embezzler often has an intricate knowledge of the internal operations of the business and will often use the very systems put in place by the company to commit the crime. The embezzler is not easy to spot, displaying few vices or work problems. He or she is often viewed as a "model employee." Because so much of this crime involves the use of systems and processes, it is there that the prevention work must begin.

Controlling Access

The first order of business is to control access to the computerized information that may be targeted. We are not referring to controlling the physical access to computer rooms—that topic is covered in the Chapters 11 and 13 of this book. In this section we are referring to controlling access to the information *on* the computerized systems. This prevention step may be summarized by the old adage of providing access on a need to know basis. Once access to a system is given, it may be necessary to subdivide or partition access according to function. In other words, secure the business system so that the criminal would have to recruit an accomplice with a different access level to complete their crime, thereby making it much less likely. For example, if one employee is responsible for both accounts payable and accounts receivable, a simple keystroke or two can create the illusion that a nonexistent shipment is being paid for. If two different people run accounts payable and accounts receivable, separating these functions would require collusion. This would be akin to the double key access provided in a physical security application. This separation is needed in any application in which functions might depend on each other. Every business has a number of these positions, and they should be examined for possible embezzlement opportunities. Accounts payable, accounts receivable, payroll, and accounting should be the first places to start separating function and access. In keeping with this philosophy, businesses should be warned against "putting all of their eggs in one basket."

I investigated a case as a young detective in which there was one employee who understood the entire shipping, receiving, billing, and payroll systems. The two business owners each had a partial knowledge of the system, but neither understood the system relationship. The company was experiencing mass losses that they immediately assumed were the result of warehouse theft. The shipping and billing practices quickly revealed that the loss was not due to warehouse employees, but rather computer manipulation. Even though the employee was caught red handed and even failed a polygraph, the owners refused to believe that this "model employee" of over 20 years was stealing from them until all the details were laid out. Had she only had access to one aspect of the system, this crime would certainly have been averted.

When reviewing the information systems, do not overlook the need to secure data and program manuals. Many individuals are computer savvy and, armed with a technical manual, could access confidential information or cause irreversible damage. Policies should require the use of password protection, rendering computers essentially locked when the employee steps away from the workstation.

Background Checks

The next area focuses on the employees or operators themselves. The first positive step to managing the operators of a business system is for the employer to do his or her homework when hiring key personnel. If a business is incapable of conducting a thorough background check for key positions it should consider outsourcing the task to skilled professionals who provide such services. Additionally, promotions into such positions should also require a background check. Even though the employee may have been with the company for years, he or she may never have been given the opportunity to steal or the added reward that the new position will provide. In a 2001 article in *American Banker Magazine*, the Fraud Examiners Association is quoted as stating, "While lower level employees committed about 80% of all corporate fraud, they only took 20% of the total amount stolen" (Thompson, 2001, p. 11).

Policies and Audits

The final layer of prevention related to embezzlement is to control systems through policies and through audits. Policies should address the requirements and accountability for data security and system integrity. Such policies should specify reporting requirements. They should require the aforementioned background investigations of key employees. An annual detailed audit by an independent auditor designed to identify discrepancies and errors should be a requirement of the business. Policy should allow for unannounced spot check audits by management of all divisions and, when possible, a computerized audit trail should be produced and spot-checked by management for breaks in the audit trail. A policy of prosecution for criminal acts should be in place and should be posted throughout the business. This policy should include when law enforcement will be called in and the requirement for employees to cooperate with investigators.

Embezzlement techniques take on many variations, so it is difficult under the best circumstances to identify means to prevent it. In cases in which embezzlement is suspected, a specialist may need to be called in to investigate and provide information as to "how" the crime was facilitated. Once the specialist is aware of the "how," he or she should be able to develop a prevention plan, after the fact, for future crimes. Regardless of what specific techniques might be employed, it behooves each and every business to take a proactive stance of addressing its existing systems, employees, and operations through effective controls and audits to increase the difficulty for dishonest employees to commit such crimes.

Pilferage

Pilferers, like embezzlers, have been given access to certain company property by virtue of their employment with the business. When such property is converted to their personal use without authorization, they have committed a crime. Our focus, for the purpose of the law enforcement crime prevention practitioner, will be on the casual pilferer. The casual pilferer is one who steals for personal use rather than to sell the stolen items. As with any other crime, the pilferer must be provided the opportunity or access to the item(s) that he or she desires, accompanied by a means of removing the stolen items. The pilferer is no more likely to draw attention to him- or herself than is the embezzler. The employee who is frequently embroiled in a controversy with management is not likely to pilfer while he or she is under the microscope of so many.

Often the question is asked, "If the model employees are the ones pilfering and the pilfered items are so inexpensive, why even consider addressing the pilferage at all?" That is a great question to ask any supply clerk for a legitimate answer. Ask the clerk what it costs the company annually to provide paper, pens, CDs, and other items for the operation of the business, and you will soon have your answer. Pilferage alone is responsible for billions of dollars in losses to businesses in the United States annually, not just in administrative supplies, but also from petty cash accounts, coffee funds, long distance services, and more. All of these are required for a business to operate freely. Successful prevention of pilferage involves controlling the use and distribution of items targeted without stifling employees' legitimate access within the work environment. Although this is a difficult task, it can be accomplished by considering needs and assignment of responsibility:

- Assign the responsibility of monitoring supplies to one employee, with an alternate if needed.
- Require that employees "sign out" administrative supplies through a charge employee, thus creating an audit trail of use or abuse.
- Have the supply charge person prepare a monthly report to be signed off on and reviewed by the unit, department, or division head.
- Require a monthly or quarterly inventory of supplies. This inventory should include a breakdown by division or unit of usage and should include a listing of newly received shipments as well.
- Businesses should offer incentives for reporting abuse, misuse, or new techniques to conserve supplies.

In addition to these techniques, the policy overview should include policies similar to those listed in the embezzlement section.

Cashier Theft

Dishonest cashiers working in retail clothing, convenience, and department stores are pocketing their employers' profits at enormous rates. Cashiers steal in so many ways that the space here is inadequate to prepare the crime prevention practitioner to address them all. The local law enforcement agency should instead focus on the most common of these techniques and recommend environmental changes, policy implementation, and procedural controls.

Dishonest cashiers steal from the cash drawer or tills, as well as stealing merchandise through collusion with others. It would be asking far too much of the local crime prevention practitioner to be prepared to address all variations as well as their other duties. Instead, we hope to prepare the practitioner to address the most common of the methods used by dishonest cashiers and the most common techniques for preventing their crimes.

The knowledgeable store manager can often detect cash thefts from the cash register till. The first step in prevention of cashier theft is to ensure that the responsible manager, assistant manager, or other employee is aware of what is "normal" for their store by way of cash register transactions. The first clue that there is a problem is abnormalities, especially when the abnormal activity is linked to one or two employees. Once the store manager is aware of the normal activity, policies can be created to remove the opportunity for theft by abnormal transactions. Most of the abnormal transactions can be identified by conducting a thorough examination of the register detail tape or of the computerized system memory. A good starting point for policy, even before a problem is detected, is to appropriately limit the following transactions:

- Cash refunds at the checkout register
- Cash voids or no sale rings without manager authorization/witnessing
- Under-rings without manager authorization/witnessing

Cashiers are not likely to steal from their till in large amounts, but rather in small increments throughout the day. The cashier might ring up a sweater valued at $35 for $30 plus tax, include the additional $5 in the amount charged the customer, and then put all the cash in the register until the opportunity arises to remove it. When the opportunity arises, the cashier consults their tracking system to see what their "take" is and pockets that amount, in this case $5. In this theft variation, the cashier needs to ensure that the customer cannot observe the amount on the cash register window.

Skimming also can occur every time the register is opened. For example, the cashier may have made a legitimate sale on the register but neglected to close the register drawer. This provides him or her the opportunity to pocket the take from a previous sale or to charge for a small item for which the tax amount can easily be calculated and not rung up. The casher can consult his or her tracking mechanism later and pocket the cash. Cashiers may overcharge customers by small amounts as well and later collect that amount, having rung up only the legitimate price but charging the customer more.

Checking registers at the end of a workday is insufficient in deterring theft because the skilled cashier tracks his or her thefts and the register will balance. In fact, the cashier who consistently balances exactly should be closely examined for theft. It is normal to be off by a few cents on occasion. The following steps are essential to preventing such opportunities:

- Require that the cash register window be visible to the customer at all times.
- Require that the cash drawer be closed after each transaction by penalty of disciplinary action.
- Conduct unannounced spot check register audits at various times to increase the risk of detecting the cashier's stolen cash.
- Prohibit the accumulation of loose change or other items around the register. To track his or her thefts, the dishonest cashier often uses these for "accounting" purposes.
- Prohibit clutter around the cash register, which may be used to conceal the cashier's activities.
- Never allow cashiers to ring up their own purchases. If a manager is available, require the manager to ring up all employee purchases.
- Never allow cashiers to count their own till at the end of the workday or shift. Instead, require that the drawer remain closed until a manager can check out the till and conduct the count.
- Managers should be required to periodically spot check the detail tapes from the registers for abnormal patterns and discuss such abnormalities with the employee responsible.

Cashiers may also steal from their employer by inaccurately charging merchandise for friends, family, or accomplices. Policies that prohibit ringing up family and friends are very effective in addressing the opportunistic thief, but the hardened thief can overcome this by acting as though they do not know their accomplice. A sharp manager will recognize shopping norms and realize that it is unusual for a person to go to a much longer line when a shorter one is available. They will soon come to recognize a repeat customer who frequents the same cashier. These are techniques that managers should be trained to be attentive to. A few additional tips for preventing cashier theft are listed below:

- Conduct a thorough background check on all employees who will handle cash.
- Install CCTV cameras with pan and tilt capability over the cash register area.
- Distribute a written zero tolerance for theft policy.
- Encourage anonymous reporting of suspicious activities by providing an incentive for reporting theft, including employee theft.

Larceny—Theft by Employee

Ask most businesses what they think their employees who steal take, and they are apt to tell you that the items are inexpensive and insignificant. I believe it might surprise them to know what items are walking out of the door with their employees. For example, it has been estimated that 90% of all laptop computer thefts are internal (*Security Magazine,* 2003). Office furniture and other equipment also are popular targets of employee thieves. Other larcenies occur by employees engaging in conspiracy with others. Most larcenies by employees can be prevented by implementation of management controls over equipment and merchandise via inventories and by implementing sound written policies. Policies remove excuses and go a long way toward increasing the risk of detection and punitive threat. For such policies to prevent crime they must be in writing, well known, and signed off as having been read by all employees. They must also be applied consistently and fairly. Some policies that are effective countermeasures to theft are:

- A requirement for employees to sign in/out while at the workplace, on or off duty
- Requiring entry/exit through a designated monitored door
- Controlling and monitoring business keys and electronic access devices
- Identifying when and how employees may return to the business after normal work hours
- Identifying a means of supervising after-hours cleaning crews

In order to control the inventories and property of businesses, they must take certain steps to ensure the items and/or the function related to them are accounted for. The practitioner may wish to consider the following recommendations when addressing internal larceny from businesses:

- The business should require an updated inventory of all expensive company assets and equipment.
- One person should be given the responsibility of adding new inventory to the list and of visually inspecting the property in question annually and updating its location or assignment to an employee.
- Record all serial numbers and any description or owner-applied numbers of expensive items.
- Identify a tracking mechanism for any equipment that has been outsourced for repairs. Identifying one responsible individual who documents needed repairs, the location of repairs, and receipt of the repaired items goes a long way in removing the common excuse by employees caught in theft that the item was sent for repairs or was declared to be irreparable. A pattern of repairs by the same individual may

reveal collusion between the individual and the repair shop. A responsible party monitoring repairs can check for needed repairs and such patterns.

- Although most businesses have a regular auditing process, I believe that management spot checks and audits in all areas are necessary to prevent employees from acting in concert to steal from the company. Regular audits are, by design, not as detailed as the random checks should be. Random checks should be detailed in the policies and should include the potential for discipline. The shipping and receiving areas spot check will ensure that items received are not stolen and later sold elsewhere on the black market. Such spot checks in the payroll area will ensure that overtime and time cards are not being padded. Audits by management may reveal accounts payable clerks paying fictitious vendors, unauthorized discounting of invoiced items, and a host of other problems.

- It is not uncommon for merchandise, company equipment, and stolen cash to be "thrown out" with the trash, only to be retrieved by an employee or accomplice. To prevent this, some businesses require that employees be accompanied when emptying trash, some require shredding and other items be separated into recycle bins, and some secure dumpsters with locks to reduce the access to the rewards, or stolen items, by the dishonest employee. Regardless of what method is used, this "Trojan horse" must be addressed.

■ Business Fraud

Having covered external crimes against business and internal crimes against business we close with the discussion of frauds against business. Fraud is defined as "intentional perversion of truth in order to induce another to part with something of value or to surrender a legal right" (*Merriam-Webster's Collegiate Dictionary*, 1994).

The reason that fraud is covered here under a separate heading is that businesses are the victims of both internal and external fraudulent activities. The most typical of the external activities involve the use of financial instruments such as checks, coupons, and credit cards. Due to the nature of the use of such instruments, each is discussed under its own subcategory.

Checks—Bad Versus Fraudulent

Not all check cases are the result of fraudulent activity. In some cases honest mistakes are made and no trickery or deception was planned. "Bad checks" are those that cannot be redeemed for cash for any number of reasons. Many of these checks are the result of mistakes, and providing an opportunity for correction is reasonable. Most states require that a process of notification and opportunity for correction be given prior to allowing businesses to seek criminal charges. Crime prevention practitioners should be familiar with what their state's requirements are. These are usually codified and may be researched in the state's penal code. This process is used to separate the honest mistakes from the fraudulent cases. Fraudulent checks are difficult, at best, to collect and even more difficult to prosecute.

Prevention of both bad checks and fraudulent checks is possible when businesses and their employees are given training and direction on what to look for when accepting a draft. This training is often available in a large retail setting from the Loss Prevention Department, but small businesses may not have this training immediately available. This is where the crime prevention practitioner becomes valuable. Crime prevention units should be well versed or have access to white collar crime units that can provide free training on how to prevent these crimes. The training should include the store's check cashing policy and a segment on clues or signs that may indicate potential problems. Each store will have a process of what to do if such indicators warrant, and the store should include those directions in the training.

Signs or Clues

Although each sign taken separately may heighten the suspicion that fraudulent activity is afoot, the clues are just indicators and should not be considered to be absolute. Just as with other clues, the more clues accumulate, the higher the potential.

- *Newly opened accounts*—New accounts are used in check kiting scheme in which money is moved around from various accounts to appear to have coverage until the criminal can ultimately make away with their money and the business's.
- *Out of state or out of town accounts*—These accounts are used in fraudulent activity due to the difficulty in verifying the authenticity of the information on the check.
- *Accounts with only a post office box address*—On checks drawn locally, a fictitious address may be identified and stop the fraud. Fraudulent check criminals prefer post office boxes. Any information on a draft that is not verifiable should be suspect. Certified letters regarding the overdraft cannot be served at a P.O. box or at "general delivery."
- *Nervousness*—Signs of nervousness may be displayed, such as the writer having difficulty signing his or her name on the draft, appearing in a hurry, or rushing the cashier.
- *Altered checks*—Regardless of other signs, the presence of any alterations to a draft is an indication that closer examination is needed.
- *Lack of identification*—The inability of the "customer" to produce acceptable identification may indicate a fraudulent check, stolen check, or other criminal activity.
- *Loose checks*—These are suspect when accompanied by other clues.

Store Policy

Check fraud prevention tips are designed around the methods and techniques employed by criminals to commit the fraudulent activities. The crime prevention practitioner should offer the following recommendations to businesses in relation to their policy development:

- The check cashing policy should be posted near the transaction area to serve as an added deterrent and to avoid excuses.
- Require and verify all acceptable identification, as specified by policy.
- Verify that all checks are "true" checks and not a counterfeit or a promotional stunt.
- Ensure that all checks are signed in the presence of the cashier. If the check was previously signed, require a second signature under the first.
- Accept only checks up to the amount listed in the company policy.
- Document on all checks the minimum information required by the store.
- Require a manager's approval when the check appears altered in any way or when the check is presented with a stamped signature.
- Never cash checks written in pencil or checks with apparent erasures.
- When rushed by the customer, slow the transaction down and call for a manager to assist.
- Do not accept postdated checks.
- Require manager approval on all starter or counter checks and on all checks with a check number less than 100.
- Adhere to the store policy regarding the cashing of third-party checks.
- Use check verification services (listed in **Table 8.1**), if available, and maintain a listing of persons who have passed bad checks to the store in the past.

Table 8.1
Check Verification Services

Checkrite	800-766-2748	Telecheck	800-710-9898
Chexsystems	800-428-9623	Scan	800-262-2771
Equifax	800-437-5120	NPC Check	800-526-5380

This information was provided by the Office of the Attorney General for the Commonwealth of Virginia.

Credit Card Fraud

Credit card fraud is a crime of enormous proportions. With the advent of criminal identity theft, discussed in Chapter 9, comes an increase in the fraudulent use of credit cards. As related to identity theft, the crime may begin with the criminal fraudulently opening a credit card account using stolen identification; in other scenarios; it may begin with the criminal actually using a stolen credit card. In some cases unscrupulous businesses or fictitious merchants have submitted fictitious invoices for payment. Acceptance of credit cards for financial transactions is almost essential for the businessperson. Their convenience ensures their continued use, so we crime prevention practitioners must adapt and identify ways to assist our businesses customers in protecting themselves from credit card fraud. Rather than trying to list the litany of ways in which credit card fraud is perpetrated, some general prevention tips are offered here to assist the crime prevention practitioner in addressing the fraudulent activities:

- When setting up accounts with credit card companies, read all crime prevention material that is provided by the company. Many companies provide a number of services to assist the merchant in reducing losses.
- When making a credit card transaction, retain the card until the transaction is complete.
- Check the card to see if the embossed letters are clear and uniform in size and spacing, the colors are uniform and well-defined, holograms appear to move when the card is tilted, the card is not expired or invalid, the magnetic strip on the card has not been tampered with, and the card is signed.
- If the card is not signed, require the presenter to produce photo ID and to sign the card. If a signature is present, it can be checked against another form of ID.
- If the card is marked in the signature box to "check for ID," the employee should require ID.
- When suspicious for any reason, the employee should require identification and should check the warning list or file.
- Require company authorization on any transaction over the required limit.
- Train employees to be cognizant of common behaviors associated with credit card crimes.

Used with permission of the Virginia Retail Merchant's Association.

Other Common Frauds

If there is a legitimate means in which to transact business, a criminal mind will find a way to use it to their advantage. A glaring illustration of this fact is the recent criminal scheme to use automatic teller machines (ATMs) to steal from legitimate users. In this scheme, the criminal designs and affixes an ATM card reader to the façade of an actual ATM. An individual then comes to the machine, inserts his or her card, and uses the machine as normal. The card reader, however, records the card information while the criminal retrieves the PIN number using binoculars or, in some cases, a video camera. Using technology available to all, the criminal then produces his or her own duplicate ATM card, uses the individual's PIN, and cleans out the account of the unknowing user. New technology to prevent this crime will be developed and sold, when a simple exercise of care will prevent the crime. As I alluded to earlier, if there is a desire and the individuals provide the opportunity, eventually the ability will be designed.

Less common frauds that officers encounter are sometimes seen as acceptable losses or not able to be prevented. I believe if the criminal mind can figure out how to accomplish a desired crime, there is certainly a way to prevent it. Some examples of frauds that are perhaps not as common but warrant at least a cursory review are as follows.

Food Stamps Fraud

This crime involves the selling or trading of legitimately obtained or issued food stamps to individuals or dishonest businesses at a reduced face value for cash or for items not authorized in the food stamp program. Some dishonest businesses have done quite well in trading for food stamps at 50 cents on the dollar. This crime affects every taxpayer. State and federal authorities are doing much better in ensuring accountability of these items, but this crime still occurs. Because this book is written specifically with the crime prevention practitioner in mind, I have chosen only to mention this type of crime, and to state that cooperation with honest businesses and citizens may be the best method of prevention. I leave the prevention to each practitioner to develop. Remembering the basics for creating a prevention program will help; that is, asking what we can do to make the crime risk, effort, and so on outweigh the rewards and benefits. I suggest that in this case the local crime prevention practitioner can do little to change the design and use of the stamps, but can best use their time in identifying ways to increase the risk of detection. Media campaigns and partnerships with legitimate businesses that offer rewards for reporting dishonest businesspersons who abuse the system will go far to accomplish this goal.

Coupon Fraud

Yes, the criminal has even taken advantage of this opportunity—individuals or businesses can accomplish coupon fraud. While I was in my late teens and in the Army military police, I had a second job as a pizza deliveryman for a national chain. The chain had a booming business on the military base and loved to hire military police because they were familiar with all of the addresses and could easily deliver the pizza within their specified delivery time. The chain put coupons in the local Sunday paper with offers such as buy one get one free, buy a certain pizza and get a free 2-liter soft drink, or simply a discount on the pizza ordered. A friend of mine in the delivery job filled me in on his way of making some additional money. While working on the base as a military policeman, he would "patrol" the residential neighborhoods, and after the newspapers were delivered, he would remove pizza coupons from the papers. On his next working day with the pizza delivery job he would legitimately grab a supply of soft drinks and take off with his orders as they came in. When he delivered a pizza, he might sell the person a soft drink—sometimes at full price, sometimes at half price. Due to his frequent "discounting" practice, people would call in and ask for him by name. He would then return to the store with the cash and turn in a soft drink coupon, pocketing the cash along with his tips. He would take an order for two pizzas, deliver them, and return with payment for one along with the buy-one-get-one-free coupon, pocketing the cash for the second pizza. He made employee of the month several times because he was constantly volunteering to take the orders over the telephone and to make the extra deliveries. He would write down two pizzas when only one was ordered and on the way back he would sell the one to some soldier for half price under the guise of the person not being home who ordered it. He would then turn in his coupon and pocket the cash. He even recruited others, not working on the base, to do the same. He provided the coupons and they provided him a cut of the night's take. This soldier, who was a supervisor, told me that he had made more from his pizza scheme than from his military pay. So far as I know he was never caught, and he saw no harm and certainly no crime in what he was doing. The reason behind this illustration is to demonstrate that when one knows how a crime is committed, one can develop prevention. In hindsight it would have been relatively simple to put in place some procedures to reduce the losses to this company:

- Institute a policy that delivery persons may not take the orders.
- Institute a policy requiring the order taker to ask if the customer has a coupon and to mark the order accordingly. As part of this procedure, ensure that coupons are marked that the caller *must* tell the order taker of the use of the coupon at the time of the order.
- To improve customer service, require the manager to periodically call customers after their orders have been received, read back what they ordered, and verify it, and ask about their satisfaction with the product and delivery.

Other fraudulent uses of coupons have made businesses very wealthy. The manufacturer's coupon is intended to be a marketing tool to get potential customers to try the product. Dishonest businesses have seen this as an opportunity for them to collect a little profit "without hurting anyone." After all, the manufacturer had planned to absorb the losses from the use of the coupon. Each time the manufacturer's losses are not offset by potential gains, the result is higher prices to absorb the losses. Because the manufacturer is rarely accessible to the local crime prevention practitioner, and not likely to prosecute the crime, the involvement of the crime prevention practitioner is limited. Corporate loss prevention officers are more often given the task of understanding the gravity of the losses and developing ways to address them. Certainly they are in the best position to influence corporate practices and prevention.

One prevention method that is being used to address this crime today is the use of coupons redeemable "after the sale." This method requires those wishing to redeem the coupon to submit the coupon, along with a UPC symbol or other proof of purchase, directly to the manufacturer who will then mail the promised redemption. Based on the rebate process, this technique ensures, to some degree, that the goal of reaching the consumer with the product is met. Although not foolproof, this is a positive step that tilts the scale toward making the crime not worth the effort.

Expense/Travel Account Fraud

One type of fraud that is prevalent in the business world but that is "winked at" is the fraudulent reporting of expense or travel accounts. In business, this crime represents one of the most abused "entitlement" frauds. Although no one would disagree that the traveling worker should be compensated for, and is entitled to, all legitimate expenses related to his or her business, this account should not become a source of a second income. The types of expense accounts that are most problematic are those based on reimbursement. The primary problem is not the reimbursement, but rather the lack of realistic expenditure controls on the employee. Often mileage is inflated because the company rarely checks mileage. The result is that the employee adds cash to his or her pocket over and above the truly deserved reimbursement. Employees also can inflate lodging costs. They may report lodging at an expensive hotel while actually lodging at a much cheaper one. Some may forge documents to support their claim; still others may use hotel letterhead from a previous stay and reproduce the billing to be submitted for reimbursement. Fraudulently submitted meal receipts are another easy means to pocket some extra cash, even with per diem amounts in place. Undated and handwritten receipts are accepted, and excuses abound as to why no receipts were available. Having described a few of the more common ways in which travel and expense accounts are used fraudulently, it remains only to address the best method of prevention: implementation of realistic controls through policy and "actual expense" reimbursement.

Mileage misreporting and abuse can be addressed by providing a company car and/or use of a company credit card to pay for gasoline. The company policy should mandate that the employee document the starting mileage at fill-up prior to departing for business and again at each subsequent fill-up, including one after arriving home. This document should be submitted with any other expense account document at the end of the trip. The last fill-up may seem like a "gift" to the employee using their own car, but in reality it will aid in creating an audit trail of the usage and mileage and actually save travel account money. The misreporting of meals and lodging may be similarly addressed. Rarely does the regularly traveling businessperson meet his or her per diem for meals. The company policy of allowed amounts for each should be supported by the use of a company credit card. The same credit card used for the gasoline would ensure the removal of excuses of lost receipts and provides an easy-to-follow audit trail of expenses. The policy should still require submission of an expense report with receipts to be attached and should identify legitimate or authorized expenses and limits.

Someone once said, "Where there's a will, there's a way." When it comes to fraud that statement couldn't be truer. Perhaps the quote might more appropriately be, "Where there is greed, there will be fraud." I have barely scratched the surface of the fraud arena, but have tried to touch on those schemes that a law enforcement crime prevention practitioner might encounter. One need only pick up a newspaper to identify others such as insider trading, insurance fraud, bid proposal fraud, and investor deception. Each of these frauds requires a greater understanding and much more time to address than the average crime prevention practitioner can devote. The business requesting this type of intervention or assistance needs to be referred to a specialist with expertise in the area in question. The role of the law enforcement crime prevention practitioner is to be aware of the types of fraud, to identify some specialists in his or her region, and to be prepared to recommend several when requested to do so.

■ Chapter Summary

Crimes against businesses are largely theft oriented. Any injuries incurred during the crime are mostly incidental to the theft, rather than being the primary motivation of the criminal. Business crimes originate from both external and internal sources. Although the majority of the prevention effort is directed at the external sources, as much as 80% of the losses are attributable to internal sources. It is the crime prevention practitioner's duty to educate the business owner of this fact and of prevention methods related to both sources.

■ Review Questions

1. Are businesses more or less likely to be robbed than individuals?
2. What does separating the management responsibility of shipping, receiving, and storage accomplish as related to storage trailer thefts?
3. What business crime is defined as taking, or converting to one's own use, another's property as a result of a relationship of trust?
4. An employee who inflates lodging costs on a reimbursement report to his or her employer is committing what type of fraud?

■ References

ADT Security Services. 2004 National Retail Survey by Dr. Richard C. Hollinger, sponsored by ADT Security Services. p. 1.

Dunn, Robert. November 11, 2003. "Mitigating laptop theft." *Security Magazine*. Available online at http://www.securitymagazine.com.

Harris, Patrick. 2005. *The Cost and Impact of Gas Drive-Off Theft in Virginia*. Virginia Crime Prevention Association. Richmond, VA (contains responses from the Virginia Petroleum, Convenience and Grocery Association and the National Association of Convenience Stores).

Jack L Hayes International. 2004. *Shoplifters and Dishonest Employees Continue to Steal Profits from United States Retailers*. Fruitland Park, FL.

Merriam-Webster's Collegiate Dictionary. 10th ed. 1994. Merriam-Webster Incorporated, Springfield, MA.

National Crime Victimization Survey. U.S. Department of Justice; Office of Justice Programs, Bureau of Justice Statistics.

Thompson, Laura. 2001. "Are small banks more vulnerable to internal theft?" *American Banker Magazine*, vol. 166, p. 11.

Frauds Against
the Individual

"Love of money is the root of half the evil in the world. The lack of money is the root of the other half."

—Unknown

■ Introduction

In this chapter we continue to look into the world of fraud—but with a twist. Instead of the victims being businesses, the victims of these offenses are individual citizens. These particular frauds are of special interest to the crime prevention practitioner because it is these victims we are most likely to encounter and to influence through education programs that will actually lead to prevention.

Frequently the victims of these offenses are the elderly, living on a fixed income or off of their hard-earned savings. During my career in crime prevention, I have been approached numerous times after presenting an educational program and been told how the tips offered prevented an individual from being victimized. On more occasions I have been told that the presentation they had attended had prompted them to report suspicious activity that may have in turn prevented others from becoming the victims of frauds, scams, con games, and swindles.

A multitude of frauds are perpetrated against individuals, so each has been separated in this chapter for separate discussion. Because most scams and frauds operate under the same premise and with the same goal, the prevention application and efforts will be very much the same. Therefore, the frauds will be described with some prevention tips unique to the crime being listed and then the general prevention tips are listed under one separate heading.

■ The Premise and Crime Prevention
Application of Frauds

Frauds against individuals are big business for professional criminals. According to research by the National White Collar Crime Center, in 2002 one in three households was the victim of white-collar crime (Johnston, 2002). One conclusion of the research is that the number of victimizations might be a sign that individuals are unaware of how susceptible they are to such crimes. It is from this research finding that the premise of preventing such crimes begins. The crime prevention practitioner, understanding the methods used and opportunities sought by the white-collar criminal, arms the citizen with information and with techniques to avoid victimization. This is accomplished primarily through education and awareness campaigns.

The con artist, swindler, or white-collar criminal creates opportunities by playing upon the greed, the need, or the desire of the would-be victim to help others in some fashion. The crime prevention application begins with educating citizens about clues or signs of potential problems, and then arming them with information and tools to verify, check, or otherwise determine the validity of the offer or proposal. As related to the four D's of prevention, this education serves to delay the criminal act, which is frequently based on a "must act now" ruse; to detect the criminal scheme through knowledge; to deny criminals access to what they seek; and to consequently make the environment nonproductive to them so that they are deterred. When the citizen is armed with information about the schemes being used, he or she becomes more aware of the clues and can employ the tools taught by the crime prevention practitioner to avoid being scammed. The tools in each of these programs are designed to increase the effort required on the part of the scam artist and to increase the perception of risk of being revealed.

■ Scams

Pigeon Drop

One of the oldest scams still active is the pigeon drop scam or some variation. It works like this: A total stranger comes up to you with a request that you assist him. It seems that he has come into possession of some valuable item (found it, had it given to him, etc.), but due to some unfortunate circumstance he cannot cash the item in. Some possible excuses are that the individual is not a U.S. citizen, that he is disabled and can't show any income, that he is in the middle of bankruptcy, or that he is being reviewed for an alimony increase. The con man then tells you how he really needs the money and how he came into possession of the valuable legitimately. He will then ask for your advice, ultimately offering to share the profits for your help. Now a third party, supposedly a stranger to both of you, comes up and claims she had overheard the conversation. She has an idea of how to help and offers to do so for a share of the profit. She tells the swindler of a method to get cash for the valuable item, and also offers a way to keep everyone "honest." She suggests that because she needs to take the item somewhere to convert the item into cash, she will give the first person (original con man) an amount of cash to hold as collateral until she returns, and then she suggests that you (the victim) put up a matching amount so that the first guy will not feel that he is going to lose the valuable. She suggests that the first person, who originally had the valuable, should hold the money and that everyone meet at some location at a certain time to distribute the bounty. Once you give the cash to the first con man, he will meet up with the second person and share the wealth—as the victim, of course, you get nothing.

The Bank Examiner Scam

In this scam, the victim receives a telephone call or is approached by someone who claims to be a banking official where the person banks. The "official" tells the victim about some crime, usually theft, that is suspected at the bank and advises the victim that the bank suspects a certain teller or employee. They praise the victim's record as a good citizen or excellent customer, and ask him or her to aid in the capture of this employee. The official asks the person to withdraw a certain amount of cash from his or her account, assuring the person that even if the suspect gets away with the crime, his or her account and cash will be protected. The official asks to meet the victim, if not already there, to make the transaction and personally ensure the funds are safe. The official asks the person to withdraw the money and bring it to him or her to use as evidence. He or she will give the victim a receipt for the amount and advise him or her that as soon as the bank is done auditing the employee the money will be credited to the account. He or she may offer a specific time when the crediting will occur, such as by 2:00 p.m. Of course, the person is not an official but a scam artist, and the money is gone.

Call-Back Scams

This scam is one in which individuals are notified of a prize or service that they have won, and they only need call to verify some information to claim the prize. These scams work in a number of ways to benefit the criminal. One is that the individual may call back and be awarded the prize for free, but the shipping and handling fees are so exorbitant that the person ends up paying more than the item is worth. The person may win something that seems valuable but is not, and the gimmick is to get the person on the line to buy something at a greatly inflated price. It is also just as likely that the victim will never see the nonexistent prize after he or she paid the "prepaid postage and handling" fees. Finally, the telephone call itself might be what costs the citizen. Be especially wary of "900" numbers. Look on the material to see if there is a disclaimer regarding how much the call will cost. Often these scams that get people to call to see if they qualify play a recorded message for callers stating that all lines are busy, please hold, or some lengthy information about how to verify this or that. All the while the clock is ticking and the victim is being charged by the minute. (See "Telephone Scams" later in this chapter for other phone-related scams.)

Telemarketing Fraud

Telemarketing crimes cost consumers tens of billions of dollars annually. American consumers lost more than 40 million dollars in telemarketing fraud in 2000 (Federal Trade Commission, 2001). These crimes may originate through a stranger obtaining the citizen's name, personal information, and telephone number by purchasing a so-called customer list, or the criminal may mail the person information to bait him or her into contacting them. Sometimes a survey may be sent out with a request that the person list his or her purchasing "tendencies" and other information; this will then be followed up with a phone call or with a request that the person call them. Once on the telephone, these slippery serpents begin to beguile. They are skilled at the gift of gab and can con and deceive the most suspicious of citizens. They con using so many different techniques that to begin to list them here would be futile. The ultimate goal, though, is to get the victim to send them cash, credit card, or bank account information. The worst part is that after they have bilked the person once he or she will become known as an easy target and they will continue calling with promises of the prize or big return for just a little more cash. Finally, they may even sell the individual's name to others or call him or her back with a recovery scam promising to get the lost cash back for a fee, only to cause a deeper loss. The AARP has an excellent presentation available and is a wonderful source of information about this type of fraud. For contact information, please see the Resources section of this book. To remove your name from most calling lists, contact the National Do Not Call Registry at 888-382-1222 or visit its Web site.

Work at Home Scams

Working at home on your own schedule sounds appealing, doesn't it? For those who do not already work from home, the promise of doing so, with good monetary compensation, leads many down a slippery slope. The con man hopes that these advertisements placed in free papers, newspapers, and other locations will generate plenty of interest. The ad may indicate the possibility of big bucks for a small investment. In some cases no investment is required, so what is there to lose? Plenty! The reality is that often the small fee to start is for materials. The materials may be nothing but a book on how to get started, how to place scam ads like the one answered, or information on how to start a home business—materials that provide nothing that couldn't have been learned at the local public library. Some of these work at home schemes may actually involve some type of work, such as assembling products, envelope stuffing, or the like, but invariably payment is withheld due to "substandard work," "lack of productivity," and so on. Translation: The worker gets nothing but tired. In these scams, like all of them, be wary of promises that are too good to be true or of anything requiring you to put up money before beginning.

Investment Scams

Investment scams target a specific type of audience; therefore, they almost always promise big profits and often actually pay small dividends in order to get new victims (word of mouth advertising) and to string out the scam. In Roanoke, Virginia, in April 2004, a federal grand jury indicted just such a criminal. This criminal had a different twist—he wasn't just a financial adviser or investment agent—he ingratiated himself to a local church and became a "financial pastor." He had scammed over 140 people throughout the United States, some investing over $1 million with him. He was, after all, affiliated with a church.

Investment scam artists depend on new victims in order to pay some dividends to their previous victims and to keep from being detected. These types of scams are typically referred to as "Ponzi schemes," named after their originator, Charles Ponzi. Brokers who legitimately invest dollars but charge extra hidden fees may conduct other investment scams. They may pocket or skim from returns by underreporting performance of investments to clients (North America Securities Administrators Association, 2004).

Charity Scams

These scams often occur during the holidays and involve legitimate-sounding so-called nonprofit agencies. These scam artists use telephone solicitation, the mail, and more recently spam e-mails. The solicitor plays on the heartstrings of people who want to help the less fortunate. The problem is that the false charities use real-sounding names and pocket all the money that is sent them. Some are borderline legitimate and may advertise, for example, that they are soliciting to provide the families of police officers killed in the line of duty with a death benefit. They do not bother to tell you that the officers have to sign up with them to get it, and that what they are actually doing is buying a term life insurance policy for the officer. By checking into the charity and finding out where the money actually goes and if the charity is legitimate, the citizen can avoid this crime. Better yet is to suggest that people contact the charities that they want to contribute to and contribute directly to them. If the charity cannot provide a citizen an informational letter, physical street address (not a P.O. box), and some time to think about contributing, the citizen should be directed to hang up the phone and report the solicitor.

Credit Card Scams

These scams begin with a victim receiving a mail solicitation, a telephone call, or more recently an e-mail solicitation. The solicitation notifies them that they have won a prize. That's great, until they tell you that the person needs to pay for shipping or needs to provide his or her credit card information because the prize was the result of the card being used, and verification is needed. When the winner gives this information to anyone who they did not call originally, they become a loser. A variation that is becoming popular is to ask for other numbers on the back of the card. These numbers can be as damaging as any others. The numbers, part of a program known as Card Verification Value, are present to actually confirm the validity of the card. The unique three-digit code is also used to detect counterfeit cards. It is important to emphasize that credit card companies will *never* ask for any such information on the phone. They issued the card, and they have all the information they need relative to it.

Another way in which credit card information is obtained is by someone calling and claiming to be from the credit card company. He or she tells the potential victim that the company suspects an error or a theft from the person's account, and he or she needs to verify the credit card number. Another method criminals obtain credit card information is by setting up a bogus Internet company (which is very easy to do) and then advertising discounted items complete with digital photographs. Then they simply wait until the credit card orders start rolling in. A variation of the Internet company scam is to offer items for sale at Internet auction sites and collect for items without shipping a thing. In an effort to combat such Internet crime, in 2003 thirty-four United States Attorneys and numerous other law enforcement agencies nationwide and abroad participated in a program dubbed Operation Cyber Sweep, which revealed Internet frauds with estimated losses of $100 million and resulted in more than one hundred arrests and convictions (U.S. Department of Justice, 2003).

Telephone Scams

A relatively new, but growing, trend that is similar to credit card scams is scams that focus on stealing long distance service via calling cards, call forwarding, or tricking victims into calling an international long distance number.

Most of the telephone scams operate similarly to other scams, with the twist that telephone service is the target. For example, in the calling card scam the criminal calls the victim posing as a telephone or calling card company representative and uses some ruse to get the victim to give him or her their calling card number. The ruse may be, as with the bank examiner scheme, to catch a dishonest employee or, as with the credit card scam, to check on unauthorized charges. In any event, once the number is obtained, it is sold to others to make long distance calls, and the victim gets the bill. The call forwarding scams usually begin with the victim receiving an automated message that he or she needs to call a number for an urgent message or to claim some huge prize that he or she has won. The victim figures that he or she has little to lose by calling to "just see" what the call is all about. Usually the directions include the victim calling a two-digit number followed by an asterisk or the pound key and then an 800 number. Even better, the consumer thinks, because it is an 800 number and will cost nothing to call. Wrong again. When the victim calls, what he or she hears is nothing. He or she has just allowed incoming calls to be forwarded to a long distance operator. The criminal can then sell, or use, the telephone number to make long distance calls and again, the victim gets the bill.

The final method of bilking the consumer by way of their telephone that I would inform citizens of is the international long distance scam, or the 809 area code scam as it is sometimes called. This scam begins as the others either with a call coming in to an answering machine, via an automated system, or by some other ruse to get the victim to call the telephone number, such as an ad or e-mail. The ruse may again be based upon greed (a prize) or upon some personal need being fulfilled (a new secret weight loss treatment). In any event, the caller is duped into calling the number. Although the amounts of loss are greatly exaggerated, the calls to these numbers can result in some fees levied and a hefty long distance bill, especially if the person is on the line for some time. The area codes frequently used are 809, 876, and 284. These codes are in the Caribbean, where the usual additional three-digit international long distance codes do not have to be used, so they lend themselves easily to this scam. Other area codes to Canada and some other locations also may not require the three-digit code.

The best defense against all of these scams is for people to know who they are calling, check to see where the area code is located, be cautious when answering ads or prize notifications, and as always, not to reveal personal information to people they do not know or did not originate the call with.

Paving/Repair Scams

Con artists of this ilk tend to almost exclusively target senior citizens. In the paving scam, a worker may arrive at the door and claim to have some leftover materials from a job just up the block, and then offer to pave the driveway at a greatly reduced price. This is also used in relation to roofing and other repairs. The criminal will usually start the job or "plan to start the next morning" because he needs to pick up some other material or it is too late in the day. He will then require a down payment; in some cases the worker never returns, but in others he may return and do an inferior job. In either case, the consumer did not get what he or she was expecting.

Another con used in repair scams is when the con artist claims to be some type of home inspector, and offers a free inspection. Who wouldn't want something for free, right? The bogus inspector returns after inspecting the wiring, the floors, the insect infestation, or the plumbing and advises the homeowner that he has detected "code violations," "fire hazards," or some other ominous sounding problem that requires immediate attention. In some cases he may claim to be obligated by law to report it to the authorities if it is not immediately repaired. He likes the homeowner though—he or she reminds him of his own parents, and he wants to help them out, so there is one thing he can do. He happens to have a friend who would do the job quick and cheap, which would prevent him from having to report it to the authorities. The trap is laid, and if the homeowner agrees, the con man's accomplice calls and then comes by the next day or later that day to complete the repair. The accomplice goes in and completes the fictitious work and collects payment, and the homeowner is none the wiser.

International Financial Assistance Scam

This strange scam turned up a number of years ago in letter form and has transitioned now to the Internet. The target is usually a small business owner, but an individual may also receive a letter or e-mail. The letter or e-mail stresses secrecy, and the writer claims to be associated with a bank or, more commonly, claims to be a government official. The letter expresses the person's distrust of his home country, a potentially toppling government, or lists some other reason for what he is about to request. Originally these letters were all related to Nigeria and have come to be known as the Nigerian Letter Scam. The writer continues in the letter to praise the recipient and then states that because of the problems in his bank or government he needs to move large sums of money into safe accounts that cannot be seized. The letter then proposes to the recipient that if he or she will allow his or her account to be used, usually in the millions of dollars, the recipient will be rewarded with being allowed to keep a huge portion of the money. The thought process of the victim often goes like this: I get to keep a large sum of money for doing nothing. . . . I am helping a struggling country. . . . This sounds good. All that is left is for the victim to arrange to help the official to wire the money into his or her account. In order to do that, he will need your account number—remember, this must be done in complete secrecy. Of course, you see the scam as it is laid out before you, but many have not. How popular are the scams? I received one of the letters in my office at the police department. My name and address were probably purchased from a business I had previously dealt with. These types of scams account for tens of millions of dollars in losses annually. The governments from which the letters come will not aid in prosecution, and so the scam continues.

Medicare/Medicaid Fraud

Medicare and Medicaid lose billions annually to fraudulent claims. Many of these claims are not necessarily those claimed by the individual, but rather are unnecessary services billed by the medical business. Any intentional misuse of these programs is fraud. Some potential clues are claims for excessive amounts of supplies, claims for unnecessary services, billing Medicare instead of other (primary) insurers, and deceptive billing. Abuse of these programs is abuse of the taxpayer. The crime prevention practitioner should encourage recipients of these programs to examine their bills and ensure that the amounts on the bills are proper. If bills are in question or fraud is suspected, they should be directed to report it to their local Medicare or Medicaid office.

Fraudulent Billing of Estates

This scam is perpetrated by criminals who read the obituaries to find and select their victims. The criminal identifies a potential victim by reading the obituary, and then sends an unwarranted bill to the address of the deceased, which they can obtain by any number of means. The bill is often paid by an unsuspecting relative in an effort to settle the estate. The recommendation is for all bills to be verified prior to paying them. Verification may include verifying the existence of the business through the Better Business Bureau, Yellow Pages, or local merchant's association, or by simply checking for a physical address for mailing a follow-up letter. Those in charge of settling the estate may wish to request proof that the charge is due. Some records to request may include previous invoices, packing slips, order forms signed by the deceased, and the like.

■ Identity Theft

Identity theft is a financial crime in which the suspect assumes the identity of the victim through use of personal information and documents, and uses the "new" identity to commit fraud in various ways, leaving the person with the stolen identity to face the financial and legal responsibility for the suspect's crimes. This is one of the fastest growing types of white-collar crime in the United States today. It is estimated that in 2004, 3.6 million households discovered that they had been victims of identity theft within the previous six months, and losses of 3.2 billion dollars were linked to identity theft in 2004. One in six victims had to pay higher interest and one in nine were denied utility services as a result of identity theft (Baugm, 2006). To use the medical field as an analogy, most frauds are like an injury that caused a great deal of pain initially, but when treated the pain went away. There may be a scar as a reminder, but the pain is gone. Identity theft is more like a chronic disease; it hurts initially, and continues to hurt over and over again. Even after treatment it may come out of remission. This crime attacks more than the victim's bank account; it attacks the victim's credit, criminal record, driving record, insurance potential, ability to open bank accounts, and more.

Personal Information

Identity theft is perpetrated in a number of ways, but requires the suspect to obtain the victim's personal information in order to be successful. This information often is obtained through stolen mail, wallets, checks, and so on. Because the primary element of the success of this crime is obtaining the personal information of a victim, it is clear that the prevention element involves guarding such information and making it unavailable. The primary information sought by the criminal of this ilk is the victim's name, date of birth, social security number, address, and/or bank account number. Much harm can be done with just one or two of these pieces of information. Armed with the victim's name and date of birth, a birth certificate duplicate might be obtained and later used to get a driver's license and credit card. The credit card will have a different address from the victim's, so the bills are not sent directly to the true holder of the identity, but to the fictitious P.O. box. Not until the harm has been done to some degree is the true holder of the identity sought and sent a bill. That is when the headache begins.

In order for the crime prevention practitioner to combat this crime, it is imperative that he or she provides literature and presentations to citizens on methods to guard their personal information and on what to do when they realize that they have become a victim of identity theft. The following are some tips unique to this crime that the practitioner might offer for guarding personal information:

- Only carry your social security card, birth certificate, passport, and other such documents when absolutely needed for a transaction.

- Limit the number of credit cards carried on your person to the minimum. Remember, each additional piece of identification moves the criminal closer to success.

- If your state allows it, remove your social security number from your driver's license and opt instead for a state license or control number.

- Order your checks without your social security number imprinted on them. If requested, you may have to provide it for the store to accept the check, but most will not require it. Your driver's license number usually will be accepted instead of your social security number.

- Be careful what you discard in the trash. Do not discard anything with personal information on it without shredding or burning it if possible. Pre-approved credit card offers, bank statements, check stubs, and canceled checks should all be treated as though they contain personal information.

- Install a lock on your mailbox to prevent theft of mail with key information enclosed. Place all mail containing personal information, such as bill payments, in a secured post office box or mailbox.

- Never give out your personal information over the telephone, on the Internet, or in person unless you initiated the contact. Always request any carbon copies of credit card receipts and take them with you.

- Remove your name and personal information from mailing and calling lists. One free service to individuals that removes your name from a number of such lists for 5 years is the Direct Marketing Association. Write to them at the following address or visit their Web site to request removal:

Direct Marketing Association
Mail Preference Service: P.O. Box 9014
Telephone Preference Service: P.O. Box 9008
Farmingdale, NY 11735-9008

The Victim's Responsibilities

If a citizen is victimized, he or she needs to know what to do. It is a most unfortunate fact that the victim bears the responsibility of resolving the issues created by the criminal. The most important advice a victim can be given is to move to stop any additional damage as quickly as possible. Each day creates additional opportunities for the criminal. The first priority is to report the crime to local law enforcement and those financial institutions involved. The victim should use a notebook to log dates, times, telephone numbers, and names of the people they speak to in unraveling this knot that the criminal has created. They should keep receipts and records of costs as well. If the criminal is caught, he or she may be held accountable for the cost of correcting the credit of the victim. All written correspondence should be by certified mail with a return receipt requested and made part of the file kept by the victim. The three major credit reporting agencies—Equifax, Experian, and Trans Union—should be contacted to report the theft of the identity, to request that any applications be verified with the victim, and to request the victim's credit report. The victim should also contact those creditors with whom their identity was fraudulently used and ask them to close the account and forward the victim a copy of all of the fraudulent transactions. If the victim believes that a fraudulent change of address has been filed, he or she should notify the postal inspector. If it becomes necessary for the victim to change his or her social security number, he or she should be directed to the local social security office for further information.

In cases of identity theft, it is recommended that victims request a copy of their driving and criminal record. If any fraudulent driving charges are on their record, they should contact their local motor vehicle bureau or division for directions on how to correct the errors. Likewise, if fraudulent criminal charges exist, they should request direction from their local law enforcement agency, state police, or the Federal Bureau of Investigation.

A final piece of information that should be given to the victim of this crime is to be prepared to endure a very frustrating and long recovery period. Often victims will be pressured and even threatened by creditors, but they should remain calm in their resolve to cooperate and to assist in correcting any problems, but recognize that they are the victims and should not be revictimized each time a new creditor calls. It will be an uphill battle, but a battle that eventually can be won.

Others scams related to vacation property, miracle cures, weight loss supplements, and a plethora of other topics exist. In fact, if one can make money legitimately from it, it is a good bet that others are making much more from it fraudulently. I have covered a number of the major frauds perpetrated against the individual, and you can see what makes them successful—the individual wants something for nothing, seeks an easier way to accomplish a normally difficult task, or is simply careless in guarding the conveniences we so enjoy. The following are some general tips to help the careful individual avoid becoming a victim of fraud:

- Only purchase from reputable sources, whether in person, on the phone, or on the Internet.
- When called on the telephone, verify by mail, and when contacted by mail, verify by phone.
- Always get a physical address rather than just a P.O. box for contacting a business.
- Don't accept a Web site as proof of a legitimate business.
- If you buy online, understand both seller and purchaser responsibilities before you buy.
- Never provide your credit card information or bank account number to anyone that you did not initiate contact with. When using your credit card to purchase items online, check that the site is secure.
- Do not complete mail-in, online, or other surveys that will add your name to a list, which later may be sold.
- Block or do not complete the profile information associated with your e-mail address.
- Request that Internet directories remove your name, e-mail address, and other information from their databases.
- Ignore any pitch that involves high pressure sales, requests bank or credit card numbers, requests other personal information, or states that you will make a lot of money while doing little.
- Read any contract carefully and wait at least overnight before making any decision.
- Never send money to callers who offer to recover money you lost from dealing with other fraudulent telemarketers.
- Never deal with anyone who asks for a donation but cannot send you information in writing. If information is sent, research the organization.
- Never make investments with a company or person that guarantees that you cannot lose money.
- Be careful of anyone who asks you to send money in advance of receiving the item that you ordered.

- Any business that offers to send a courier to pick up your check or cash, or that asks you to wire the payment, is almost always involved in a scam.

- Offers that play on weaknesses or emotions—promises of a quick cure, quick and easy weight loss, easy debt correction, and so on—should be avoided.

- Monitor credit card bills closely for any items not charged by the cardholder.

- Discard any document that appears to be from the government claiming that you won a prize or that requires you to pay a small fee to receive a "refund." The government does not solicit in such ways.

- Be careful of "double deal" checks that, when cashed, enroll you for services that you may not desire.

- Never hire a person to inspect or repair your home without a contract being given to you and your having time to review it prior to making a decisions. The minimum recommended time for reviewing a contract is 24 hours.

- Never pay for information on working at home; if it is legitimate the information will be free.

- Check out any door-to-door sales company before buying. Remember, by law, if the consumer changes his or mind about any purchase over $25 within 3 days, he or she has the right to cancel the purchase without penalty. The cancellation must be in writing to the address on the bill; make sure there is one.

For additional information on frauds and prevention, people can be directed to national state resources, or they may wish to contact the following organizations:

Federal Trade Commission
Bureau of Consumer Protection
Office of Consumer and Business Education
1-877-382-4357 or 1-877-438-4338 (ID theft)

AARP
601 E St. NW
Washington, DC 20049

National Fraud Information Center
1-800-876-7060

■ Chapter Summary

Frauds against individuals succeed for two reasons—the skill of the criminal and the need, greed, or desire of the victim to help in some way. Usually the criminal emphasizes a sense of urgency to push the would-be victims to make a decision without taking time to think through what they are deciding or consulting with others. This urgency is often prefaced on their need to act now or miss the chance. The crime prevention practitioner must educate potential victims to slow down and check out the offer. A simple understanding that the con artist's goal is financial rewards, frequently while playing on the victim's hope of the same, will help the citizen to withhold their up-front money and reduce the losses suffered. One goal of the education programs related to these frauds is that the victims will not be ashamed to come forward when they have suffered losses, and thus can limit their own losses while helping others.

■ Review Questions

1. The AARP has estimated that more than 50% of the victims of what type of fraud are over the age of 50?
2. Which scam or con artist almost exclusively targets senior citizens by claiming to have "leftover material"?
3. Who bears the responsibility of resolving bills and expenses created by an identity thief?
4. A credit card holder typically has how many days to dispute questionable charges on his or her credit card bill?

■ References

Baugm, Katrina. April 2006. *First Estimates from the National Crime Victimization Survey–Identity Theft, 2004*. Published by National Center for Justice, Doc. # 212213. Washington, DC.

Center for Social Research. July 2003. "Privacy and American Business Survey." Available online at www.pandab.org/id_theftpr.html (accessed April 26, 2006).

Federal Trade Commission. October 2001. *Ditch the Pitch: Hang up on Telephone Hucksters*. Federal Trade Informational Packet. Washington, DC.

North America Securities Administrators Association. 2004. *State Securities Regulators Release Top 10 Scams, Schemes, and Scandals*.

Johnston, Brian. January 2002. "The battle against white-collar crime." *USA Today*.

U.S. Department of Justice. News Release. November 20, 2003. *Justice Department Announces Operation Cyber Sweep Targeting Online Economic Fraud*. Washington, DC.

Violence Prevention

"Outside of the killings, Washington has one of the lowest crime rates in the country."

—Marion Barry, Past Mayor of Washington, DC

■ Introduction

As absurd as the quote may seem, some people actually view violence as a minor problem that is perpetrated against others and not a danger to them. It is not until one stops to think that much of the violence in the United States is actually experienced by innocent parties rather than persons engaged in criminal activity that the importance comes to light. Violence is a problem that touches us all, and that should be addressed by all. Between 1981 and 1991 assaults increased by more than 47% (National Crime Victimization Survey, 2004). There were an estimated 1.7 million aggravated assaults in 1990 alone, and murders topped the 24,000 mark nationally for the first time in 1991. It became clear that something had to be done to curb the violent trend that was on the increase. Clearly, the statistical reality of the increase led to the anti-violence initiatives that continue today. Violent crime has steadily decreased since 1994, reaching its lowest point ever in 2002. This is due, at least in part, to a better understanding of the motivating factors for crimes of violence within the prevention community.

■ Violence Prevention Measures

As I have stated before, once the motivation and the crime are understood, prevention measures can be developed to counteract those motivators. It is here that we begin to examine the premise of violence prevention programs.

The Premise

To understand the premise behind violence prevention we must adopt a definition of what is meant by the word *violence*. I define violence, in the most simplistic terms, as an intentional act initiated to injure or inflict harm upon one or more victims. Since the first Biblical murder of one man by his own brother, man has been motivated to settle disputes through violence. Wars have been fought out of greed, the lust for power, and land. Violence has constituted a major element of entertainment, from the arenas of Rome to the ring of Madison Square Garden. Most adults can understand that violence should not be used to settle disputes, but some are ill equipped to settle them otherwise. Motivators for violence vary from emotional distress to entertainment to everything in between. As with other crimes, potential victims can do little to address what motivates the offender, but they can do a great deal to remove their opportunity to become a victim. Violence prevention programs that are developed or initiated by law enforcement crime prevention practitioners must first identify the motivation of the offender of a particular type of violence and then endeavor to educate those potential victims who meet the motivating factors of the criminal. Education will focus on changing the behavior, situation, and opportunity that allow offenders to recognize those individuals as an attractive target of their particular brand of violence.

Crime Prevention Application

In violence prevention programs we not only address the opportunity arm of the crime triangle, but also attempt to address the desire arm to some degree. This is especially true in certain types of violence, such as domestic and youth violence prevention programs. In these programs the offenders are "treated" to lessen or remove the motivating factors that they possess. Although this is more of an intervention program, when successful it may be considered to prevent future attacks. One might say that these programs address the crime of violence by removing the reward, that is, the satisfaction gained from the violence. You will see as we examine different types of violence, some programs address the attack by increasing the risk of detection, many increase the effort required to be successful, and almost all involve changing the potential victims' habits, all of which lead to deterrence, detection, delaying access (thus increasing risk), and finally denying access to their target altogether. Much of the prevention aspect depends on a change in the potential victim's behavior and in some cases a change in the physical environment.

The Process

In order to adequately address the more common violent crimes through programming it is helpful to discuss them separately. In this chapter I have identified five major categories for discussion: general personal safety, violence against women, youth violence (which includes school violence and gangs), and workplace violence.

■ General Personal Safety

Law enforcement crime prevention practitioners depend on cooperation from those they serve if their prevention programs are to be successful. Many times practitioners are called upon to present a program on personal safety. I am not a great fan of teaching physical self-defense as part of law enforcement prevention programs. There are many other avenues for obtaining that type of long-term instruction within every community. Our focus must be on reaching the masses with something that any person—old or young, fit or frail—can use to prevent attacks. The problem is that, although the information is well researched and proven to accomplish the goal, it requires the potential victim to actually apply the information. The approach taken to overcome this issue is to educate large audiences regarding the research and techniques and hope that at least a small percentage of the large group will practice the techniques. This would make it more difficult for offenders to select a target or would force them to alter their modus operandi, which may lead to their arrest. It is difficult to convince people to change their habits and behaviors, even with the threat of attack, but the practitioner should realize the importance of this task.

One point that I emphasize in my education programs regarding personal safety is "convenience kills." Target selection by an offender is no different than that of a beast in the wild. The target that meets the required needs of the criminal, based on his or her particular motivation and opportunity, will become the victim. In prevention, we address potential victims' behaviors and shift the scales in their favor. Convenience often clouds logical decisions regarding safety. For example, it may be more convenient to park behind the workplace because few others park there and it is closer than the regular lot. The facts that make it convenient, however, may very well be the same facts that make it unsafe. There may be a reason few others park there—perhaps it is dark or requires one to walk through an alley. When the risk of detection is reduced, the effort is reduced, and the right motivation or reward is available, the potential for attack in this area is substantially increased.

A survey conducted in 1998 to evaluate the importance that safety and security played in citizens' choices of shopping locations revealed that 67% of those surveyed stated that security was an important factor in the choice of where they shopped. Fifty-two percent of those surveyed refused to shop at sites where they perceived a lack of security (Mattson, 1999). Based on the behavioral issues discussed and research into violent attacks, the following are some general tips that you may want to include in presentations to reduce the probability of a successful attack:

- Always lock car doors as soon as you enter the vehicle.
- Park in populated areas, even if a short walk with co-workers or friends is necessary.
- Park in well-lighted areas if there is any chance that you may be returning to your vehicle after dark. Most violent victimizations occur in large urban areas between early evening and early morning hours (6:00 p.m.–6:00 a.m.), and the most likely site in which to become the victim of violence is in an area such as a parking lot (National Crime Victimization Survey, 2004).
- When walking to your vehicle, have your keys in your hand to expedite entry into the vehicle. Your attention should not be drawn into a search for keys. Plan in advance; have your keys in hand.
- When approaching your car with keys in hand, scan the area surrounding and even under your car. Look inside the car before entering.
- Limit travel after dark and try to have a companion along when you must travel at that time.
- If a co-worker or friend is departing around the same time as you, wait for them and walk out together. You may leave 10 minutes later but you will arrive home safe.
- Avoid overburdening yourself with items. An overburdened person makes an attractive victim because he or she is less likely to be able to react as quickly or abandon his or her packages.
- If you observe people you feel suspicious of, return to where you came from or go to another preplanned location. They may be up to nothing, but it is always better to be safe than sorry.
- When traveling by train, bus, or air transport, visit the restroom immediately upon arrival. This is the time when the restrooms will be most populated and provides the safest time in this private location.
- Keep a flashlight with fresh batteries in your car. Keep your vehicle well maintained and your fuel tank full. Some sage advice that my father-in-law gave his daughters was that it costs no more to keep your tank full than it does to keep it empty. A full tank, filled during the daylight hours in a safe location, prevents a breakdown at night in an unsafe or unfamiliar location.
- If you do break down, do not exit the vehicle. Call for help from the vehicle. Should a Good Samaritan offer help, open the window slightly and ask him or her to call the police.
- Avoid flashing cash, expensive jewelry, and other valuables that may identify you as a potentially profitable target.
- Walk or jog in more populated areas; avoid alleys and shortcuts that tend to be more isolated.
- When walking along the street, walk closest to the curbs to avoid recessed doorways. If a vehicle approaches you, move away from the vehicle and keep your distance.

- Always plan your actions and behaviors to allow you to control the environment, the time, and the activity and to increase the effort and risk of the offender. After only a short time of thinking things through before you take action, the actions will become habitual and you will become safer.

■ Violence Against Women

In this section our focus turns to a specific target of the violent criminal. The crime prevention practitioner will be called upon frequently to present on the topic of women's safety. Although many of the same tips listed under general personal safety will apply, additional steps must be taken to evaluate the unique motivation behind this type of violence. In this section we will look at sexual assault and rape and briefly touch upon domestic assault. An estimated 223,290 women were raped or sexually assaulted in 2003. (National Crime Victimization Survey, 2004). About seven in ten women raped identified the suspect as a friend, acquaintance, or intimate partner. (National Crime Victimization Survey, 2004).

The statistical data provided not only help us to identify the size of the problem of violence against women, but also are beneficial in evaluating possible causes or contributing factors leading to such victimization. For example, the statistics mentioned above indicate that drugs and alcohol were at least part of the equation that may have led to violence. These data are supported by street officers, who know that there has been a recent upturn in the usage of date rape drugs. These drugs, such as gamma hydroxy butyrate (GHB), rohypnol, methylenedioxymethamphetamine (MDMA), and ketamine, have been used to incapacitate women to facilitate sexual assault and rape. When investigating such crimes, the law enforcement community must be careful not to "blame the victim" by asking why she frequented a certain location or dressed a certain way. At the same time, the law enforcement crime prevention practitioner must recognize that there is indeed a correlation with such behaviors and attempt to educate women before an assault occurs.

It is true that sexual assault may occur anywhere, including the workplace, but statistics reveal that as much as 50% of rapes occurred within the victim's home. A December 2000 study of the sexual victimization of university women revealed that 9 out of 10 of the victims knew their assailant (Fisher, Cullen, & Turner, 2000). Armed with the knowledge and information gained from these statistics and the knowledge of crime prevention, practitioners have developed awareness programs that focus on removing the advantage of the assailant, reducing the opportunities for such assaults, and improving the victim's chances for escape when assaults do occur. These programs concentrate on the planning and mental aspects of prevention rather than on the physical defense aspect.

The awareness programs encompass those tips mentioned in the previous section, but also include the following:

- Install a motion sensor light in a location where a vehicle entering the driveway or a person approaching will activate it. This simple step allows a woman returning home to scan the area prior to exiting the relative safety of her locked running vehicle.
- Leave a light on when there is even a remote possibility of returning after dark. This will not only will provide the illusion that someone is home, but also will allow the resident to recognize that something might be amiss if the light is not on.
- When first moving into a new apartment or house, the resident should have all exterior doors rekeyed, even if it is at her own expense.
- Any women residing alone should take steps to create the illusion of others residing in the home. It is believed that at least half of rapes are planned, including the

choice of victim and location. Remember that at least half of these attacks occur within the victim's home. Some ways to create the illusion of other residents are:

- Have a male friend record the voice mail message on your machine.
- When recording your own voice mail message, do not use your name; instead, state, "You have reached 555-5555, we cannot come to the phone right now. Please leave a message."
- Place a large pet bowl outside your residence to imply that you have a large dog.
- List only your last name or just the address on you mailbox.

- If you do not want an unlisted number, list your name in the telephone directory by last name and first initial only. Ask the telephone company to list no address in the directory for your number.

- Never reveal to a caller on the phone or an unknown visitor at your door that you are home alone. If an individual come to your door requesting medical or other help, do not open your door. Inform them that you will call the police to help them, then do so.

- Always verify repairmen or service persons' identity through a locked door prior to allowing them to enter. Such workers generally carry business identification for just such instances. While they are inside, leave your door open if possible to provide an easier escape or allow shouts for help to be heard.

- Ensure that all exterior doors are substantial and equipped with deadbolt locks and peephole viewers. (See Chapter 12 for specifications.)

- Do not reveal your telephone number or address to new acquaintances; instead, take their number or give them your cellular telephone number. Do not allow new acquaintances to pick you up at home; instead, offer to meet them somewhere public until you are satisfied that you can trust them.

- When going out alone or on a date, tell someone where you will be and with whom, especially if going on a blind date or going out with a new acquaintance.

- Develop and always have a plan to quickly remove yourself from situations that make you feel uncomfortable or uneasy. If your date is becoming aggressive, implement your plan. Tell the person that your brother is waiting at your home for you to help him, or anything else that gets you away from the situation.

- While out on the town alone, or preferably with a friend, guard your drink to avoid it being drugged with a date rape drug. Have your friend watch your drink while you are away, and do not accept drinks from anyone other than wait staff unless they are in a sealed bottle.

- Don't accept invitations to parties from people you don't know unless a friend accompanies you or is familiar with the people.

- When going to parties, assess the situation. Notice if is there an extreme inequity in the ratio of men to women; whether people are already inebriated, aggressive, or excessively rowdy; and whether you feel comfortable.

- In addition to the general tips regarding walking provided in the previous section, walk with confidence with your head up and make eye contact with others in passing. The crime of rape is very much about control, and a confident woman can be a deterrent.

- When using an elevator, position yourself near the floor buttons. If attacked on the elevator, do not push the alarm button because it often is designed to stop the elevator; instead, push as many of the floors as possible. Each time the door opens represents another opportunity for escape, an opportunity for a witness to hear your screams for help, or an opportunity for others to come to your assistance.

- Avoid using stairwells alone. Stairwells by design are often fire resistant and therefore virtually soundproof, which creates an ideal location for an attack.
- Although it is indeed a woman's choice of how to react, statistics have indicated that it is almost always prudent, absent the presence of a weapon, for the woman to do whatever it takes to avoid being taken to a secondary location.
- Once an attack has begun, the emphasis should be on surviving the incident and reporting the crime immediately before showering, changing clothes, or cleaning the rape scene, which may disturb valuable evidence.

For more information on sexual violence against women, contact the National Sexual Violence Resource Center at 877-739-3895.

Domestic Violence

Having mentioned the unique environment and motivation of the sexual assailant and rapist, I should also mention that domestic violence has its own unique motivating factors. Guided by power and control, the person who abuses his domestic partner, cohabitant, or spouse has been proven to have long-term issues leading to such actions. The cycle of abuse has clearly been recognized by experts, and in order to intervene the cycle must be broken. This is more difficult than one might imagine because the victims are often afraid to leave the relationship because of a feeling of isolation, a lack of support from their family, a feeling of shame, a lack of financial support to sustain themselves, and a feeling of dependence. It often takes repeat incidents to motivate the victim to take steps to break free.

Preventing domestic violence begins before a woman becomes involved in such abusive relationships. The crime prevention practitioner can best serve the prevention role by educating young women about the warning signs of a potential batterer and of actions that they can take to remove themselves from the relationship before it escalates to violence. Warning signs include when a significant other is overly possessive, jealous, and controlling; verbally demeaning or abusive; has a history of violence; and is prone to violent outbursts.

Once armed with the warning signs, the practitioner must emphasize to his or her audience how manipulative and skilled the batterer can be. The practitioner should develop a resource list and be prepared to advise the victims of how to break the cycle. To begin, the practitioner may refer the possible victim to the National Domestic Violence Hotline at 888-799-SAFE. An excellent resource for additional information on domestic violence issues is the Web site for the Office on Violence Against Women.

The final role of the law enforcement crime prevention practitioner is to educate law enforcement about the issues related to women's victimization and how to conduct a tactful investigation, as well as to provide resources to which officers may refer victims. Without a specialized domestic violence specialist, the practitioner should coordinate efforts within the courts and the community to address intervention. In order to do so, the practitioner should become very familiar with state statutes, local ordinances, and resources related to this topic. An additional resource of value is the *Toolkit to End Violence Against Women*, available from the National Advisory Council on Violence Against Women and the Office on Violence Against Women mentioned above.

■ Youth Violence Prevention

Prevention of violence by and against youth has been given a lot of attention, and rightly so. Not only are younger people more likely to be victimized, but those 12–24 years of age also have demonstrated a tendency to actually be more violent than the rest of the population (National Crime Victimization Survey, 2002). The National Center for Injury Prevention and Control (2004) lists homicide as the leading cause of death among African Americans between 10 and 24 years of age. More than 750,000 youth of this age bracket were treated in emergency rooms in 2004 for violence related injuries. It is because of such alarming facts that many fine national and local programs have been developed over the years.

Those not truly understanding the programs' approach have unfairly criticized some of these programs. It is not enough to say that this program or that program is not successful because it does not meet one, or even any, of its original goals. Ask any person who has ever initiated a new program through federal grant funding, and he or she is likely to tell you that often a program developed to accomplish a certain goal will inadvertently accomplish a totally unexpected, but equally valuable, result. This occurred with the Drug Awareness Resistance Education (DARE) program. Researchers may be unable to prove a nonentity (that which was prevented and never occurred), but when evaluating such programs one should examine all results. For example, in the above mentioned DARE program, it can be proven that a unexpected result was that students are more likely to have a positive impression or more trust of law enforcement and an increased knowledge of the harm that drugs may cause. Youth violence prevention programs are by design multifaceted and often involve education as their foundation. In this section we will attempt to overview some steps to follow when developing a violence prevention program.

One of the first steps to take when developing a prevention plan is to identify the risk factors facing youth today. We must understand that young people act out violently, and are victimized violently, for numerous reasons. Some of the reasons are their lack of social skills, their parents' discipline styles, their home environment, their family's economic status, and substance use or abuse. It is interesting that time and again researchers are finding that the same risk factors that cause youth to act out violently are those that result in others becoming chronic victims of violence. Without actually conducting an in-depth analysis of the theories surrounding juvenile delinquency and victimization, we should recognize that there is indeed a correlation between the risk factors listed and the incidence of violence, and therefore the factors are a key part of any prevention program. This is why partnerships are of crucial importance to a successful program. Partners such as the Boys and Girls Clubs of America, the local schools, and community outreach programs address the diverse risk factors, each using a different approach.

Alternatives to violence must be taught, modeled, and reinforced, and certainly law enforcement is ill equipped to handle such a monumental task alone. Law enforcement may act as the catalyst, but there are many resources that will be more than willing to help make a youth violence prevention program successful. Some provide mentoring and modeling of positive behaviors, others provide education in conflict resolution skills, and yet others may provide a safe and positive environment where a young person may spend time away from home. All such partners are needed. The law enforcement crime prevention practitioner's role is to coordinate these efforts and to facilitate directing the at-risk youth to such programs through a court liaison or other means. The practitioner also participates in the education aspect by providing valuable information to youth and parents on conflict resolution skills training designed to alter the behavior leading to violent victimization, bullying, gang violence, abduction, Internet crime, and other violence-related issues.

Another very important role for the practitioner is to be involved in conducting school safety and security audits. Such audits should be conducted by those trained in Crime Prevention Through Environmental Design (CPTED) to identify locations and environmental issues creating vulnerabilities within the school and surrounding area. The trained practitioner should then make appropriate recommendations for actions or changes that would reduce the vulnerabilities identified. Each state and school system will require different changes and may have a set format, see Appendix 10.1 for an example of how one aspect of an audit, the exterior physical design, may be documented. A complete audit will review and address many more aspects including the interior design, policies, and critical incident procedures or plans. In the example, notice the people listed on the cover page as being involved in the larger complete audit. An audit cannot cover all of the necessary points without those most knowledgeable being involved; one or two individuals alone should never conduct an audit.

Having already discussed generally the incidence of victimization as related to the offender and the need for potential victims to alter certain behaviors that make them attractive as victims, I have provided the following list of tips that a practitioner may wish to use in presentations or program development for young children:

- Ensure that young children know their full name, address, and telephone number.
- Ensure that children know to call 9-1-1 or 0 if they need help.
- Teach young children to go to a store employee, a security guard, or a police officer if they become separated form their parents in a store or mall.
- Teach all children that they should not talk to or take gifts from strangers, even if they seem nice or ask for help.
- Educate parents to identify a password with their children that must be used by anyone who is sent to pick them up. Teach the children that if the person does not know the password, they should not get close to them or go with them, even if they do know their name. Once used, the password should be changed.
- Teach children to keep their distance from cars slowing down near them. If your jurisdiction has a safe house program, such as the McGruff House program, teach children to look for the house designation for help.
- Educate children who must enter an empty house to immediately lock the doors and call either a parent or a person designated by the parent to advise them that they are home. Parents and children should develop a plan of where the child should go if they arrive home and find the door open or something suspicious.
- Educate children never to reveal to anyone on the telephone, on the Internet, or at their door that they are alone and never to open the door to people who they do not know well. Practice ways that the children may appear not to be alone, such as advising the caller, "Mom is in the shower. She said you should call back later."
- Check with schools for after-school programs that allow so-called latchkey children to remain late on the school property at a program until a parent can pick them up, rather than send the child home alone. This is often an excellent way to address socialization issues that have been linked to future violence tendencies and victimization potential.
- When playing outside, even in their own front yard, children should not relax safety rules.
- Teach children to trust their feelings. If something feels wrong or unsafe, they should get away and notify an authority.
- Remind youth that if anyone ever tries to grab them, touches them in a way that makes them feel unsafe, or tries to force them into a car it is okay to scream, fight, and run away.
- When left in a car by a parent making a quick stop at a store, doors should be locked, the ignition turned off, and the keys taken with the parent. Children should be told that they should not unlock the doors for anyone other than the parent or guardian who they are with.
- Educate parents as to the importance of checking references of babysitters, reviewing daycare certifications, and familiarizing themselves with their children's teachers and school policies.

- Parents should always have updated photographs of their children and know their child's personal identifiers such as the existence of birthmarks or scars and their blood type.
- Teach children that no one, not even a teacher, minister, Scout leader, or family member, has a right to touch them in their "private areas" or in a way that makes them uncomfortable. Teach the children that if this happens they should get away and tell a parent or trusted adult.
- Children should be taught that they have a right to privacy when changing clothes or using the restroom.
- It should be emphasized to adults that if they suspect child abuse, even if they do not think it "means anything" they should report it to the police, the school, or anonymously to child protective services for investigation.

Sexual Offenders on the Internet

Sexual offenders are no longer just lurking in the shadows of parks and playgrounds. Today parents and kids invite them into their homes. The offenders create a digital mask and communicate freely with anonymity. A pedophile on the Internet does not use force, or even threats; he or she simply develops a relationship and seduces the children over time. Some research has revealed that one in five youngsters using the Internet have been approached for inappropriate sexual activity online (Finkelhor, 2004). What is worse is that many times the parent is oblivious to what is going on. Often the computer is in a child's room and not controlled by parental controls or filtering software, even when they are available free of charge. Prevention tips for this type of seduction and molestation crime are really the same as they would be for the offender in the playground. Some specific tips that the practitioner may offer to prevent the Internet from being a door into a child's room are:

- Do not allow children to complete profiles on Internet sites and chat rooms. Pedophiles access this information and can easily identify the sex, age, and interests of a child and then create a similar profile for themselves to get close to the children.
- Place the Internet-accessible computer in the family room, kitchen, or other room in which private viewing is limited. As a parent we monitor what movies our children view and music they hear; we should also monitor what sites and chat rooms they are accessing.
- Use parental controls provided by your Internet service provider. If you don't know how to set them up, call the provider and get directions. If a child truly needs to access a site for school reasons, advise them that you will sign on under your password and allow them to do their research while you are home and able to monitor the access.
- Purchase filtering software to block certain sites and verbiage. A parent can search the Internet for a list of the various types of filtering software available and costs. Some packages filter access through a third-party server and others simply block the sites. There is also "spyware" available that allows parents to see the sites that their child is accessing without the child realizing that their digital trail is being tracked.
- An excellent prevention tool is for parents to become familiar with the language of shortcuts used by children and Internet users. For example, if a parent is passing by and their child is chatting with a friend, it would be beneficial for the parent to know that "pos" means parent over shoulder. What are they hiding? It could be typical teen behavior, but at least it gives the parent the option to inquire further.
- Educate children about how people can pretend to be someone else on the Internet and that things are not always as they seem.

- Teach children *never* to give their name, telephone number, address, school name, or parents' information to anyone who they do not know personally from face-to-face conversations.
- Forbid children from sending photographs of themselves or their friends to anyone over the Internet unless first approved by a parent.

Youth Gangs

If time allowed us to learn enough to prevent all crimes completely, we certainly should have eradicated the youth gang problem long ago. Frederick Thrasher (1927) initiated a study of youth gangs in Chicago in 1927 and documented his findings in his book *The Gang*. In the 1960s more than 20 U.S. cities reported having gangs. At that time it was estimated that the United States had over 700 gangs (Wexler, 1997). By the 1990s, the estimated number of gangs had grown to 2300 nationally. It was in the 1990s that an alarming trend began to surface—gangs becoming active in smaller jurisdictions. By 1995, the Office of Juvenile Justice and Delinquency Prevention Programs conducted a national survey examining the trend reported that more than half of the agencies responding that gangs were active in their jurisdictions were those with populations less than 25,000 (National Youth Gang Survey, 1995). It is speculated that this migration may have been due to population shifts or to the freedom with which the gangs could operate in jurisdictions unaccustomed to dealing with this unique problem. Of course larger cities also continue to experience problems with such gangs. The 1998 National Youth Gang Survey findings reported that every city with a population of 250,000 or greater reported the presence of youth gangs, as they did in 1996 and 1997. In addition, the number of gang members increased 43 percent in rural counties from 1996 to 1998.

Gangs concern communities because of their activities. Gang activities are related to vandalism, drugs, and other youth crimes. Most of the victims of youth violence are juveniles. Gang violence leads to intimidation of citizens and often can result in closed businesses, residents fleeing the community, and localities losing populations and the tax base that supports community-provided services. It may be because of this fear that jurisdictions historically have denied the existence of gangs. The powers that be may deny the existence out of some misguided belief that their lack of admission will retain the residents and businesses, or they may deny the problem for some political reason. One major factor that contributed to the denial of gangs was the lack of a standard by which to substantiate or refute what a gang was. When asked about the existence of gangs in their jurisdiction, most people would answer based on their individual belief of what constituted a gang. Opinions and interpretations varied within a jurisdiction, and therefore it appeared that the jurisdiction was hiding something.

In recent years, legislators across the nation have recognized the value of having a standard measure by which a gang may be identified. Law enforcement has welcomed this definition, and armed with such a standard can now apply the elements required to determine whether a gang exists. A typical codified definition of a gang will include some language that defines the number of participants, some means of unified identification, and the presence of ongoing criminal activity. The number may simply be three or more, and the unified identification may be nothing more than a group name, insignia, common color scheme, and distinct style of clothing or hand sign. Couple these with the ongoing criminal activity, whether vandalism or drug sales, and the definition would be met. Absent the criminal element, the Boy Scouts or National Guard might meet the definition. It is the criminal element that makes a group a gang.

It is interesting that many gangs did not begin originally with a criminal activity in mind, but rather formed out of a common need. Some form out of boredom, some from a need to belong to something that they felt a part of, and some out of common interests. The bond that began from this initial contact or need leads to shared activities and a sense of family. Some believe that it is the lack of guidance that leads the group from this stage to criminal activity to gain status within the group. In fact, the group takes on a family-like quality to the members and they strive to impress their brothers or sisters. They get the attention that they seek, they get recognition for their gang activities, and the gang provides them protection and physical needs, often from ill-gotten means. Understanding this transition is crucial in developing gang prevention and intervention programs. It is essential that the attention and recognition sought by the youth be provided, but through positive peer mentoring, family involvement, or community outreach.

The following are three proven effective responses to gangs. Each response may be appropriate in certain instances, but not appropriate in all.

Law Enforcement–Rule Keeping

Certain gangs and hardcore members will be so entrenched in the gang lifestyle that the only effective way to curtail their activity will be law enforcement and incarceration. Legislators have recognized this and have provided for enhanced punishments for those hardcore members and those that recruit youth into gangs. The enforcement option allows officers to identify active members; establish their territories, hierarchy, and activities; and then target the leaders with selective enforcement. As part of a larger approach, charges against upstart or newly recruited members may create an opportunity to force early intervention on an unwilling participant. Some useful tools for the enforcement approach are curfew ordinances and parental accountability laws such as child neglect and truancy programs.

Officers throughout the agency should be trained in identifying gang characteristics and membership, intelligence gathering, reading of street gang signs and graffiti, and the desired reporting procedures. In medium to smaller jurisdictions in which gangs have not yet gained a foothold, specialized units are undesirable. It is much better that the gang-related dollars be spent on training and intelligence gathering hours at this juncture. The creation of a gang member database and means of accessing the information are important tools in controlling gang activity and in enforcing gang-related statutes that have been created to control the related violence and spread of the gang.

Gang Intervention

Once a young person is suspected of becoming involved in a gang, quick action is needed. The longer the youth is involved in the gang, the deeper his or her loyalty is likely to become. Likewise, when a gang is beginning to form, intervention and enforcement are more likely to be successful than after the gang is established.

Gang intervention begins with the initiation of the problem-solving process. Whether one chooses to utilize the SARA process (scanning, analyzing, response, and assessment) as described in this book or some other process, the issue must be researched and analyzed in order to properly identify the direction that the response should take. If boredom and intimidation are leading youth to criminal acts as a group, then the response may differ than if the motivation is the need to be accepted or to receive recognition. After the motivation, or reward, for gang membership or creation is known, a response may be developed that replaces the illegitimate reward with a positive legitimate one. The crime prevention practitioner's role in the intervention stage is to identify such motivations and to bring together the resources to address the needs through coordination. The successful practitioner will introduce those participating in providing resources and create a coalition that eventually will accept the responsibility of managing the intervention program, with the practitioner then becoming a resource for their efforts.

Prevention

As with intervention, the most important element in preventing gangs from being formed and from growing their membership later is to understand the factors that led the individuals to the gang in the first place. Although there are still those who would argue that youth join gangs because of economics or for financial reasons, most experts now agree that the primary underlying reasons for joining a gang are not financial. The most cited reasons are the need for recognition and for a sense of belonging or acceptance—in other words, to receive positive attention that they are not receiving elsewhere and to be recognized for their achievements. The gang provides that acceptance and recognition for achievements, albeit criminal or illegitimate ones. Many youth who are unsuccessful in the primary activities of their peers, such as academics or sports, turn to illegal acts to find their niche. The creation of other legitimate activities in which young people might excel, the encouragement and recognition by schools and community organizations for achievements that are not necessarily those often recognized, and the simple act of positive involvement in the life of a youngster may be all that are needed to steer that child in the proper direction.

Social intervention by agencies identifying at-risk youth who are apt to be recruited or targeted by gangs is the first step of prevention. The crime prevention unit should partner with social workers, school counselors, student outreach programs, parks and recreation agencies, and the like to redirect the at-risk youth to a legitimate means of receiving recognition or to act as the surrogate family that the youth seeks. The at-risk youth may be receiving little encouragement or self-worth from his or her home environment, and it is essential that someone build a positive framework if that child is to avoid finding his or her self-worth from the gang. Some programs that the practitioner may wish to begin to coordinate and gain partners for are organized after school activities, mentoring programs, church-sponsored activities that focus on building self-worth, summer and after-school jobs programs, and job training courses. In short, by spending some time and effort assisting the at-risk youth to participate in some activity that he or she may find rewarding and be successful at, we can prevent him or her from seeking the recognition and self-worth from the surrogate family relationship provided by a gang.

The crime prevention practitioner also should take the message of gang participation and membership to the parents and community through education. At a minimum, the education program should provide an overview of why youth join gangs, and provide parents with information on how to recognize that their child may be participating in, or being courted by, a gang for membership. Some signs of potential recruitment or gang interest are:

- Consistent wearing of the same colors
- Associates or friends all wearing the same clothing style or colors (for example, all wearing the same professional football team jacket)
- Graffiti on school books, notebooks, in the child's room, or in a "clubhouse," especially if the same graffiti or work is found
- Photographs of the youth in a group apparently posing and presenting unfamiliar hand gestures or signs
- Comments about how their friends care more about them than the parent or how they would do anything for their "boys" or "girls" (friends)

The education program should also include certain actions that members of the family and the community can take to combat gang recruitment. Some tips for what the family and community can do include:

- Teach youth to respect themselves and to respect others, regardless of the talents or lack of talent they may display.
- Talk to children about the consequences of violence and gang activity and emphasize that violence may not just lead to death, but also can lead to physical and mental incapacitation.
- Try to know your teen's whereabouts and friends at all times. Take the time to find out about where your teen's friends live and learn more about them.

- Support youth programs and hobbies. If a young person wants to brag to you about his or her activity, show a genuine interest and reinforce their pride in what he or she is accomplishing.
- Assist in organizing alternative programs for youth within the community. Volunteer to staff the activity, even if you can give only a few hours a month.
- Avoid humiliating youth for their shortcomings, but rather praise them for their strengths. When providing praise, provide it for specific things, not general praise. Always take steps to build the self-esteem of children for any positive acts, whether sports or a good deed that they did for another.
- Be a good role model by avoiding violence and by encouraging others.
- Always monitor the television, movies, and music entertainment that children are involved in and discourage, or if a parent prohibit, any such entertainment that glamorizes the gang or violent lifestyle.

Finally, as the crime prevention practitioner attempting to prevent gangs and gang recruitment, it is your role to work with the schools and local media to provide anti-gang messages. Contact the local office of the Bureau of Alcohol, Tobacco and Firearms for assistance in providing the Gang Resistance Education and Training (GREAT) program that the organization will sponsor free of charge to the locality. Work with the media to ensure that they do nothing to glamorize gangs when reporting about gang violence, thus elevating the status of the gang. A good agreement is to ensure that when reporting gang violence, the media should refer to the violence as criminal acts and always include a paragraph about the positive steps being taken to eliminate gangs in the community, such as suppression and intervention measures.

School Violence

Parents have always depended upon schools to be a safe haven for their children. Even when children live in communities infested with violence and drugs they have found solace in the local school. The unfortunate reality is that drugs and violence are now a very common problem, even within the school environment. Violence has escalated from the common fistfight to use of weapons and even mass murder. The school resource officer (SRO) program, created to build student–officer rapport, has out of necessity become relegated to a role of enforcer. School violence can, and must, be addressed. The law enforcement crime prevention practitioner may be required to take the lead, but more often the local SRO or school administrator will initiate the process. If a jurisdiction does not have an SRO and wants to start such a program, it can learn how by contacting the National School Safety Center at 805-373-9977 or by visiting its Web site.

Behavior Indicators

Much work has been initiated to identify the causes of bullying and violence and to profile those with the potential to act out violently and who need early intervention. These efforts have led to the creation of numerous programs designed to prevent violence and to ensure early intervention. The programs vary in scope, but most build upon the profile data, identify some process (school-based or otherwise) to create a positive outlet in which potential offenders can vent their anger, and address the physical environment and policies of the schools. It is to this end that the crime prevention practitioner or the SRO should direct their efforts.

The following violence indicators, gained through research in the field by experts, may aid in identifying students susceptible to acting out violently (Olweus, 1993). As with any such list of indicators, the presence of one or more indicators in a youth suggests that closer scrutiny may be in order, and the accumulation of indicators increases the youth's potential for violence. The list should be used only as a gauge for potential violence and to focus intervention efforts.

- Sudden anger outbursts, especially if this is a new characteristic of this student
- Extreme interests in weapons
- Declining grades and behavior
- Change in companions or friends or isolation of oneself
- History of bullying, including ostracizing, name calling, and mean-spirited teasing
- Refusal to comply with rules
- Threats to others' or their own welfare
- Violent thoughts, drawings, or stories (verbal or written)
- Cruelty to animals
- Glorifying violence or associating fame with violent acts
- Overly controlling of or overly submissive to others
- Lives in a home characterized by negativity, lack of rules, and extreme use of corporal punishment as discipline
- Admission of, or bragging about, violence against others

In evaluating the indicators of violent tendencies, it becomes obvious that the influences that lead to the tendencies may originate from any number of sources. The home environment, peer social status, various entertainment venues, and experiences contribute to how a student acts or reacts in a given situation. Prevention of violence must therefore be multi-faceted and involve a variety of partners if it is to be successful. Interestingly, the same measures that are suggested to address the potential for violence and bullying are likely to also address the potential for victimization; that is, a very fine line exists between what influences the creation of a bully and what influences the creation of a chronic victim (Unnever, 2000).

Some things schools can do to help prevent violence among schoolchildren include the following:

- Focus on children revealing problems to authorities as "good citizenship" rather than as "snitching."
- Sponsor peer conflict resolution programs and other such programs that educate youth in positive ways of handling conflict.
- Sponsor an anonymous telephone or Internet tip line for students to report crimes and violence in advance and to identify suspects after they occur.
- Educate students in methods of identifying signs that a friend might be the victim of bullying, suffering from depression, or on the verge of acting out themselves.
- Educate students about the harm caused by drugs and violence. If your schools have no program to focus on substance abuse harm, the school or law enforcement agency may wish to contact DARE America.
- Establish a reward program for recognizing good behavior and positive conflict resolution.
- Sponsor a peer mentor program to welcome new students to the school and help them to assimilate quickly.
- Encourage teachers, staff, students, and parents to compliment others for accomplishments, no matter how seemingly insignificant. Low self-esteem has been identified as a significant contributing factor in both bullying violent behavior and chronic victim behavior.
- Involve parents and law enforcement in addressing school-related issues and in presentations of awards to youth.

- Provide a safe physical environment in which students may learn. Have a law enforcement officer or other professional trained in conducting school safety assessments conduct such an assessment to examine the physical vulnerabilities of the school, to assist in developing critical incident plans, and to assist in creating other pertinent guidelines.

School Policies Contributing to Safety

In the midst of an incident is not the time to decide what to do to address the incident. Law enforcement, military, and all of groups that are involved frequently in critical or emergency situations know that the key to success is preplanning and training. Policies are preplanned directives that guide our actions in situations when they are occurring. In other words, they have been developed in a calm environment for use when the environment is often anything but calm. Policies also guide the decisions of the administrator regarding unusual circumstances that are infrequent and therefore require guidance in handling them properly. Each school has policies for handling student misbehavior, grades, and the like; schools should also have policies that guide actions and activities related to the prevention of crime and violence. The following are a representative sample of some recommended policies, but the list should not be considered to be all-inclusive:

- All schools should produce and distribute a student handbook that contains information pertinent to the expected behavior and responsibilities of the students. The handbook should be required reading and acknowledged by the signature of both the parent and the student.
- All schools should establish in writing a zero tolerance policy for weapons, drugs, and gangs, and should specify in the guidelines what actions will be taken with each occurrence.
- The schools and the local law enforcement agency should identify and agree in writing upon what information will be shared and how the information is to be shared or disseminated.
- A graffiti policy should be established that specifies s a process for immediately reporting, recording, and removing graffiti to avoid "tagging wars" and instigation of other groups.
- All school staff should be required to attend training provided by the jurisdiction on the following key issues:
  - Conflict resolution
  - Anger management
  - School-required crime reporting
  - Identifying at-risk youth and reporting procedures/requirements
  - Physical aggression intervention policy and procedures
- Schools should have a policy that requires a critical incident plan and annual review, including a mock practice of the plan.
- Schools, in cooperation with law enforcement, should have a policy for capturing violent encounter data and for conducting regular analysis of the data to determine any contributing factors such as location in the school, proximity to other activities, common time occurrences, and the like.
- A policy designating what may be stored in school assigned lockers, the right of random inspection, and other such pertinent information should be in writing, and all students made aware of its content and the consequences for violation.
- The school dress code or uniform policy should be provided to all students prior to school.

- All policies for on-campus behavior should also be made applicable off-campus at school-sanctioned functions, such as the bus stop, on the school bus, at school dances and sporting events, and so on.

Disorderly and Violent Youth in Public Places

Schools are certainly not the only place where young people congregate, and as with adults, the larger the assembly, the more likely that an argument or violence will occur. Young people in a social society are bound to congregate, and law enforcement must realize that congregating in and of itself may not warrant our attention. In fact, such assembling is an act of social interaction important to normal development in youth. Law enforcement is often put in a precarious position when the local political figure or business leader complains about the assembly and demands officers "do something about it." I always caution officers to remember that the "APE" (acute political emergency) on your back does not justify the violation of the rights of any citizen, even if they are not of voting age. In cases in which the youth are not disorderly or violating a local ordinance, they may be directed to other locations more accepting of their assemblage or, more often than not, the complaining party must be made to understand that his or her rights are no more valuable than those of the young people peacefully enjoying their gathering. In many such cases it is the perception rather than the reality that is the cause for concern. Generational gaps, new clothing styles, music choices, and lack of understanding contribute to this misperception. Although not a true crime problem, it is one that the true community-oriented officer will want to address through the creation of favored activities in an alternate location or by acting as a catalyst to foster a better understanding of the real rather than the perceived people involved.

The truly disorderly youth who require our stronger hand and attention are those who interfere with commerce by blocking sidewalks, business entrances, and parking lots and those who purposely intimidate or harass others. The intimidation or harassment may be by nature of the assembly or by the size of the assembly, which contributes to the belief of members of the group that they can act with virtual anonymity, blending in to the assembly. The problem groups are those that create fear within the community and have the potential to act violently as a mob. The worst approach that an agency can take is often the one most taken: wait and see. The wait and see mentality is one that focuses on responding to calls, followed by officers threatening the youth and arresting when necessary. This reactive approach is not likely to solve any problems, and may even make the assembly or location more popular.

A better approach for the law enforcement crime prevention practitioner is to view the issue through a filter of cause and effect. Understanding that there will always be those people who thrive on violence, the practitioner should endeavor to bring together forces that redirect the majority of those assembling into a legitimate location with legitimate inexpensive, if not free, activities. By demonstrating an interest in the youth, the agency may realize that the group is very likely to police their own, especially if area officers are sympathetic to the youth and encourage them to anonymously call if someone creates issues that might endanger their continued use of the site or activity. Another approach to discourage assembly in certain areas might require the alteration of the design of the area contributing to the assembly. For example, if the assembly is outside a business near the business's sign, it may be that the wall surrounding the sign creates a comfortable location on which to sit and spend time. By removing the wall, increasing the lighting upward, and planting thorny shrubs, the site may no longer be a desirable location for assembly and the youth will relocate on their own naturally. More emphasis on these techniques is discussed in this book in Chapter 12.

■ Workplace Violence

An act of aggression, whether verbal or physical, is going to cause problems in any workplace. Whether the aggression is directed at a person or the property of the business, it must be addressed for the harm it will ultimately cause. In law enforcement, we have come to accept that violence is an ever-increasing problem. In recent years the increase in violent physical acts in the workplace has directed attention toward the need to train employees in conflict resolution, to address the non-acceptance of violent or hostile behavior through policy, and to address the physical environment to ensure that it is not conducive to violence. In recent years studies have demonstrated that the need to address this problem is enormous. In 1992 the Centers for Disease Control declared "workplace homicide" a serious health problem (*Homicide in U.S. Workplaces*, 1992). In fact, in recent years homicide has been noted as the second most common cause of death in the workplace and the leading cause of death in the workplace for women (Pearson, 1998). Each year close to 1 million people are the victims of violence at work. Some studies have shown that one in four workers have been threatened or attacked on the job. A University of North Carolina study related to "uncivil workers" revealed that 53% of the 775 workers studied lost time from work because of an "uncivil person." (Pearson, 1998) The human and financial consequences alone should be motivation enough for companies to desire to diligently address this problem. In many cases information regarding the prevalence and potential problems are not known, and it is the responsibility of each crime prevention practitioner who works with businesses to encourage them to take steps to address this problem. If the human and potential financial losses are not enough, then the employer should be made aware of its obligation under the federal Occupational Safety and Health Act of 1970 to provide a "safe workplace" (OSHA, 1970). The provision known as the "general duty clause" requires that employers take steps to remove or address "recognized hazards that are causing or are likely to cause death or serious physical harm to employees." Although the clause falls short of guaranteeing a workplace free from violence or making the employer shoulder all of the liability for all criminal acts, it has been used by the Occupational Safety and Health Administration (OSHA) to force employers to address potential violent acts, and employers have been held liable for acts of violence that the courts deemed were preventable. Many employers argued that the general duty clause did not apply to criminal acts. In 1992 OSHA issued a memorandum that finally settled the argument stating, "There is no reason to exclude from the list of hazards criminal acts of violence which are recognized as part of the nature of doing business" (U.S. Department of Labor, 1998).

It is the responsibility of businesses to ensure a safe workplace, and it is the responsibility of crime prevention practitioners to assist in accomplishing that goal by understanding the potential for violence, the motivations for violence, the underlying causes of violence, and the opportunity afforded to the violent offender to accomplish that act of violence. When the practitioner understands these topics, the prevention efforts may begin with the practitioner acting as the catalyst and cooperative partner of the business.

Crime Prevention Application

Research has provided us with a great deal of information about the motivation and the potential profile of a violent offender, as well as the reasons why violence may occur in a workplace setting. Workplace violence may originate from internal or external sources. Each source must be addressed differently due to access and other control issues. Therefore, this section separates the prevention recommendations according to the originating source. Typically, the externally generated violence is prevented or controlled by the initiation of preventative policies and procedures and the implementation of physical security measures—the measures best suited to control access to the facility and the violent offender's intended target. In other words, these steps prevent the crime by deterring the offender through delaying their effort and allowing more rational thinking to prevail; by completely denying access to the target, thereby frustrating the attempt; and by strategically designing a facility that allows for quick detection and intervention. On the other hand, internal offenders often must have access to the area of their potential target, are less likely to be deterred or delayed by virtue of such access, and require different measures. Internal sources must most often be addressed by management skills, hiring practices, and intervention techniques. These will be addressed a little later in the chapter.

External Violence Sources

As stated earlier, the external violent offender can usually be addressed with much less training and effort than the internal one. Although most crime prevention practitioners feel confident in addressing the external offender, they must continue to hone these skills due to the changing work environment. External sources of violence may include clients, customers, vendors, delivery workers, employee family members, or strangers. Any of these external sources that interact with workers may act out violently against an employee of the business, with varying degrees of determination for achieving their goal. Some violence is the result of frustration, as with a client who feels she is not receiving all of the attention she deserves. Still other violence may result from a rejected boyfriend or spouse determined to speak with the source of their rejection. Regardless of the motivation of the external source, their attack may be prevented at the workplace by controlling their access to their target. This access control involves a systematic approach of implementing well-thought-out policies that limit access by anyone other than the workers required to be in an area. It also involves information sharing and use of physical devices that frustrate the efforts of the offender, as well as the creation of written policy guidelines for dealing with potentially violent incidents. All businesses should, at a minimum, have policies that address and give guidance to employees in how to handle key control, bomb threats, robberies, and disorderly persons.

A method of surreptitiously alerting others within the business of an in-progress dangerous incident should also be addressed. Model policies for these situations are widely available from government agencies and business organizations. Up-to-date bomb threat policies and information are available from the Bureau of Alcohol, Tobacco and Firearms (ATF). Robbery information is available through the Retail Merchants Association and local crime prevention agencies. The availability of this information should prompt the local crime prevention practitioner to obtain, study, and have this information available when assisting businesses in workplace prevention.

Communication within a business is a key tool for identifying and addressing potential hazards. The method of reporting hazards among peers, supervisors, and subordinates must be addressed to ensure that steps are taken proactively to prevent a potential violent act. For example, if a certain employee is being threatened by a customer or estranged spouse, the supervisor may be able to take steps to temporarily move the employee to a different location or store where the offender will not know his or her whereabouts. Employees should feel compelled to report any situation to their supervisors that may pose a threat to their or their co-workers' safety. The supervisor must understand the need to develop a relationship conducive to such reporting, supported by trust and confidentiality when necessary. Failure to develop this trust may result in the employee failing to report the potential; this lack of knowledge could lead to an unknowing co-worker "bending" policy for a spouse to allow access to the target.

Physical environment changes are another method of reducing the potential of violence from external sources. A design that requires all people entering the business to pass a centrally staffed position enhances access control to the facility and creates another source of risk and effort for the would-be offender. This staffed position does not need to be an armed security person, but rather any staff member who serves to put all visitors on notice that they have been observed and can be recognized.

In conclusion, if the business has foreknowledge of potential threats, if policies to guide the actions of staff during violent incidents are in place and understood, if threats of violence are taken seriously and addressed through planning, and if access to the facility is controlled through personnel and security devices, the business will be well protected against external violence.

Internal Violence Sources

An internal offender may be defined as someone who, by nature of his or her employment relationship, has access to employees at their workstations and within the workplace. This includes supervisors, subordinates, and co-workers. These offenders have been psychologically researched for years, and researchers have developed a profile of the employee prone to violence. As with all profiles, this description is not absolute and does not claim to guarantee total accuracy in predicting violence; instead it is offered to allow the supervisor some forewarning that closer scrutiny might be justified and quicker intervention may be appropriate when warning signs are observed. The more the characteristics are observed, the stronger the potential for the profiled individual to become violent. The characteristics of the violent offender in the workplace are listed in the following profile (Kinney and Johnson, 1993):

- *Male*—Until the 1990s, all reported workplace homicides were committed by men. It is suspected that with more women maintaining leadership roles in the workplace and being promoted over their male counterparts, jealousy and a sense of unfair treatment may cause an increase in male perpetrated attacks unless steps are taken to properly address violence by businesses.
- *Caucasian*—A number of theories have been floated as to why race may be a factor but I have found no scientific research supporting any primary cause.
- *Between the ages of 25 and 50*—This characteristic may change as well, due to workers remaining on the job much longer than in past years.
- *Poor self-esteem*—It is easy to imagine that a person with little self-esteem in his personal life might gain much of his self-worth from their position or job at his place of employment. He may view his value as diminished if he is disciplined, passed over for promotion, or reassigned without having requested to be reassigned.
- *Tends to be a loner*—By keeping to himself, the individual has no real support system to assist him in coping with stressors. It is easy to see how a person with low self-worth who is overlooked for a promotion is less able to deal with the situation if he internalizes the incident because of a lack of a support system.
- *Overreacts and is irrational*—The profile reveals that the individual prone to violence is an angry person, tends to lie, does not accept responsibility for his own actions, deals poorly with rejection of any sort, and has a history of confrontations with supervision. He may express feelings of being targeted or persecuted.
- *Has family problems*—He may have a history of domestic violence and consequently an unhappy home life, leading to his basing his self-worth on his work performance.
- *Gun enthusiast*—Guns are sometimes seen as a symbol of power or of control, and the individual may brag or talk frequently of his ownership and skill with firearms.
- *Substance abuser*—Substance abuse is very common in violent workplace encounters.
- *Complains about any changes*—These complaints may be observed through hesitance in taking on newly assigned tasks and may be related to job stress. Again linked to the self-worth gained at the workplace, the individual may feel that due to

his being unfamiliar with the new changes he is not as "important" to the business. This stress may lead to sick time usage as the added stress leads to physical illness.

The Hiring Professional's Responsibility

Once the crime prevention practitioner understands the profile of the potentially violent offender, he or she should emphasize to the businesses he or she serves that those responsible for hiring must check for these indicators during the hiring process. An exhaustive screening process may seem like an unnecessary expense, but it is likely to save the business in the long run through overcoming the resulting lost wages, bad publicity, and liability suits filed citing negligent hiring practices. The language of suits proves the importance of this process: the employer knew, or should have known of the violent tendencies. In other words, failing to adequately recognize the potential and address it in some way could be the difference in a ruling for or against the business. There are, however, certain legal limitations to which the hiring screener must adhere (Perkins Coie Law Firm, 1997). However, screening tools are available that might reveal violence-prone individuals without violating these limitations.

The screening process should always begin with the recruitment of good applicants. This is best accomplished by using one of the best resources a business has at its disposal, its current employees. By encouraging other employees to recommend applicants, the business ensures that the new employee will have a mentor to assist him or her in acclimating to the company and is more likely to get an employee who requires less scrutiny. The recommendation of friends or acquaintances does not remove the need to conduct a thorough screening, but it does give the employer a starting point.

Applicant screening should include a close examination of the information provided. Any paperwork provided the prospective employee should be retained for as long as the state requires under its records retention guidelines. The following tips are offered for screeners of applications:

- *Ensure the application is completely filled out*—Unexplained blanks or comments questioning the business regarding its need for the information should be viewed with suspicion.
- *Check for accuracy*—Each listed reference and address should be verified. Conservative estimates show that one third to one half of applicants lie on their applications.
- *Check for obvious gaps in employment and residences*—Require that the gaps be explained either prior to or during the interview process.
- Obtain a release to allow previous employers to disclose information about the applicant and reason for resignation or termination of employment.
- *Check credit and military history, if one exists*—These histories may reveal poor judgment, poor self-management, financial needs that might lead to theft, problems with authority or in taking orders, and other such issues.
- *If applicable, obtain a driver transcript*—Driver transcripts may reveal poor judgment and decision making, and most importantly, substance or alcohol abuse. An applicant with three previous DUI charges may warrant closer scrutiny for alcoholism.
- *If applicable, require submission of a criminal history*—These histories may be obtained by the applicant authorizing in writing that his or her history be released or by requiring that the applicant go to the local law enforcement or state police agency and obtain a certified copy themselves.
- If applicable, the business may wish to contract with a reputable company to conduct psychological or polygraph testing.

- *Conduct an open and unrushed interview of the applicant*—Much is revealed in the interview process that may not be legally asked. The skilled interviewer knows to:
  - Ask open-ended questions. This allows the screener to get a feel for the thought processes of the applicant, interject a degree of stress to evaluate their stress management, and evaluate the applicant's verbal skills.
  - Allow the applicant to speak uninterrupted for as long as he or she desires. Take copious notes on key issues that may indicate he or she meets the potential violent offender profile.
  - Watch for hot-button topics that may reveal anger and ask follow-up questions. Note any questions that provoke a visceral reaction.

The Manager's and Supervisor's Responsibility

Once an employee is hired, the responsibility for preventing violence shifts to the management and supervision team. Liability against management is generally based upon negligent training, negligent retention, and negligent supervision. The standard often used remains that they "knew or should have known." A good defense tool used for the training aspect is training records and signed documents indicating that they have been issued, or at least that the employee read the policies and understands them. Training lesson plans, video of the material, and the like further support the defense related to training. Crime prevention practitioners should not be offended when asked for a lesson plan of a prevention presentation that they are providing. I have been asked to videotape a shoplifting presentation that I provided for potential use in future litigation. These requests are not unreasonable and, if allowed by your agency, should be granted.

The negligent retention and negligent supervision questions are much more difficult to address. In order to address them in a workplace violence context, a supervisor and/or manager should be able to demonstrate that they did not know, nor should they have known, of the potential violent acts of the employee. In other words, the supervisor and/or manager did not have any indication of any displayed danger signs and their supervision style was close enough to have observed such signs. They should be able to show that they are proactive in dealing with violence issues when they arise and do not tolerate violent behavior. The supervisor/manager and business may begin to demonstrate their responsible handling of such situations by providing a written policy of not tolerating violent behavior in the workplace and requiring that any violent activity be reported to supervision for action. The documented actions taken relative to the case in question, as well as any others that may have been taken, may strengthen the case that management and supervision took positive steps when made aware of the potential for violence. Likewise, uninvestigated or ignored complaints and indicators will be used to demonstrate a lack of concern and support the claim of negligence on the part of the manager or supervisor. Some of the indicators that have been identified as precursors to violence and that should be effectively dealt with when observed or reported are:

- An employee meets the profile characteristics of a violent offender.
- An employee displays sudden irrational beliefs or emotional outbursts.
- An employee makes written or spoken threats.
- An employee is observed or reported to be overly stressed.
- An employee indicates that he or she is contemplating suicide or hurting others
- An employee is apathetic about safety and appears to be committing unsafe acts.
- Co-workers are unwilling to work with an individual or express fear about working near him or her.

- A downturn in the quality of an employee's work may indicate depression or feelings of not being appreciated.
- An employee has recently experienced rejection in his or her work or some other aspect of life.
- An employee expresses feelings of hopelessness or of having nothing to lose.
- An employee blames others for work problems rather than taking responsibility for him- or herself.
- An employee has a negative change in hygiene habits.
- He or she is unable to concentrate on tasks, possibly resulting in increased accidents or mistakes.
- The employee has experienced a recent trauma in his or her life, such as a loss of a loved one, a divorce, or another traumatic event.
- He or she intentionally destroys property.
- Verbal outbursts or physical violence toward co-workers or supervisors are noted.

There are three basic strategies for addressing potentially violent employees. The appropriate strategy will depend on several factors such as the employee's history, the employee's needs, and potential future harm. Strategies for addressing acts of violence are usually implemented in the following order: intervening to diffuse, referral to address underlying issues, and if deemed appropriate, discipline.

Intervening to Diffuse

All members of supervision and management should be equipped, through training, to manage conflict and to de-escalate potentially violent situations. Techniques used to de-escalate such situations include (Bolton, 1979):

- *Be cognizant of nonverbal communication*—Nonverbal communication is often interpreted by an unreasonable employee as being hostile. Avoid staring, pointing, standing as though frustrated, or placing your hands on your hips.
- *Do not attempt to rush a resolution*—Encourage the employee to vent verbally; avoid interrupting him or her, and use active listening skills.
- *Listen closely*—Practice active listening by restating what is being said in your own words for clarification, and acknowledging that you can understand the employee's point. Treat the employee's points with seriousness; never laugh or undermine their points.
- *When the employee is emotional, deal first with the emotion and then the problem*—Project calm by speaking in a soft, normal tone of voice to encourage the employee to do the same. Encourage him or her to explain the problem and only interrupt when the employee starts to get emotional again. Indicate that you are starting to understand in the same soft tone of voice.
- *Once emotions are out of the way, deal with the issues*—Explain the problem, as you understand it. If there are consequences for the employee's actions explain them, but do not use them to threaten. For example, "Our policy says I have to report this incident and I would like to report it as having a positive outcome."
- *Explain the supervisor side of the issue and brainstorm with the employee(s) a resolution to the underlying issue*—Always be honest, repeat what has been identified as the underlying problem, and ask what would resolve the issue to both or all involved's satisfaction. Get agreement if possible, then repeat the agreed-upon solution and remind the employee of any action that you must take. Close by thanking the employees for resolving the issue themselves.

- *Make notes of all that occurred and any agreements with dates and names of those witnessing the incident or involved in it*—Retain the notes in the appropriate location designated by the business.

Employee Referrals

If the supervisor or manager determines while diffusing the situation that the employee is displaying warning signs or indicating difficulty coping with problems, a referral to some type of counseling may be warranted. (See the precursor indicators listed previously.) Many businesses have a policy of when such a referral is warranted, and the crime prevention practitioner assisting in educating the business about workplace violence issues should recommend that the supervisor follow the company policy. Referrals may be to a peer counseling team, a company employee assistance program (EAP) coordinator, or directly to a counselor. In any event, counseling is an option that should be utilized when the potential for violent acts is recognized. All supervisors should familiarize themselves with their individual policies concerning referrals. If none exists, the business should be encouraged to consider implementing an EAP program.

Discipline

After diffusion, if a review of the situation reveals that the employee must be disciplined for his or her actions, every effort must be made to ensure that the discipline is perceived as fair and consistent. There should always be an appeal process, even in termination cases. All discipline, including termination, should be done using positive language. When disciplining, it is important to praise the positive attributes of the employee, praise his or her willingness to agree on steps to resolve the issue (see the "Intervening to Diffuse" section earlier in the chapter), address the discipline, and complete the meeting on a positive note.

If terminating an employee, do so early in the workweek to allow the employee to exercise his or her rights immediately rather than to stew on his or her perceptions over a long weekend. When termination actions have been decided upon, prepare all paperwork and have in hand any owed pay to give the employee at the termination meeting. Policy should state that all terminated employees must be immediately escorted to obtain their personal belongings and then off the property. Also dictate by policy that all terminated employees who need to return to the premises must first call for an appointment. Remove all excuses for the ex-employee to return to the premises.

Workplace violence can be reduced by taking necessary steps to identify potential offenders, by addressing offenders and situations fairly and expeditiously, and by designing the workplace in such a way as to avoid the potential of violence.

■ Chapter Summary

Preventing violence and crimes against people should be the most important task of the law enforcement officer. Property can be replaced or easily repaired, but people are fragile. As with any crime, if we have a clear understanding of the motivation to commit a particular type of violent crime, we can prevent the opportunity from occurring.

■ Review Questions

1. According to the National Crime Victimization Survey, what one factor is violent crime victimization dependent upon?
2. Around what percentage of rapes occur in the victim's home?
3. What age group has demonstrated a more violent tendency than the rest of the population?

4. Does the Occupational and Safety Health Act of 1970 cover criminal acts of violence in the workplace?
5. What is the race of the typical violent offender in the workplace violent offender profile?

■ References

Bolton, Robert. 1979. *People Skills—How to Assert Yourself, Listen to Others and Resolve Conflict.* New York: Simon & Schuster.

Center for Disease Control and Prevention, National Center for Injury Prevention and Control. 2006. Available online at www.cdc.gov/ncipc.

Finkelhor, David, and Mitchell, Kimberly. 2004. *Highlights of the Youth Internet Safety Survey.* 2004.

Fisher, Bonnie, Cullen, Francis, and Turner, Michel. 2000. *The Sexual Victimization of College Women.* Washington DC: U.S. Department of Justice, National Institute of Justice.

Homicide in U.S. Workplaces. September 1992. Morgantown, WV: National Institute for Occupational Safety and Health.

Kinney, Joseph, and Johnson, Dennis L. 1993. *Breaking Point: The Workplace Violence Epidemic and What to Do About it.* Chicago, IL: The National Safe Workplace Institute. pp. 40, 41.

Mattson, Beth. August 1999. "A sense of security." *Access Control & Security Systems Integration.*

Occupational Safety and Health Administration. Title 29 United States Code.

Office of Juvenile Justice and Delinquency Programs. Section 4 (A)(1) Title 29. United States Code 654 1997. 1995 National Youth Gang Survey, Program Summary. Rockville, MD.

OJJDP Fact Sheet. March 2004. Office of Juvenile Justice and Delinquency Programs. Rockville, MD.

Olweus, Dan. 1993. *Bullying at School—What We Know and What We Can Do.* Cambridge, MA: Blackwell Publishing.

Pearson, Christine. 1998. Uncivil Workers University of North Carolina at Chapel Hill. Chapel Hill, NC.

Perkins Coie Law Firm. 1997. *Practical Suggestions for Preventing and Coping with Workplace Violence;* 1997 Executive File: Hot Employment Issues. Brentwood, TN: M. Lee Smith Publishers.

Thrasher, Fredrick M. 1927. *The Gang.* Chicago, IL: University of Chicago Press.

U.S. Department of Justice National Crime Victimization Survey. 2004.

U.S. Department of Labor, Occupational Safety and Health Administration. 1998. *Recommendations for Workplace Violence Prevention Programs in Late-Night Retail Establishments.*

Unnever, James, et al. 2000. *Roanoke School-Based Partnership Bullying Study.* Bureau of Justice, Office of Community Oriented Policing Services. Washington, DC.

Wexler, Sanford. March 1997. "Gangbusters." *Law Enforcement Technology.*

Protecting the Physical Environment with Devices

"There are costs and risks to a program of action, but they are far less than the long range risks and costs of comfortable inaction."

—John F. Kennedy

■ Introduction

Along with the overall design of an environment comes the use of devices that are designed to physically inhibit the criminal from successfully completing his or her crime. This chapter covers target hardening, which addresses the use of security devices and practices to limit vulnerability. Chapter 12 will discuss Crime Prevention Through Environmental Design (CPTED), which examines the overall design features with an eye toward limiting opportunities for the criminal. Neither of these are stand-alone crime prevention programs; however, they are instruments used in almost all successful crime prevention programs. These techniques are based on physically and psychologically influencing the criminal's motivation and opportunity.

■ Target Hardening

The Premise

Target hardening is the concept of protecting vulnerable areas by means of physical security devices such as locks, alarms, fences, and the like. Target hardening is limited by proper application and understanding of the crimes to be prevented. If you think about target hardening in the context of protective clothing, it becomes easier to recognize that the application may be either directed or general. For example, the cowboys of old wore high boots to protect their legs from snakebites. When working in high brush they wore leather chaps to protect their legs, and they wore a wide-brimmed hat to protect themselves from the rays of the sun. You can see that each item of clothing protected a separate vulnerable area as needed, but not all were necessarily needed all of the time. Target hardening works similarly. One would not install an expensive high security system on every door in a building, but may choose to install a high security system in a particular office to protect that especially vulnerable area. Costs must always be a consideration when assisting the public with recommendations, and the practitioner's goal should be to accomplish the protection of the area within the budget of the citizen.

Recognizing the techniques and motivations of the potential criminal element, target hardening assumes the rationale that if the target is a formidable one, the criminal will choose another target or, at least, avoid the hardened one. This is supported by the "rational choice" theory described by Ronald Clarke (1977). The topic of target hardening includes doors, locks, window security, electronic access controls, alarms, lighting, and securing facility openings.

Crime Prevention Application

Target hardening is largely based on the opportunity reduction technique of increasing the effort for the criminal to be successful. In other words, the target becomes more difficult to overcome as it is psychologically and physically hardened. Although target hardening does not guarantee denial of access or complete prevention, it does make the crime more difficult. If a target is more difficult to overcome, then the criminal is more likely to be physically delayed, detected, and, in many cases, denied access.

In order to provide a more usable reference, I will discuss the security and prevention devices under separate headings below. It should be noted that these devices are usually part of a larger system and not addressed individually. However, in this book I am merely attempting to address the most common vulnerabilities encountered by the law enforcement crime prevention practitioner, and I hope that I will provoke the practitioner to think creatively to address any other vulnerability that he or she might encounter. Anything that is likely to make the criminal act more difficult, no matter how simplistic, is a positive target hardening measure. However, always make sure that recommended measures do not violate any building or fire codes for your jurisdiction.

Door Systems

A door should actually be considered a system of various devices, all working together to create one smooth function. To strengthen one part of the door without strengthening the others would be akin to a doctor repairing a lacerated hand while leaving the broken bones in the fingers untreated. The patient may not bleed to death, but the hand will be practically useless and certainly weakened. Therefore, we need to view all parts of the door system as important when examining it for vulnerability. The door system typically consists of five individual parts: the door, the hinges, the strike, the frame, and the latch and lock.

Because the door works as a system, each individual part must be examined for weakness. One should use common sense to determine how much protection is required in each situation. For example, a coat closet in a business may need no protection, but the payroll office probably requires a great deal of protection. In order to make recommendations, the practitioner needs to understand the weak versus strong device.

It is generally recommended that all exterior doors be of solid core construction, a minimum of $1\frac{3}{4}$ inches thick, and fit snugly into their frames.

Doors

Hollow Core Doors. Certain doors are at the bottom of the food chain in terms of security. The hollow core door, sometimes referred to as a luan or panel door, has absolutely no application as a security measure. These doors are constructed of veneer panels glued over a framework of fir strips or cardboard. The only acceptable use for these doors is for a closet that requires no security. While conducting assessments I have encountered these doors equipped with heavy locks, and the owners were certain that they had a good secure door. These doors are so weak that a punch by a youngster can penetrate them.

Solid Core Doors. The next step up from the hollow core is the solid core door. These doors are constructed of glued pieces of wood covered by a veneer panel. These doors are quite strong and are not easily penetrated. Solid core doors are often used for exterior doors and are usually the minimum recommended thickness of $1\frac{3}{4}$ inches.

Solid Wooden Doors. These doors are constructed throughout of solid board, but in reality may be no stronger than the solid core doors because the boards are glued together, and the joints tend to weaken over time, especially if susceptible to weather conditions.

Wooden Panel Doors. Wooden panel doors are frequently found in older houses. These doors consist of four to six panels within a wooden framework. The panels are much thinner than the door framework and are tapered on the outer edges, where they are inserted into a slot within the framework and glued in. Over time the panel glue often deteriorates and the panels can be moved slightly in the slots. These doors are easily defeated by attacking a panel, which will usually pop out of the slot or split in half, and can be removed from the slots. The criminal then reaches in and unlocks the door, or in some cases actually crawls through the opening.

Metal Core Doors. Much like the solid core door, the metal core door is constructed of glued wood pieces, foam core, or a steel grid, but instead of being covered by veneer, it is covered by metal. These are formidable doors and are in frequent residential use. The construction and popularity of these doors make them a less expensive alternative for exterior applications.

Doors with Windows. Whether a nine-lite kitchen door or a decorative wooden door with an oval glass panel, a "window door" poses some difficulty in securing. Obviously the favored method of entry is to simply break the glass and reach in to unlock and open this door. Often fire codes restrict controlling the entry with a double cylinder lock (discussed under locks later in this chapter). Therefore, the only recommendations for strengthening this type of door are the following:

- Cover the window with a wrought iron decorative grate in a close-together design that makes it difficult to reach in through the broken glass.
- Install an additional single cylinder deadbolt lock near the floor, or as far from reach as possible from the window opening.
- Replace the glass with a break-resistant polycarbonate glass or purchase a newly designed stained glass door, which provides some protection with the stained glass framing.
- Install a polycarbonate glass panel on the inside of the existing glass.

Sliding Glass Doors. Sliding glass doors and windows are treated in the same way as window doors because they pose the same vulnerability. Typically the slider has three very distinct vulnerabilities. First, the glass construction itself is problematic for the same reasons mentioned for doors with windows. It is not practical to attempt to grate or cover these with polycarbonate; therefore, those wishing to have a sliding glass door must accept a certain amount of risk. This vulnerability can best be addressed by applying CPTED principles, discussed in the following chapter. The second weakness that the slider poses is the critically inadequate lock. The typical lock is practically useless unless augmented by another locking device. Small deadbolts are commercially available for sliders. Finally, the sliding door or window, by nature of its slide function, requires a certain amount of "play" in the track. This play makes the door susceptible to being lifted up, tilted, and taken out of the track. To combat the locking problem and to address the lifting issue to some degree, a hinged commercially available bar should be installed midway up the door on the stationary side. The bar can be hinged down into a U-shaped receiver mounted on the active slider. Lacking a commercial device, a wooden or metal dowel rod may be cut to fit snugly into the track of the slider to prevent it from being forced open. Keyed track locks also are available, but may violate fire or building codes in your locality. To specifically address the problem of the door or window being lifted out, the owner may wish to insert additional screws into the track and leave them protruding enough to prevent the door from being lifted; typically, $\frac{1}{4}$-inch screws will work.

Double Doors. French or double doors pose much the same problem as the doors with glass discussed earlier. An additional recommendation to address this type of door's vulnerabilities would be to include a tight-fitting flush bolt that is attached to the stationary leaf of the door and slid into a reinforced strike in the top of the frame and the floor. The slide should lock into place and not be able to be shaken loose. Often an astragal (a metal covering over the bolt strike from the lock) will prevent the locks from being slipped or compromised.

Roof Hatches.   Roof hatches are often overlooked. These are generally well constructed of metal or heavy wood framing and equipped with a hinged door. These hatchways should be protected by a heavy-duty hasp and a case-hardened padlock. Skylights to a facility should be constructed of safety or polycarbonate glass.

Frame and Strike Plates

A typical residential door construction involves placement of a header (usually 2 × 6) and studs (2 × 4) to frame the door. The actual door is then "hung" in that space using shims and filler to level and nail the door facing, usually 1 inch or less of wooden material, to the studs. As a result, the door may or may not be secured completely to a solid stud. In most cases the door facing is secured to the studs. The problem more likely comes from the weakest point of the door system, the strike plate. Police officers have long known that this is the weakest point of the door system, which is why, when forced entry is necessary, they kick the door at the strike rather than at the hinges. Most locks come equipped with their own strike plate and screws for installation. Unfortunately, the screws are usually too short to secure anything but the strike plate itself. Remember the door construction described above, and you can see that the half-inch screws usually provided only penetrate the door facing and are of insufficient length to effectively strengthen the door strike area. In order to combat this problem, the strike plate should be installed with screws at least 3 inches in length that go through the trim (facing), through the air or filler, and into the studs. For added security, full metal security strikes are available commercially, to replace the open type that comes with most locks.

Hinges

Another often-overlooked element of the door system is the hinges. Hinges for out-swinging doors that are exposed to tampering from outside are an important security concern. Regardless of the quality of the lock, door, or strike plate, an exposed hinge may offer easy access by removal of the pins. Removing the pins essentially creates a reverse door. In order to prevent the hinge pins from being removed, the practitioner may recommend remortising the door and frame, replacing the door and frame, replacing the hinge pin with a headless nonremovable hinge pin, or installing a studded hinge system that prevents the door from moving. You can also create your own studded hinge system by backing one of the screws out of each hinge approximately ¼ inch and sawing the head off of the screw. On the opposite side of the hinge remove the adjacent screw (if one exists) to create a receiving hole for the created stud. If no adjacent screws exist, the hinge should be marked and drilled to create a receiving hole for the created stud. When the door is closed the created stud enters the hole, and even with the hinge pin removed the door will not easily move.

Locks

At the outset, it should be stated that a latch and a lock are not the same, but many people confuse the two. The device shown in **FIGURE 11.1** is often called a lock, but in reality it is a spring latch. Even though it has a keyway it is not necessarily a lock. This device is often found in residential applications on exterior doors. Latches are constructed of low-grade metal, which can be wrenched with something as simple as a pair of channel lock pliers. Nothing should be recommended for an exterior security door other than a deadbolt lock with at least a 1-inch throw for the bolt. When engaged, the bolt should not be able to be

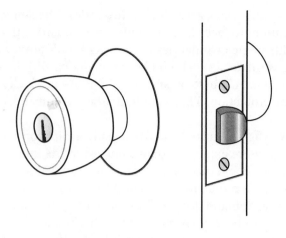

FIGURE 11.1
A spring latch.

manipulated without using the thumb latch or key. In other words, it should be "locked." The homeowner may choose moderate-quality locks, but at least the practitioner should ensure that he or she is using a deadbolt. Not all deadbolt locks are created equally. Just as with practically anything on the open market, deadbolts come in varying levels of quality, ranging from the inexpensive store brand to the high-end deadbolt manufactured by a company specializing in high security. Depending on the application and what is being protected, locks can be defeated by prying, wrenching, picking, using an ill-gotten key, drilling the lock, or other methods. It is up to the owner and the crime prevention practitioner to determine what needs to be protected against and just what it is worth to the owner to protect that asset or property.

Deadbolts come in a variety of styles, each with a different application. The area containing the keyway, tumblers, and pins is known as the cylinder. The most frequently recommended and used lock contains one keyway and a thumb latch on the opposite side; it is known as a single cylinder deadbolt. A lock with two keyways is known as a double cylinder deadbolt. A lock with a keyway on one side and a removable thumb latch that acts like a key and can be removed by using the key or a combination is known as a captive deadbolt or child safety deadbolt. An older type of deadbolt is a flush-mounted vertical deadbolt (**FIGURE 11.2**). The crime prevention practitioner should be cognizant of the differences and the applications. The captive deadbolt is ideal for an application within 40 inches of a window. The lock can be used as a double cylinder when the home is not occupied but as a single cylinder when occupied. The double cylinder deadbolt may be applied in residences where there are other access/egress points; applicability often depends on

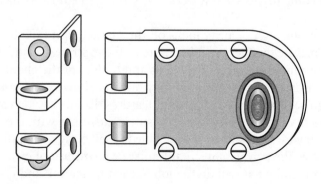

FIGURE 11.2
Flush-mounted vertical deadbolt.

travel distance to emergency exits, according to fire codes. The single cylinder deadbolt is appropriate at any location; in fact, the hotel industry standard is that all hotel/motel doors be equipped with single cylinder deadbolt locks and door viewers. As a law enforcement practitioner, the word *deadbolt* should be synonymous with lock. Other devices such as the spring latch, so-called chain lock, and slide bolts are not locks and offer little more than a ¼-inch screw as protection. They should not be recommended.

High Security Locks. High security locks are usually an appropriate recommendation for a business. Although more expensive than standard residential locks, the protected assets warrant the extra cost and quality associated with higher security measures. The law enforcement crime prevention practitioner should therefore have a basic knowledge of the differences in lock application and design. Only the client can relay the need or degree of protection that they wish to have at entrances and other private controlled space. Just as an inexpensive department store mountain bicycle will suffice for the casual cyclist, so may an inexpensive deadbolt lock suffice in certain applications. The serious cyclist will require a higher quality precision-built machine, and likewise the serious protection of an asset will require a precision-built lock constructed for the primary purpose of security.

A high security lock is identified by having passed Underwriters Laboratory (UL) testing. In order to achieve the UL 437 those standard, a lock must pass a number of timed tests of typical ways that a lock might be compromised. Among the tests are tests for prying, pulling, drilling, and picking. Only the locks that pass these tests are recognized as high security and listed as meeting UL 437 standards. Certain features found in some high security locks are:

- Design patents
- Interchangeable cores
- Key duplication controls. These are essential in protecting assets. It does little good to install expensive quality locks if the keys are easily duplicated and the potential for extra unaccounted-for keys exists. Keys are controlled in a number of ways such as stamping "do not duplicate," but the ideal control is through a utility patent that allows only authorized dealers of the particular lock to duplicate keys within a specific set of guidelines.
- Six- or seven-pin tumbler design

A good example of quality high security locks are those manufactured in Virginia by the Medeco Corporation. This corporation has produced high quality locks for many years and is known for the protection provided by their angled key cut design and duplication controls through patents. They have partnered with law enforcement in our area to educate officers about their product as well as others that are available. If any law enforcement agency has a similar manufacturing company in its area, it should at the very least approach the company to see if it would be willing to educate officers about locking devices.

There are numerous high security locks on the market, and each has its own strengths. The consultant in private business will be aware of those strengths and can determine which company's product best meets the needs and budget of the client. By policy, the law enforcement crime prevention practitioner may only be allowed to recommend a type of lock, such as a high security lock with certain features. In this case, a list of high security lock manufacturers may be provided to the business customer with the specified feature identified, and the business would be responsible for selecting a lock that meets the needs recommended. Just as the private consultant must be cognizant of cost, so should the practitioner. Recommend what will do the job needed by feature and give options to the consumer. A few high security locks that are frequently recommended are:

- Schlage Primus™
- Best™
- Assa Twin™
- Medeco Keymark™

Because high security locks are expensive, the practitioner may need to recommend a less expensive locking mechanism in some locations of a facility, in order to ensure the highest security available in a more critical area of asset protection.

Although high security locks are typically found in business applications, more and more homeowners are recognizing the value of such locks and trusting their home security to them. The practitioner in crime prevention owes it to his citizen and business clients to be prepared to give sound advice regarding their use.

Electronic Access Locks/Controls. In the not so distant past, electronic access devices were found only in facilities with top security. The reason they were not used more often was the expense. With the cost of computers and the accompanying technology decreasing, some form of electronic access is now common in almost all commercial facilities. Most end users of these systems initially are more concerned with access rather than using the devices for security. Often there will be some other form of security in place. Electronic access has developed today to a point where it is now being recognized as providing security and is being used as a primary source of security.

Even though electronic access devices differ, most have a common basic operation. That is to say, they all have the following:

- Something that gives authorization to a user
- Something that receives the authorization and verifies it
- Something that sends the verified authorization or denial to the locking device
- The locking device itself

Although these devices may have additional features, they will have the above as a minimum. Extra features sometimes include interconnectivity with other devices, use of duplicate mechanical and electronic access controls, and the ability to produce reports of entry or audits. To demonstrate the basic electronic device features, consider the electronic access that most law enforcement officers are familiar with—the electromagnetic lock typically found in a detention facility or police station. What gives authorization in this case is recognition of the officer's face, uniform, or badge. The clerk, dispatcher, or other person observes the authorization and then verifies it as being authentic. He or she then pushes a release button to send a message to the electromagnetic lock to open, and the locking device releases. Although this may seem to oversimplify how such systems work, it is necessary to do so in order to draw a comparison for the practitioner and to remove any fears about understanding the more complex systems. Once one can draw a familiar comparison, he or she has a frame of reference for understanding how the other systems basically work. Drawing on the above example, consider the steps of other more complex systems:

1. A device such as a key fob, a proximity card, an identification card, or some other means gives authorization.
2. The reader receives the authorization and sends the information to a computer.
3. The computer checks to see if the authorization is verified and current.
4. Once checked and found to be authorized, the computer sends an impulse to the magnetic strike or locking device to release, and the process is complete.

This all occurs within seconds, and because it uses a computer, reports can be generated demonstrating date, time, access point, which user gained access, and so on.

Authorization devices that are used in electronic access control vary in shape, size, and operation. The practitioner should not become overwhelmed by the variety and methods of operation, but should strive to familiarize her- or himself with the devices and recognize that, like mechanical locks, each has strengths and weaknesses. There is no one perfect electronic access system for all applications any more than there is a perfect lock for all applications. Some types of authorization devices are manually operated keypads, insertion cards, magnetic strip cards, punched cards, retinal scanners, fingerprint scanners, voice scanners, and computer microchips (within a key head, for example).

Except for the keypad device, each of the devices listed will require a corresponding reader, and each may be used in conjunction with other devices. Use of electronic devices is not an all or nothing proposition. The practitioner should examine the need for the device before settling on one, or for that matter before settling on such a device as a stand-alone security system. For example, an office building that allows only certain staff in one wing of the building but allows all employees to access other areas may choose to use an electronic access control device in the one wing and use mechanical keys for the rest of the building, or the company may choose to install electronic access throughout with different amounts of access assigned to different levels of staff. As you can see, the versatility of the device is significant.

When using electronic access devices in a security application, the ability to produce a so-called electronic signature for each individual and thus produce an audit trail is an essential feature. Another essential is a secondary power source for backing up the device and the computerized information. The audit trail allows the facility to prevent criminal activity by significantly increasing the probability of detection and risk of capture, while increasing the difficulty in overcoming the electronic system. Many such systems even allow the facility to create a tracking map throughout the facility.

Although these systems provide an excellent prevention and investigatory tool, they are of little use when the business does not have a policy in place that requires immediate reporting of lost or stolen electronic authorization credentials, with a significant penalty for failing to do so. A lost credential is not serious if reported and cancelled immediately. In most electronic access systems being used in security applications, the lost credential can be "locked out" within seconds. In fact, this ability is one of the cost-efficiency measures provided by electronic devices. A facility protected only by mechanical locks that experiences a lost key would need to replace or recore the lock and replace all assigned keys to authorized personnel. The unreported credential has the potential for severe consequences to the business in losses and in cost over time.

Windows

Windows pose a unique challenge to the practitioner. We must keep in mind that citizens want to reduce the opportunity for crimes to occur while also avoiding a fortress appearance and, more importantly, the locking down of escape routes from the building in case of fire. There are a number of different window types, and each must be evaluated from a vulnerability standpoint for any recommended protection. In this section I will try to cover some of the more common window problems to consider when making recommendations.

Window Glass

Only a limited amount of effort is required to break glass and, depending on the window size, locks might do little good. Window protection is often accomplished only by neighbors observing and being alerted to the sound of glass breaking and then calling the suspicious activities in to police. The criminals are aware of these support mechanisms and adjust accordingly by choosing less visible windows and using methods to muffle the sound of the glass breaking. The practitioner must be especially cognizant of the most vulnerable windows when recommending protective steps.

In addressing the window glass itself, there are many choices of replacement glass that are less vulnerable to breakage, and some are even impervious to that method of entry. In the more vulnerable areas of a residence or a business, the practitioner may recommend replacing the normal window glass with safety glass, polycarbonate resin, tempered glass, or some of the newer protective glass on the market. Another method of dealing with a particularly vulnerable window is to install grating (**FIGURE 11.3**). For residential applications, decorative grating styles constructed of wrought iron are available. Some decorative iron bars for windows are mounted on a hinged frame with a substantial locking device. These are ideal for an occupied office or a residential application.

Windows that have air conditioning units in them also may be protected by having grating or metal bars formed to fit snugly around the unit on the exterior and secured through the wall with round flush bolts, or for less protection with square head screws. The grating or bars also provide support for the window air unit and therefore serve a secondary purpose.

Air ducts, although not windows, are treated in a similar way. Many industrial facilities are equipped with large air ducts that can easily provide access. Installation of steel grating, as demonstrated in Figure 11.3, is recommended for all such air ducts. An alternative is installation of steel bars spaced no more than 6 inches apart.

Window Style

Security problems for many of the hinged window styles are addressed similarly to their counterpart discussed in the door section, so I have chosen to address the three major styles of windows briefly below.

Sliding Windows. The sliding window is a smaller version of the sliding glass door, which was addressed earlier. The measures suggested there also apply to sliding windows. The bar mechanism, a dowel rod, and commercially available locks are the typical improvements.

Crank-Out Windows. The one advantage of a crank-out window is that it typically secures very tightly. Unfortunately, the locking mechanism is not very substantial and may need to be supported with a secondary lock of some sort. In the average residence using

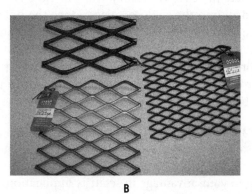

FIGURE 11.3 A, B
A. Window grating used at the rear of a warehouse area, not occupied by employees. This was a particularly vulnerable area that was not visible to the public or to patrols. **B.** The various gauges of grating available for window coverings. Some of these grates are angled and sharpened to an edge similar to that of a knife.

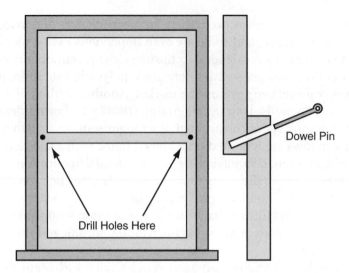

FIGURE 11.4
Pinning technique. Note the downward angle of the drilled location where the dowel pin or nail will be inserted.

this style window, an easy way to prevent the window from being used as a burglary entry point is for the resident to simply remove the crank when he or she is away. The window may still be broken and a pair of channel locks may do the trick for cranking it open, but, as stated time and again in this text, the average burglar is not going to put forth that much effort and subject him- or herself to that much risk of detection.

Double Hung Sash Windows. This is the window found in most homes today. Older homes are usually secured with a single crescent latch, and newer homes generally have two similar flat latches. The crescent latch is easily defeated, especially if the window is loose in the sash. The newer windows and replacement windows have a much better system to ensure that the windows are tight and that the latches secure the window in place. Every crime prevention practitioner is aware of what to recommend for reinforcing the security of these style windows. There are commercially available locks to provide a secondary locking mechanism, but the practitioner generally will recommend a technique known as "pinning." In order to provide extra protection the window is closed and then a hole on the right and left side is drilled through the top corner of the bottom window (where the two windows join). The hole is drilled at a downward angle, being careful not to drill into the enclosed glass. Once the hole is drilled, pins or nails of a slightly smaller size than the drilled holes are inserted to reinforce the existing lock (**FIGURE 11.4**). The pins allow for quick escape in case of fire; the downward angle prevents the pins from being vibrated out. If desired, the window can be raised slightly (3–4 inches) and drilled through the existing first window and again into the second window to enable the window to be secure when it is open.

Lighting for Safety

Although lighting is one of the most inexpensive ways to provide security for a facility, it is often overlooked or improperly used. You do not have to be a lighting designer to use lighting to your advantage in security applications. All that is required is a little understanding of the types of lights and their characteristics, and some good old-fashioned common sense. Lighting is a very effective and important crime deterrent; any law enforcement officer or investigator will quickly attest to that from experience. I learned the importance of lighting as a young detective. Several young men had been arrested and confessed to a huge string of thefts from cars. During the interviews, one comment struck me about their tactics. They stated that they always hit late at night after following their victims from a local cruising strip where the sharpest cars would frequent. The thieves watched the cars as they parked, and if the area was not "lit up good" they would return later and break into them. When I asked why they were concerned about the lighting, the answer was so obvious that I felt stupid for posing the question: "People might see us." Those interviews taught me a valuable lesson about lighting that I later applied to prevention programs and recommendations. Lighting is merely an aid for allowing observation of an item or area. If there is no observation of the area, lighting provides little benefit for security.

Lights and Their Purposes

Lighting should serve to enhance or provide for observation. This section will concentrate on how the law enforcement crime prevention practitioner can use lighting toward that end. Because I am not a lighting designer or expert, and because this book is intended for use as a practical guide, I will not be discussing lighting from a technical viewpoint, but from a practical, plain language position, and I will include some of the more common lighting terms and definitions.

Let's begin with a look at the most commonly used lights and their standard applications:

Incandescent Lights. These are the lights found in most homes. They are good at rendering color but are not very cost-efficient to operate, and therefore they are not often used in security operations.

Fluorescent Lights. Fluorescent lights are most commonly recognized by their long tubular bulbs. They are used frequently in schools, stores, and businesses. Due to the technology and how the bulb operates, they do not operate well in cold weather and therefore should not be used in exterior applications in areas that experience such weather conditions.

High Intensity Discharge (HID)—Mercury Vapor. These emit a bluish tinted light and are very inefficient to operate due to the shortness of the bulb's life. They are occasionally found in old street lights, but are more likely to be used by landscapers.

HID—Metal Halide. These lights are easily recognizable because they burn very white and have excellent color rendering qualities. Therefore, retail establishments for which "roadside appeal" is important frequently use metal halide lights. They may be used by jewelers, in boutique windows, and especially in car lots.

HID—High Pressure Sodium. The high pressure sodium light is a popular choice for street lighting. These lights are efficient, have fair color rendering qualities, and are relatively inexpensive. The change in wattage allows for increasing or diminishing the output of the light with relative ease.

HID—Low Pressure Sodium. Low pressure sodium lighting has an easily recognizable quality when burning. The light emits a yellow tint and depicts objects as monochromatic yellow and black. It may be of benefit in an area monitored by black-and-white closed circuit television, and has been said to discourage gathering due to the sickening emission of the yellow light. This light might be useful for discouraging street drug sales and prostitution, both of which involve the customer wanting to examine the product prior to purchase.

Lighting Fixtures

Now that I have discussed the most commonly encountered types of lights, we need to examine the fixtures, or luminaires, that are available. Along with the fixtures we need a basic understanding of the types of controls that activate the lighting fixtures and their common usage.

FIGURE 11.5
Shoebox fixtures.

In most modern retail parking lot applications the more attractive "shoebox" style fixture is generally used (**FIGURE 11.5**). The size of the fixture, mounting height, and wattage vary, depending on the usage and needs. However, an issue that has become rather prevalent with this type of fixture in recent years is the undesirable spilling of light from one property to an adjoining property. This is referred to as "light trespass," and has resulted in changes in light wattage, de-lamping, and even removal. There is, however, a better way to deal with this problem. Fixtures are available that actually shield or block the light from spilling into a certain area. These light blocks are sometimes retrofitted to existing fixtures as well. These "cut off" devices are available on most types of commercial fixtures.

The most common residential application of lighting is the dome style "dusk to dawn" fixture. This fixture is activated automatically by a light-sensing photocell positioned on the fixture that measures the amount of light available. These fixtures also are available with a cut-off design to control light spillage, as demonstrated in **FIGURE 11.6**.

Pedestrian-level street lamps are often found in tourist attractions and up-scale neighborhood developments. The height of the poles and fixtures allows the illumination to be unobstructed by thick tree foliage, because they are generally beneath the tree canopy.

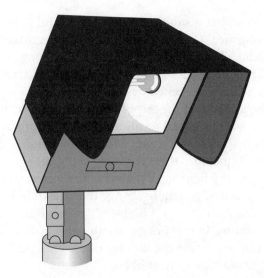

FIGURE 11.6
Fixtures that control light trespass by design of a cut-off shroud and housing, or both.

Of course, there are many other styles of fixtures that are not discussed here, each with a specific designed use. Flood lights are designed to cover a wide area with light; spotlights are designed to intensely illuminate a specific smaller area. There are walkway lights and landscape lights, and there are even lights for underwater use. It should be noted that each light is designed with specific uses in mind, and the bulbs are not necessarily interchangeable.

Each light fixture may be activated using one of a variety of methods. As with the choice of the type of light and the fixture, the activation method is an important choice that needs to be made while keeping the desired result, especially when the result is the prevention of crime.

Architects and lighting engineers have developed certain recommended light levels for the various applications one might encounter. Although many law enforcement crime prevention practitioners have educated themselves about these levels, which are measured by a light meter in foot candles (FC), most members of the law enforcement community accept the standard of being able to recognize facial features from a distance of 30 feet as a measure of adequate lighting. Some use another rule of thumb of being able to read the smaller headlines of a newspaper. The professional consultant may actually use a meter to get complete and accurate readings throughout the area, but most in law enforcement are satisfied with their rules of thumb being "close enough for government work." Indeed, I have rarely seen the need to be as precise in evaluating lighting as a light meter would allow. Being knowledgeable of the recommended measurements might be more beneficial in designing lighting for a new facility than in evaluating existing lighting. Specific recommended standards for lighting a variety of applications may be obtained by contacting the Illuminating Engineering Society of North America.

Proper Usage

As a practitioner in the law enforcement community I find that that proper usage of lighting is much more important than applying the exact recommended light level. Some of the pitfalls caused by improper usage follow.

Over-lighting. A common mistake made by the inexperienced practitioner is to recommend that a customer "increase the lighting." This translates to the erroneous belief that more is better. I had an experience in which I had recommended lighting changes, along with other types of changes, that resulted in a very successful reduction in street drug dealing in a public housing area. One of the other housing managers in the area was aware of this and decided to reduce his similar problem by "improving" the lighting. He increased the lighting throughout his facility to 400 watts and actually added fixtures. We were all surprised when he didn't get cited by the Federal Aviation Administration for confusing the pilots as to the location of the airport, because it was certainly bright enough to land aircraft there. Joking aside, the end result from over-lighting is that residents and even businesses close their shades and blinds rather than opening them to encourage observation on the street. Remember the old adage, "Too much of anything is bad."

While discussing increasing lighting, I should note that the usual method is to increase the wattage. One cannot generally change the type of light without changing the fixture. In other words, you can't change a high-pressure sodium fixture to a metal halide light simply by changing bulbs. In most cases, reading the two-digit decal on the fixture and then adding a zero can determine the wattage of the existing light. For example if a "20" is displayed, the light wattage is most likely 200 watts.

Lighting Without Cause. From a crime prevention perspective, the primary reason for lighting is to enhance observation by better revealing the area or persons in it. If there is no opportunity for observation, then lighting rarely has a crime prevention benefit. One might use a motion-activated light to reveal to a security guard that something is behind a building that warrants investigation. In this case, the light becomes more of an alarm.

Creation of Shadows or Dark Spots. Ensuring that applied lighting does not produce sharp contrasts but rather is uniform and allows for a gradual eye transition is an extremely important factor when recommending lighting improvements or changes. It takes longer for the eye to adjust from light to dark than from dark to light; therefore, the desired effect in a late-night establishment would be to slightly over-light the inside in order to create what is known as the "fishbowl effect." This allows those outside to view inside activities. The lighting should be a gradual transition to the exterior and then back into the neighborhood or larger community.

Improper Mounting/Directing. Lights that are misdirected and create horizontal light (glare) are a detriment to those approaching and actually prevent visual observation into a facility or an area. Glare can be used positively, however, as at a facility entrance guard shack, but the practitioner should be certain that glare is a desired goal when examining the facility for lighting issues.

Poor Maintenance. Poor maintenance of lighting and the foliage surrounding it lessens the desired effect of the lights. Often an area may appear to be extremely dark and in need of upgraded lighting when in fact the lighting should be adequate but is inhibited by foliage or by dirty or bug-filled lens covers. On occasion the lenses have become yellowed with age and need to be replaced, a proposition much cheaper than upgrading completely. A final maintenance issue is that of relamping, or changing the bulbs. In most cases a cherry picker–type machine has to be rented to change the lamps, and it is just not cost-effective to change them as they burn out. Therefore, it is recommended that relamping of all lights, burned out or not, be done on a scheduled basis.

The Impact of Lighting

Lighting has been studied for years and has been linked to reducing vandalism and burglaries (Clarke, 1997). Numerous lawsuits related to injuries incurred during a crime have been filed based on lighting issues, some resulting in millions of dollars in awards. A 1988 study proved the value of lighting to retail when it revealed that 67% of respondents named security as an important factor in their choice of malls and 52% said that a perceived lack of security was their top reason for not shopping at a specific mall. More than 80% of the respondents in this study identified well-lighted parking lots as the most important security measure at the mall (Mattson, 1999). Based on the growing amount of litigation related to facilities and their lighting as related to crimes, it is essential that we law enforcement crime prevention practitioners inform our citizen business customers of the potential for crime and civil liability related to lighting.

Closed Circuit Television

To begin this section, I must first apologize for any personal bias against closed circuit television (CCTV) in a crime prevention application. I want to make clear that I am not saying that CCTV has no preventative effect, and I am in no way detracting from CCTV's value as an investigative tool. CCTV does have a preventative value in deterring crime. The deterrent, however, does not necessarily come from the television itself but rather from the potential of being discovered. This is where the discussion usually becomes argumentative. CCTV, like any other tool, when used improperly will prevent nothing. It may contribute to prevention when applied properly in the appropriate setting and when monitored. I will discuss this in more detail shortly, but first I want to point out the advances in technology that have made CCTV such a popular tool.

Modern CCTV has a much wider choice of applications than in the past, and due to its popularity it is very cost-effective to use. The modern system makes tracking of an intruder or suspicious person through a facility unobtrusive and relatively simple. Using multiple cameras with pan/tilt capabilities and a multiplex system, one operator can track the target to any location that the camera covers. In addition, most systems are equipped with digital or VHS video recording capabilities. Video may now be enhanced using special equipment to clarify features or better observe objects. This capability is invaluable to facilities in protecting them from false injury claims, providing documented proof to aid in recuperating losses from insurance carriers, and identifying suspects and suspect actions during an investigation. The video may also assist in some limited capacity in preventing future similar incidents from occurring due to planning implemented after the first event.

Monitoring of CCTV is sometime considered to be a preventative measure as well. I concede that monitored systems provide a timely response to an active event if an alert employee observes the event. The timely response may lessen the injury, loss, or damage and may result in an improved outcome of the event, but even the monitored event has not been prevented. Additionally, often the monitoring agent is responsible for monitoring numerous screens for long periods of time, is responsible for other tasks as well, and honestly is not apt to recognize any but the most obvious active crimes. Due to this reality, even the likelihood of intervention is decreased. The presence of CCTV camera systems and signage indicating their existence are the primary prevention value of the CCTV system. Creating a perceived risk may cause the would-be criminal to choose another location or another target.

The existence of CCTV places responsibility upon the facility to monitor the cameras. The existence of the camera is apt to lull the customer or facility user into a false sense of security out of the belief that they are being monitored and that should an event occur, help will be on the way immediately. Videotaping a system without monitoring may subject the facility to liability resulting from injury or losses from a crime on their property. On the other hand, hidden cameras take away any crime prevention aspect that the CCTV may provide by way of perceived threat. How does the law enforcement crime prevention practitioner resolve this dilemma? Some suggestions from practitioners in the field are:

- Honestly explain the strengths and weaknesses of CCTV to the business considering using it.
- Determine in advance what the business expects to gain from using CCTV.

- Identify alternatives to accomplish the same goal if monitoring while the facility is open is cost prohibitive. Such alternatives will be discussed in detail in the next chapter, but may include relocating staff and policy changes.
- If the facility insists on using a system that will not be monitored constantly while the facility is open, suggest saturating the facility with signage indicating that the facility is "periodically monitored" by video surveillance equipment.
- As in the previous tip, saturate the facility with signage but use hidden video surveillance systems and change the signage to read "monitored periodically with hidden video surveillance."

Using CCTV Systems Effectively

Once expectations are clear and the business customer has expressed an intention to use CCTV, the practitioner should be prepared to offer some sound advice as to the type of CCTV system to use and appropriate signage, as discussed above. If a CCTV system is to be used, the practitioner should attempt to assist the business in using it in the most effective way.

Recommendations for usage of CCTV by a crime prevention practitioner working in the public sector are apt to be very general. The business or facility should be directed to seek its own vendor to meet the specifications required of the system. The practitioner's role is to assist in drafting those specifications and policies related to the CCTV.

If the system's desired purpose is to be a deterrent, then the presence of cameras should be well known. The cameras should be easily observable and acknowledged through the posting of plenty of signage announcing their use. As mentioned previously, if these measures are taken, trained employees must physically monitor the cameras whenever anyone is legitimately on the premises.

Liability potential also leads us to suggest that a policy and practice of checking each camera for operability daily be put in place, and that the checks be documented. Any cameras that are found to be inoperable should be reported in written form and removed or repaired as soon as possible. This procedure will afford some defense in the event of civil litigation.

Inoperable or "faux" cameras should never be used to give the appearance of CCTV monitoring.

Signage should not be overly specific; for example, instead of stating that the premises are monitored by CCTV 24 hours per day, state that the premises are monitored by CCTV. This technique will provide the deterrent desired, while affording some "wiggle room" in the event of litigation. Other phrasings for signage that are more suggestive rather than absolute are "This facility is periodically monitored by CCTV" or "Please be aware that you may be monitored by CCTV while on these premises."

Even with monitoring of cameras, a videotaping system is recommended. The video will provide evidence not only in criminal cases, but also in civil litigation. In some cases, the tape has enabled a business to refute claims of negligence, and even if this occurs only once, the system has proven its value as compared to cost.

Implementing CCTV

The business or facility using our services is our customer, even though we are public employees. As such, we must give due consideration to providing them valuable information and assisting them in implementing systems that accomplish the goal of crime prevention while being cost-effective. The facility insisting on using CCTV or requiring CCTV out of necessity should examine the following:

System Costs. The costs of a CCTV system go far beyond the initial purchase price and installation of the equipment. The practitioner should make sure that the facility requests detailed costs of maintenance and monitoring. If monitoring is to be done in house, the business should consider the cost of a monitoring site setup, the number of employees needed to monitor the system for the period of time required, the salary and benefits cost, and the training cost.

Monitoring the Site and Security. In some cases it will be necessary to have off-site monitoring whereas in others the monitoring may be placed on site. The location must be decided strategically in order to ensure that security is not compromised by casual observation and that the exact angle of the cameras can be determined by outside sources.

Ideal Location of the Cameras. The practitioner's interview with the facility manager should identify the purpose or goal behind implementing CCTV. The camera locations are very dependent upon this identified goal. If the only purpose of CCTV is to monitor the main entrance to the facility, the practitioner need only determine the most advantageous angle and location near the entrance for installation. The locations of cameras must be determined based upon the goal and the most advantageous angle.

Continuous Record or Time Delay. Time delay will extend the recording time before the tape has to be changed in a VHS system, but will provide only sporadic shots of the activity and may miss the best angle for an identification. Continuous recording systems require more frequent tape changes and a storage space for the tapes. However, the continuous recording system will allow investigators to have the tape enhanced and the best frame frozen for a still shot because the entire activity is captured on the tape. A digital system offers the best of both worlds. These systems record the continuous action, allow storage in a computer hard drive or on a DVD, and are generally of better quality. The drawback with this system is the initial cost and the maintenance.

Having given a very limited overview of the systems, I caution the practitioner against choosing for the facility or encouraging the facility manager to choose one. Remember, as a public employee we want to provide good information to the business and answer questions for them, but unless we have specialized training we should leave the decision making to the end user.

Video Reuse. VHS video declines in quality when it is used over and over, and this issue should be addressed. A policy should be implemented to identify and track the number of times a video is to be used and what is to be the disposition of it once it has met the threshold usage level. I generally recommend that a tape be used no more than three times, but other crime prevention specialists may recommend a few more or less.

Video Storage. The practitioner should be aware that it is not uncommon for some time to pass before a claim is filed or a crime is discovered. Therefore, the facility using a VHS system or other removable video medium must provide for safe storage of the video recordings. Safe storage means a climate-controlled location that is access controlled. Remember that the video may become evidence, so it is important to be able to demonstrate that few persons had access to tamper with the video. A policy should be put in place that defines the retention period for tapes before being put back into reuse. Retention periods are sometimes covered by individual state mandates on records retention; the practitioner should research his or her state's regulations prior to recommending any retention period. If not covered by state record retention standards, a minimum retention period of 30 days is recommended. Even if the tape has been destroyed after a retention period, if the policy exists to demonstrate the regular destruction and the tape destruction is documented, some doubt as to the claim might be planted in jurors' minds. At worst, the policy and documentation remove the belief that the tape was simply destroyed to remove evidence that would support the litigant's claim.

Time of Day or Night to Be Used. It is certainly important to know if a camera is expected to operate in low light, bright light, or both when drafting specifications to be addressed by a vendor. This will generally be learned during the interview process with the facility or business customer.

Accessibility of the Video Device. One should never rule out the possibility of a complicit employee causing losses or criminal activity. The video system should be in a secure cabinet or other location inaccessible to the monitoring employee. Generally the employee responsible for removal, reviewing, and storage of the video medium should not be in the organizational chain with the monitoring employees.

In my opinion and experience, CCTV applications hold yet untold value in investigations. CCTV systems are currently being used in public applications to monitor public space. They are used in downtown centers, in airports, train stations, and beachfronts. The advancements in CCTV have resulted in their usage in homeland defense applications as well. Facial recognition technology is among those advancements and is improving. Such advancements are indicative of the possibilities of CCTV use in future applications to investigate crimes and even to prevent them.

Security Alarms

If I appeared cold on the prevention potential of CCTV, then I may be perceived to be at least chilly on certain types of alarm systems. I hasten to reiterate that I am in no way devaluing alarm systems per se, but find certain applications limited in their capacity to prevent crime. The prevention value of alarms comes from the deterrent effect created by increasing the perceived risk of detection. Depending on the type of system used, the hidden sensor may also contribute to the preventative value by increasing the effort required by the criminal for success. It appears that alarm systems have lost much of their prevention value with the demise of the so-called one-stop local alarm shop. The one-stop alarm company sold the system, maintained the system, monitored the activations, and often had local guards to respond to the activations. Later on in this section I will discuss how the business of alarms and the technological advances have, in my personal opinion, resulted in less effective systems.

I again intend to simplify the understanding of alarms to terms that I prefer, rather than attempting to speak in technical terms that should be reserved for the expert alarm technician. I will overview the alarm's purpose, its basic functioning, false activations and ordinances, overall effectiveness, and the basic alarm components.

Alarm Systems Overview

With most members of the household at work or school, the natural guardians of the past are not available to alert police to the suspicious activity or attempted break-in of a residence during the day. In fact, in many neighborhoods the community practically empties during the day. Just the opposite occurs during the evening and night when business districts and downtowns empty of workers returning home. Absent these guardians or an implementation of the new urbanism mixture of residential and business use property, a different guardian mechanism is needed to alert police of attempted entry. That mechanism is the electronic alarm system. The primary purpose of an alarm is to alert someone of a change in the environmental norm. The changes in the environment may be a change in temperature, sound, air pressure, or a host of other measured standards. This is where the crime prevention practitioner is of value.

The practitioner may assist the customer in determining which environmental factor would be most advantageous to monitor. Of course, the private alarm company representative is fully equipped to make this recommendation to a potential customer, but one must recognize that the possibility for economic gain sometimes wins out over sound recommendations. It is for this reason that reputable alarm companies are advocating government licensing and controls over their own industry. The vast majority of alarm companies are honest and reputable, but the few disreputable ones lead me to encourage the law enforcement crime prevention practitioner to become acquainted with alarm systems, if for no other reason than to be a sounding board for the customer or to act as a checks and balances system for the private sales recommendation. In some states, government agencies oversee the licensing and operation of alarm technicians and companies. Not only does the alarm industry support such oversight, but they also support the use of alarm ordinances that tend to hold alarm owners and alarm service providers accountable for false activations.

Alarm Operations

To understand the commonly used sensing devices that detect changes in the environment, we will begin by reviewing how a common alarm system operates. A simple alarm system is made up of a primary power source, a backup power source, sensors, a controller (brain) to evaluate signals sent by the sensor, and an annunciator (bell, whistle, ring down, etc.). To draw an analogy with Neighborhood Watch, the sensor would be the watcher observing something that appears abnormal; it would then process what it sees and interpret it as being suspicious (controller). The watcher would then act as the annunciator by calling the police to give the alarm. Just as some improperly trained Neighborhood Watch members find everything suspicious and are problematic, so are faulty alarm systems that are improperly installed or set. Both of the examples are problematic to the police and have to be addressed to avoid wasting resources and time, and to ensure proper response when they give the alarm.

Most unnecessary alarms are not actually false alarms but rather false activations. In other words, the alarm actually did what it was designed to do, but what activated the alarm was not a burglar, but someone who forgot to key in the code to deactivate the system or an animal that got inside and activated the motion sensor.

Alarm Ordinances

Chronic false activations not addressed by the alarm owner or, in some cases, the alarm company have resulted in the growing use of alarm ordinances. Alarm ordinances typically charge an incrementally larger fee for each false activation that generates a police response. The ordinance is not designed to generate income but rather to improve the quality of alarm installations and thus reduce the time wasted by patrols responding to false activations. The support from the National Burglar and Fire Alarm Association for such ordinances demonstrates its commitment to providing quality products and services and to reducing false activations. The alarm industry and law enforcement realize that large numbers of false activations lead to the "boy who cried wolf" scenario and may ultimately lead to severe consequences.

Alarm Services

Another issue related to the effectiveness of alarms is linked to the evolution of alarm services. The early alarm systems were often audible activations or ring-down systems to a local monitoring station. In either case the activation was almost immediately called in to police. Once called, the police, and in many cases an alarm company guard, responded to the alarm site. These systems were quite effective in addressing alarm calls. The audible system had a very real crime prevention application and rarely was anything taken, unless the business displayed items in a show window and a "snatch and run" burglary occurred.

Some claim that the audible systems fell out of favor because the criminals started removing the audible sounding device, but I suspect that economics played a larger role in their decreased sales and usage. One drawback of the stand-alone audible alarm was that an inexperienced person often would install the system, which might yield more false activations than those professionally installed. Also, in some cases, because a novice had installed the system, police would arrive to find a broken window or door and have no emergency contact to call to secure the business or deactivate the alarm. The best system was the professionally operated alarm company with a local station. These companies generally sold the system, installed the system, monitored the system, and maintained the system. This type of local monitoring station held many benefits over the modern systems, which have different subcontractors selling, installing, monitoring, and maintaining them.

Today the selling agent has little communication with the installing technician or station, which makes it difficult to facilitate repairs of faulty systems. The advent of the modern system with independent operations results in poorer customer service due to lack of accountability. Additionally, today's technological advances have allowed central monitoring stations to actively monitor alarms several states away. This is truly more efficient for the alarm company, because it can place all of its operations in one building with fewer employees, but the effectiveness is reduced by this setup. With a local monitoring station, the operator would be aware that the area was experiencing an electrical storm or mass power outages, which might be relevant to the increases in activations. The local guard system would have dispatched a guard to check the property for a breach or for suspicious activity, and if none was found often the police would not be dispatched. Additionally, the guard could reset the systems without bothering the keyholder. Often the local station developed a close relationship with police and would ask for assistance in checking businesses whose alarm systems were out of service. That relationship is not present with the modern out-of-state systems. The common procedure for response to alarms activating to a central monitoring stations are as follows: The central station receives an activation, and then calls the subscriber (customer) at the business. If the call is answered the company requests a password; if the person answering doesn't know the password or if there is no answer, the company calls the local police, who in turn dispatch a responding unit. This system is so time consuming that in many law enforcement agencies alarm calls are a low priority because even when there is a burglary, the burglar is rarely still on the scene. The old guard system sent a guard immediately and, as mentioned earlier, the guard was usually there before the police.

Unfortunately, a single operation alarm company is rare today. I would recommend to any business or individual shopping for an alarm to clarify in their contract who will be responsible for repair of the system and all components including wiring, determining the cause of and addressing false activations, and maintaining the system.

Sensing Components

Although technological advances may have reduced the effectiveness of alarm companies, they have greatly improved the reliability and variety of alarm components. Sensing devices for a variety of applications are currently available, and the knowledgeable technician will be able to custom fit an application to the desired use. The technician will be able to provide sensors for perimeter, area, or even specific object protection. We have come a long way from foil window contacts. Some of the most common sensors encountered and used by alarm technicians in security operations are the following.

Door/Window Contacts. These consist of two contacts mounted on a door or window and its frame. The frame contact is usually hard-wired and the alarm activates when the magnetic field between the two contacts is broken (i.e., when the door or window is opened). Because these devices are surface mounted, over time they will require adjustment or replacement as they become worn. Problems sometime occur when the contacts are used on doors or windows that are loose, exposed to strong winds, or near heavy truck or other traffic that might result in the contacts being vibrated. Door contacts are an example of a perimeter control.

Pressure Mat or Pad Contacts. Although these are not used often, there are still some applications for which they are appropriate. The contacts in the mat measure the pressure or weight on the pad and activate when a pressure increase is detected (someone steps on the mat).

Motion Sensor. Motion sensors are examples of space or area protection devices. Motion is detected in a number of ways using different types of sensors. One motion sensor operates by the transmission of a photoelectric beam. When the beam circuit is broken, the alarm activates. Problems encountered with this type of sensor include animals, unsecured papers, or even balloons that are moved by circulating air. Infrared sensors, also referred to as PIR or passive infrared sensors, measure the heat or radiation changes. Problems sometimes occur when large animals intrude or heat is generated from unexpected sources such as computers, skylights, or windows.

Noise Sensors. Noise sensors measure sound in a variety of ways and sound an alarm when a variance from the norm is detected. Some common problems encountered with noise sensors are air drafts or turbulence, loud exterior sounds, machinery and HVAC systems cycling off and on, ringing telephones, and incoming facsimiles. An amplified sound sensor measures the sound level, and when a loud noise or sound above the tolerance is detected the alarm activates. A microwave sensor projects a radio wave over the protected area and when the wave is broken or disrupted the alarm activates. A high-pitched frequency sensor protects the area with a frequency projected too high for human detection.

Dual Sensing Systems. The dual system is a combination of sensors designed to combat the problems associated with false activations in a single sensor system. The dual system requires a change in two measured environmental factors to activate. For example, a system with both a photoelectric beam and a PIR will require both movement and a change in the radiation measured to activate. A disrupted stack of papers would not activate this system nor would a small animal, as long as the PIR was set high enough to detect only the amount of radiation emitted by a large body.

Although there are more sensing devices than those discussed here, the types listed are a good basic representation of what is in widespread use today. I close this section by reiterating the two most important points that the crime prevention practitioner should be aware of: The majority of false activations are due to user error rather than technology failure, and alarm ordinances are a sure way to get the attention of alarm subscribers and companies and to address faulty systems and careless employees.

Safes and Vaults

In all honesty, I have rarely found a true vault in my career in crime prevention within law enforcement, other than in banks. I am confident that most businesses who need a vault consult with a paid consultant. I have, however, encountered numerous safes of various types and sizes. In this section I will be referring to burglary-resistant safes as opposed to fire-resistant ones. Safes, like other security devices, are rated by the Underwriters Laboratory based on the amount of security that they provide. Table 11.1 lists some of the more common classifications.

TABLE 11.1
The common TL (tool resistant), TR (torch resistant), and TX (torch and explosive resistant) classifications that a law enforcement crime prevention practitioner might encounter. The number accompanying the letter generally indicates the time in minutes that the safe is resistant to the entry method.

Classification	Resistance
TL-15	A safe weighing 750 pounds or more with 1-inch-thick steel is tool resistant (common tools) on the door and front for 15 minutes.
TL-30	Same as above, with the addition of certain cutting tools for 30 minutes.
TRTL-30	Same as TL-30, with the addition of resistance to gas cutting and welding torches for 30 minutes.
TXTL-60	This classification is for a safe over 1000 pounds; the entire safe is resistant to tools, torches, and explosives with an impact equal to 8 ounces of nitroglycerine for 60 minutes.

As with all applications, the practitioner must keep cost in mind. In the case of the above-classified safes, one must realize that the expense of the safe is proportionate to the protection afforded. Each of the listed safes has specific uses. To recommend a safe with additional resistance that is not needed for the particular asset will result in inefficient use of the citizen's or business's security dollars. The practitioner should keep in mind that the customers he or she serves are not as likely to be the victims of a safe burglar as other types of burglars. In fact, there are few "professional" safe burglars, and those that do exist are not likely to attack a small business. That is not to say that the common burglar may not attack a safe, but rather to say that they are unskilled in the attack.

The common burglar is likely to attack a safe by one of four methods:

1. *The removal method*—The burglar, realizing his or her limitations, may attempt to remove the safe to another location where he or she can spend time trying to gain entry. This is generally addressed by affixing the safe to the building by some means, such as chaining the safe using a heavy chain or embedding it into the building floor with concrete. (Think of the common floor safe as an example.) In reality, and by definition, a safe affixed to the building is a vault rather than a safe, but most practitioners consider a vault to be something that a person can actually enter.
2. *Beating or "punching" the dial inward*—Although this is rarely successful due to the construction of modern safes, it is nevertheless a method attempted.
3. *Using tools on the side of the safe to create a hole large enough to remove the contents*—Frequently, safes that have been removed from the premises and recovered by some means are found to have been entered this way or the final way.
4. *"Peeling" away the layers of the safe in order to expose the locking mechanism, or bolt*—This is known as the "peel" method. Once access to the bolt is gained, tools are used to overcome the mechanism and gain entry.

Recommendations

Armed with the knowledge of how the common burglar might attack a safe, the practitioner should quickly realize the importance of policy, proper placement, proper additional protection, and proper combination controls to create the layered effect desired to make the safe burglary attempt more difficult. If the safe or vault is not to be encased in concrete, affixed to the building, or chained, at a minimum the wheels or casters should be removed and the safe secured to the building with bolts.

Placement of the safe depends on numerous factors, but if it is not to be installed behind several other layers of security such as locked doors and alarms, most likely it should be located in an area that can be viewed by patrols. If the cash is stored in the safe and dealt with throughout the open hours of the business, the safe should probably be placed in a locked office to avoid casual observation of safe transactions.

More safes are likely to be defeated by careless operation or poor controls on the combination than any of the prior forced means. A clear policy of who is to access the safe must be in place. A good method of controlling access to the safe is to issue keys to one employee to access the office or room the safe is in and to provide the combination to a second employee. This would then require collusion to enter the safe without force. The store or business policy should mandate that the combination be changed when any employee with the safe combination severs his or her employment for any reason or when the combination is revealed in any way. The policy should require that when the safe is locked the dial be turned two complete rotations. Some employees will want to take shortcuts and dial in the first few digits so as to only have to dial the final digit for access; criminals are aware of this shortcut as well.

The practitioner should caution the business customer to view the safe as a temporary secure holding place for valuables. The safe provides additional security, but without the proper controls losses may still occur. Safes left unlocked, those to which numerous employees have the combination, and those that are not properly placed or installed offer little more protection than a locked cash drawer. The layered and planned installation will provide a secure location for valuables to be temporarily secured.

■ Chapter Summary

Use of devices to protect property and to enhance visual or audio surveillance is often a less time consuming and less expensive proposition for preventing crime than other methods. The prevention value of such devices comes from the resulting outcomes, such as delaying the criminal act or improving observation by potential witnesses. Devices are most useful when working together with other programs and are successful because of their relationship in enhancing detection.

■ Review Questions

1. What term is used to indicate the process of protecting vulnerable areas by use of devices?
2. What type of lighting is the most popular high intensity discharge (HID) choice for government street lighting?
3. What vulnerability is created when a door is hung with the hinges exposed to the exterior?
4. What part of an alarm system senses a change in the environment that ultimately results in alarm activation?

■ References

Clarke, Ron V. 1997. *Situational Crime Prevention—Successful Case Studies*. Guilderland, NY: Harrow and Heston Publishers.
Mattson, Beth. August 1999. "A sense of security." *Access Control & Security Systems Integration Magazine*.
MSI National Security Study. August 1999. *Access Control & Security Systems Integration Magazine*.

Crime Prevention Through Environmental Design

"He that will not apply new remedies must expect new evils."

—Francis Bacon

■ Introduction

Humans have long recognized that they can provide safety for themselves and their families by manipulating their environment. Ancient civilizations built cities on hills to provide observation and make attack difficult. Cities were walled and access controlled with formidable gates. Castles were surrounded by moats, with their sole access being controlled by a drawbridge. Even the earliest settlers of the United States built fortifications with towers to keep watch over the surrounding countryside. Although those practicing these measures probably didn't realize it, what they were doing would come to be a much studied phenomenon known as Crime Prevention Through Environmental Design (CPTED).

■ Crime Prevention Through Environmental Design

Because the focus of this book is one of "practical application," I have opted to forgo providing a detailed history or analysis of CPTED. I will include some insight, and at the end of this chapter identify a recent work by some very skilled CPTED practitioners that should address these topics in more detail for those with an interest. I do not believe that one needs to be an expert in the field of criminology or architectural design to apply CPTED successfully.

The Premise

Without detailing the history, I will state that most practitioners believe that CPTED began because of a discussion by Jane Jacobs (1961) in her book, *The Death and Life of Great American Cities*, and a 1970 study on the premise of "defensible space" by architect and urban planner Oscar Newman (1972). It was criminologist C. Ray Jeffrey, however, who in 1971 coined the actual phrase "Crime Prevention Through Environmental Design." Jeffrey (1971) had conducted a series of interviews with inmates to learn why they had chosen certain locations for their crimes and what made those locations attractive. Since this early beginning, the body of work has grown immensely, but the basic understanding of CPTED has remained essentially the same. As defined by Jeffrey, "The proper use and effective design of the built environment can lead to a reduction in the incidence and fear of crime, and an improvement in the quality of life" (1971). It is certainly less expensive and much easier to apply CPTED strategies to new construction, but much success can still be realized by retro-fitting solutions in existing environments.

Crime Prevention Application

In the simplest terms, CPTED is a belief that understanding the criminal mindset of what makes a target attractive and then designing structures that are unattractive for the commission of crimes may prevent crimes. In other words, one builds prevention into the design. The best measure of a truly successful CPTED application is whether it accomplishes the prevention goals without the users being aware that prevention measures are in place. The measures previously detailed regarding applying the four D's and Dr. Clarke's *Situational Crime Prevention* help explain why CPTED works. As we discuss basic CPTED principles, it becomes evident that each principle contributes to deterring crime, delaying the criminal, detecting the activity, or denying access. Additionally, each of the CPTED principles makes the commission of the crime more difficult by creating more risk of being observed or questioned due to policies and design that remove excuses and reduce rewards that lead to successful completion of the crime.

The Process

At the risk of being shunned and censured by the crime prevention community for over-simplifying CPTED in law enforcement, I must state at the outset "this ain't rocket science." I believe that any practitioner can understand the basic principles and premise of CPTED and that only through use and application can one become advanced in this field. I encourage law enforcement crime prevention practitioners to attempt to apply CPTED principles at every opportunity where a crime problem exists. Police are very astute at understanding people, and CPTED has at its core the assumption that people are creatures of habit who desire routine and regularity in their life. This need for regularity is no different in the criminal. Investigators realize that criminals typically "sign" their crimes. It is here that we begin to examine how law enforcement may benefit from CPTED principles. These principles are territoriality, which focuses on creating a sense of ownership; surveillance, which attempts to maximize observation of the area; and access control, which directs potential victims to safe locations.

Before we move on to fully define and apply the principles, it is imperative that you understand the intended use of the structure or environment. Remember that a key element of the definition of CPTED is the "proper use" of the environment. All too often practitioners apply the principles to examining the design while totally disregarding the important use component. By keeping use in mind, the principles may be used to:

- Support the intended use by legitimate users
- Reduce the potential for conflicting or improper uses
- Maximize effective use through design planning and features

Having achieved an understanding of the desired use, the law enforcement crime prevention practitioner is at an advantage when applying the next step—reading the environment through the criminal's eyes. Police officers and investigators can apply their experience to this important step, whereas others may gain knowledge through academic study and research. Most law enforcement officers already think like a criminal. Actually, many people are capable of thinking like a criminal, which might account for the popularity of the current crime scene investigations programming on television. Test yourself by considering a place that you "feel" is unsafe. After considering the site, ask yourself the following questions:

1. What is this place designed for? (What is its purpose?)
2. Is the designed purpose or activity taking place, or is something else happening there?
3. What is your perception of the site? (Is it attractive, uncared for, etc.?)
4. By whom is the space intended to be used?
5. Who are the actual users of the space?

6. Would you feel safe at this site alone or at night?
7. Who is observing the space, and what is their purpose for observation?

This process might be addressed in another way as well. Some practitioners, such as Virginia's CPTED Committee of the Virginia Crime Prevention Association, recommend using the three D's of CPTED:

- *Designation*—What is the intended use of the area? What behavior is allowed?
- *Definition*—Are there physical limitations to the area or site? Are borders between the area and public spaces defined? Is it clear which activities are allowed and where?
- *Design*—Does the physical environment safely and efficiently support the intended use?

By answering these few questions, we should be better prepared to see CPTED as a process in which one principle complements the others with the ultimate result of reducing the incidence and fear of crime. I hope to demonstrate in practical terms how this occurs in order to equip the reader of this book with some expertise in addressing crime by examining and manipulating the physical environment.

■ Territoriality

Territoriality or territory reinforcement asserts that we, like other animals, are territorial creatures. As such we are more apt to protect our own turf or territory than territory that belongs to others. The ownership of the territory or property need only be perceived, rather than actual, to invoke our protective care. How does this apply to crime prevention? It implies that when someone has a sense of ownership or belonging, not only will that person willingly protect that property, but others also will intuitively sense his or her willingness to do so. Likewise, someone with ownership is more likely to maintain and keep the property in good repair, which in turn indicates to others a willingness to protect the property. Wilson and Kelling (1982) supported this theory in their article, "Broken Windows." The now famous article demonstrated how unaddressed problems sent a message that the property was not cared for, and therefore welcomed attack.

Individuals extend their monitoring of space to the areas that they perceive or exercise some control or ownership over. For example, individuals are much more likely to intervene through calling the police or confronting a person tampering with their car than if they observe that same individual tampering with a stranger's car. There is an innate sense of indignation when the attack is personal. Territorial reinforcement takes advantage of that fact to involve individuals passively, actively, and psychologically to increase the perception of ownership and thus extend the protected space beyond the norm.

Creating a Sense of Cohesiveness

Ownership or territoriality is created in a community or other environment by forming a sense of cohesiveness or, as one person put it, a feeling of everyone being in the same lifeboat. This sense is well known to the law enforcement crime prevention practitioner. The practitioner has dealt with this first hand, whether he or she recognized it then or not. For example, a vicious crime or series of crimes occurs in a neighborhood. The neighborhood's response is one of feeling under attack and outrage, and leads to one or more citizens forming a group to bring their plight to the police or governing board for the jurisdiction with a call to "do your job." Often a result of the group coming together around one common problem is the formation of a Neighborhood Watch or other such organization. You have just witnessed the power of territoriality, of cohesiveness, and of a group working together to keep the lifeboat afloat. Catch the criminal before the group becomes "as one" and you will likely see the effort to organize die quickly.

Techniques

CPTED identifies ways to, at a minimum, expand the scope of ownership beyond the norm. There are many techniques for creating territoriality.

House Design. In the 1960s, the design of single-family residential homes began to phase out front porches. The new design often moved the driveway to the rear of the property, making the front entrance attractive aesthetically, but rarely used. Such designs essentially cocooned the residents and eliminated the opportunity for daily interaction with one's neighbors, thereby making neighbors basically strangers and limiting the feeling of cohesiveness among them. It was then that we began to see residential street crime increase. The return of the front porch improves neighborliness and increases the opportunity, perceived and actual, for observation of criminal activity.

Tenant Associations or Community Watch Programs. Essentially, community or business organizations draw together groups around an existing common concern or activity. These groups form an alliance to protect one another's interests through regulation, observation, and monitoring and through the power of speaking with one voice. They encourage, or in some cases force, proper care and maintenance of properties to prevent the perception of inviting crime and to create a visible sign that the property and area at large are protected by someone who cares. When assisting these organizations, practitioners should take care to prevent the organization from creating regulations or policies that actually discourage people from claiming ownership or personalizing space. I was involved with a tenant association that wanted to allow residents to plant flowers in front of their apartments in a small patch of space, but the management wanted to deny it for fear that some might plant flowers that were not as attractive as others and thus create a potential argument. Absurd as it was, I have heard worse.

Community Gardens or Parks. I alluded to this in the previous point. Remember that any space that is unclaimed is space that has the potential for being claimed by an illegitimate user. Community gardens are often best placed in open space claimed by trespassers, loiterers, or street drug users. Provide some good soil and an organized cleanup, and allow residents from nearby neighborhoods or a local garden club to take over. The unclaimed space that used to be garbage-riddled will now become attractive, the space will be claimed and protected by legitimate users, and the area will create a social gathering for building a cohesive group. In the case of a community park, place benches facing toward the play areas to improve monitoring of youth.

Neighborhood Beautification Contest. This technique may be undertaken by a tenant's association, on a neighborhood level, by a local property management company of numerous properties, or by local governments. This technique may be an annual event, quarterly, or even seasonal. The concept is simple: Have each participating resident, business, community, or complex enter the contest to be awarded a prize. This not only encourages improved maintenance, already mentioned as important, but also encourages wide-scale participation at a low cost. In the case of a community award or complex competition, the prize might be a cookout event, which would create another opportunity for residents to get to know their neighbors and may extend their perceived sense of responsibility to all the properties that are participating. This event is especially beneficial in a community attempting to prevent chronic vandalism.

Regular Meeting Rooms for Organizations. There are literally hundreds of organizations that meet regularly without a set space. Some meet in restaurants, but often must buy meals to use the room without a fee. This technique creates a legitimate use for space that is often sitting vacant and affords monitoring of the property, if only for the meeting times. Many of the organizations meeting in the provided space may become a customer of the owner of that space due to a feeling of comfort and kinship with the space. A single parents group meeting in a church may net new attendees at the church; professional organizations who meet at an apartment complex may have members who decide that the complex has much to offer from their passive observation and opt to become a resident.

Signs Announcing the Entry into a Neighborhood or Community. The signs indicate that this area is claimed and cared for by residents of a common group who have joined to identify themselves as one. Entry into the area sends a message that one is entering a "semi-private" space in which public behavior might not be acceptable. The individual is likely to feel that he or she will be noticed as an outsider, and certain actions of residents, such as looking at passing vehicles or speaking to strange pedestrians, reinforce the concept.

Border Definition. Like welcome signs, each border treatment defines the area as "owned" and psychologically, if not actually, clearly demonstrates a transition from public to semi-private. The behavior expected in a public space is much less restrictive than that in a semi-private or private space. The transition from public to semi-private to private is an important one. Each step increases the likelihood of the criminal being discovered and found to be without excuse for his or her actions. Some barrier-type border methods are use of gates, thick or thorny shrubbery, bollards, or walls. Other than physical border definitions, the property may be defined by psychological or symbolic methods. These methods define the border without creating a barrier to passage; some examples are using different textured or colored sidewalks, low-growing or ground cover plantings, floral plantings, or planters. The means of defining the border are endless. The choice of application depends on the need. The technique should be chosen after carefully considering the other principles of CPTED, surveillance and access control (discussed later in this chapter), and the use of the property.

Adopt-A-Space Programs. These programs are quite popular and allow groups to claim ownership through their caring for and maintaining a blighted area. Of course, if the group adopts the space and labors to maintain it they will be vigilant about monitoring it in passing, not only for the return of garbage or vandalism, but also for interlopers who may be suspicious. After all their work, how likely do you think these groups would be to call to report loiterers, drinking in public, or others littering the area? The addition of the Adopt-A Space sign strengthens the preventative power of the program by putting others on notice that the area is indeed cared for.

Proper Placement of Pay Telephones. Payphones placed on the fringes of business lots indicate lack of control and thus lack of ownership. These telephones have frequently been crime generators used for drug deals and other illegal activity. They also provide legitimacy to the criminal who may be loitering to case the business for an appropriate time to rob it or to enter and shoplift items. The more control over the telephones that the business can manage, the safer the business, and surrounding community, will be. I differ somewhat from some of my colleagues in the proper placement of pay telephones. Some assert that it is better to have the telephones on the fringe of the establishment where the clerk can see all around them. I disagree. Control, or perceived control, of a space equates to ownership, and control in this case is substantiated by observation and proximity.

Proper Placement of Trespassing Signs. Trespassing signs put illegitimate users on notice that the person who owns the property will call the police if necessary. Legitimate users are rarely affected by the use of trespassing signs. The signs indicate someone may be watching and, most importantly, they remove the illegitimate user's excuse that they were unaware the property was private.

Identification Programs. These programs require users to display appropriate identification; they foster a sense of family or belonging and remove excuses for the presence of unauthorized people. Often businesses, schools, and even residential properties employ this technique for access control, which is beneficial, without realizing the added benefit of territoriality that it provides. The success of such programs depends on the policy requirement that legitimate users display identification on their outer garment and that they present the identification when requested. It also requires that all visitors receive a visitor's pass or be escorted by an authorized person while on the premises. These programs force legitimate users, out of habit, to look for the identification and to report those not displaying identification or, in some cases such as at a school, question their needs and escort them to the office.

Appropriately Placing Legitimate Loitering or Break Areas. Surveillance, or observation opportunities, is a key principle in CPTED applications, especially when it is used to create a legitimate use for an abused or uncontrolled area. In some CPTED circles, this use is called activity support. In essence, the strategic placement of planned observation opportunities is what this process is all about. For example, if a break area is going to be created, then an ideal location would be one that affords surveillance of a rarely used area or an area that may be opportune for illegitimate activity due to its seclusion. Rarely does an individual visit a break area alone, and the constant traffic discourages any criminal activity. Another example might be the creation of smoking areas, which are typically outdoors. Placing these designated areas in locations that overlook employee parking or some other key site has a preventative effect.

Expand Authority. Give owners responsibility for a particular area by providing additional space to be controlled by the private user. For example, in many business districts the size of setbacks has been reduced, and businesses have been authorized to create on-street dining and balconies. Each of these changes translates to increased density or space for the business, which in turn means more cash. In addition, the expanded control benefits the crime prevention effort by creating more observation on the street and even more ownership of public space. In some downtowns, open-air dining is allowed only during the evening, due to high sidewalk traffic during the day. In this case the businesses designate the dining area each night with a removable chain. In the areas that I have visited with open-air dining, street crime is almost nonexistent.

In a school situation, this ownership and thus increase in surveillance may be accomplished by assigning teachers or staff bulletin boards for displaying their students' work. This will extend their ownership or control beyond their classroom to "their" bulletin board. Likewise, assigning them zones of responsibility within the school will create a sense of ownership within their zone as well as a more thorough knowledge of locations of potential problems within their zone.

Ownership Opportunities. Create ownership opportunities while addressing other crime problems. This process represents the proverbial killing two birds with one stone approach. Often one crime will generate another, and so on. Much like the Adopt-A-Space program, we may wish to address some crimes by creating a community building program that addresses the remnants of the crime while creating ownership of the space to prevent future such occurrences. This approach is ideally suited for vandalism and graffiti crimes. Research has revealed that graffiti that is removed quickly is much less likely to be reapplied. Additionally, if we increase the number of owners who monitor the location, we are creating more opportunity for prevention. Now add to this the fact that the monitors are most likely peers of the vandal, which increases the vandal's potential of detection, and you can see how successful this prevention effort might be.

Basically, the effort is to identify favored targets for graffiti, identify a source for donating paint, and possibly apply sacrificial coatings that will allow any reapplication to be removed by washing the area. The next step is to find an incentive to get youth to volunteer to participate in painting over the graffiti, such as creating a party atmosphere with music, pizza, or whatever. An alternative to this process might be to get permission to allow a local art class to paint a preapproved mural over the graffiti. The artists, due to their contribution as well as their pride, will certainly monitor this location for some time to come.

Police–Community Interaction. Create programs to encourage police–community interaction. Officers paid to protect citizens in a certain area are not always loyal to that area. I recall an older officer in my early days on the force commenting each time there was a burglary in his area, "I don't own anything over there." Creating ownership for their patrol beats is an important step that crime prevention practitioners, and more importantly police executives, need to be concentrating efforts toward. Some successful programs toward this end are community substations, cop-next-door programs that place a resident officer in the community, and residential requirements. Officers who are part of the community are more likely to be aware of problems in the community, be observant to crimes in the community, and be apt to initiate action to prevent or solve crimes in a community of which they feel a part.

■ Surveillance

The next principle is surveillance, which perhaps may be more appropriately identified as observation opportunities. Although I mentioned surveillance previously in the discussion of territoriality, surveillance techniques can be used either separate from the other principles or to enhance them.

Removing Anonymity

Any experienced officer or crime prevention practitioner knows that most criminals prefer to operate with anonymity. Witnesses lead to interference, increased effort, and a much higher degree of risk. In short, criminals don't want to be observed. The surveillance principle of CPTED concentrates on increasing the opportunities for observation or for the perceived possibility that observation opportunities may occur. Observation can take many forms. It may be formal, as with the use of citizen patrols or security guards, or it may be achieved through the use of mechanical devices such as CCTV. Finally, surveillance may be achieved through casual means such as one might find by other legitimate users, as described earlier in the discussion of territoriality.

Techniques for Enhancing Observation

As we begin to delve into this principle, you may notice that anything that enhances observation is a positive step. You should also begin to see how steps to enhance or improve one CPTED principle often improve or enhance another of the principles. These complementary steps demonstrate the "process" that is CPTED, and lead to a successful implementation. Surveillance strategies that the law enforcement crime prevention practitioner should become familiar with are those that concentrate on creating an open environment with plenty of observation opportunities, especially around key vulnerable areas. Following are some strategies commonly used by practitioners, along with explanations of why they might be recommended. This list of strategies is by no means intended to be all-inclusive. In fact, each environment, design, and use will be different and will require creativity on the practitioner's part. However, hopefully the list will demonstrate the process behind the principle of surveillance.

Installation of Proper Adequate Lighting. This is essential in creating observation opportunities during the hours of darkness. Lighting that is too bright may result in residents closing off surveillance opportunities to avoid the light, thereby contributing to crime rather than preventing it. Lighting outside a business that is much brighter than the inside lighting may create a better opportunity for attack due to the time it takes for the eye to adjust when leaving the business into the brighter light. Improperly mounted lighting may create a blinding effect (glare), which can prevent desired visibility into a business. Used properly, lighting can enhance surveillance; used improperly, it may hinder observation opportunities. (See Chapter 11 for more on lighting.)

Ordinances. Create observation opportunities and compliance through the use of ordinances. Some jurisdictions have been very successful in their use of ordinances to create surveillance opportunities. For example, an ordinance that requires newly constructed businesses to include a certain minimum percentage of glass or windows will go a long way to creating the potential for surveillance. Some ordinances require certain businesses to install a specified percentage of front or side windows only. Regardless of the amount, any surveillance increase is better than none at all. Windows, in general, create potential for surveillance, but they do not guarantee that someone will use them. However, the window does create a perception of a threat to many criminals that they will be observed. When the practitioner is able to facilitate some type of ownership beyond the window, the use and crime prevention value increases significantly. The desired "fish bowl" effect, in which the interior is overlighted and windows allow observation into the business, is sometimes hindered by uneducated business owners. It is the practitioner's role and duty to educate the business as to how to assist in protecting their property by retaining the opportunities for surveillance rather than hindering them with displays and posters covering the windows.

Although practitioners often review business construction for windows and surveillance opportunities, we must not neglect residential construction. Residential construction often includes windows to let in air and light but may not consider the placement of the windows as important. For example, some contemporary homes have windows placed near the ceiling or make use of skylights, which work against creating surveillance opportunities. Ideal window locations in a home are in areas where residents may tend to spend much of their time. Large family room windows and windows placed in the meal preparation area of the kitchen are examples of this type of placement. Care should be taken to ensure that the design creates surveillance opportunities that overlook the rear of the house, especially in urban structures, where casual observation of vehicular and other alley traffic and of neighbors' back yards might not otherwise be possible. Ordinances may again address this, or an ordinance may require the police department to review and recommend changes in plans to address the issue on an individual basis.

Zoning. Encourage zoning and other such waivers to allow for mixed use application. The current trend toward creating what some have termed "smart growth development" is encouraging. The trend involves creating neighborhood villages or centers with businesses and most needs within walking distance of the residences in the area. This philosophy attempts to place convenience marts, grocery stores, community parks, and the like within the community to cater to the individual community's needs. The mixed use creates "eyes on the street" while walking to the local amenities, "eyes on the residences" by businesses while residents are at work, and "eyes on the businesses" while businesses are closed and residents are home, while also creating a sense of cohesiveness (territoriality). Other benefits are the reduction in vehicular emissions and congestion and economic opportunities for small business growth.

Downtown business centers, including in my own city of Roanoke, are encouraging downtown living, and many business owners who serve the downtown are seizing the opportunity. Downtowns are also granting waivers to allow for outdoor dining, which enhances the area as well as creating surveillance opportunities, which crime prevention practitioners desire. The key is to examine land use and zoning to see if such mixed uses are allowed and then begin to develop interest in taking advantage of them. Obtain information from local planning and zoning departments and seek their cooperation in implementing the changes that need to be made. Changes may be as simple as a change in the size of setbacks or density levels, or may be as complex as changing the zoning for an area.

Identifying Vulnerable Areas.
Identify potentially vulnerable areas in the planning process and locate them near active space. This particular technique takes full advantage of the surveillance principle. Unfortunately this is an often-overlooked principle due to financial factors taking precedence. A prime example is the placement of a playground or play area in an apartment complex. The apartment building developer is in business to make money, and his or her money comes from rent, so the playground is usually not considered up front in the planning process. In fact, it is usually given little consideration at all until the buildings are all planned and any unused space is available. Usually the unused space is found in a back lot with little visibility. The placement of the play area in such a location is sure to result in it receiving little use. When the play area is not used in the way in which it was designed, it will eventually be claimed for some other use, possibly an illegitimate one. Placing the play area in a location in which it may be observed easily, perhaps even by residents as they relax on their porch or balcony, not only encourages surveillance but also improves the safety for the youth using the area.

Another example of placement problems that is commonly known to law enforcement crime prevention practitioners is the placement of a cash register in a business. The practitioner knows that placing the register near the front of the business not only provides surveillance by those outside the store in passing, but also removes any excuse that an individual caught attempting to shoplift had not left the store with an item and had intended to pay for it. Restrooms in malls are another commonly observed problem area because their placement is driven by economics. The restroom often is located down a hall or in some out of the way location that would not be appealing to a business. The relative isolation of the restrooms means little opportunity for surveillance for loitering potential criminals. In some cases I have seen malls address this problem by giving space near the restrooms to a nonprofit organization or by creating a security office nearby.

Legitimate Use.
Make an area that has been claimed by criminal elements a place with a legitimate use. As mentioned earlier, if the design has created a problem, sometimes the least expensive fix is to replace the illegitimate use with a legitimate one that encourages lots of activity around the site and thus lots of observation opportunities as well as territoriality. It's this simple: Legitimate use provides legitimate users. One of our local schools had a problem with fights in the courtyard and another problem with teens loitering just off the property at a school sign. The resourceful school officer (SRO) found that those hanging out at the sign were seniors not wanting to be bothered by underclassmen and that the fights were due to the remaining seniors and underclassmen clashing. He implemented physical changes that rendered the sign undesirable as a location to hang out and had the courtyard classified as the senior courtyard, which allowed only seniors to assemble there. This remedied the problem by creating a legitimate controlled use of the area.

Placement of Staff. Encourage observation by proper placement of staff. Placing a receptionist in a center workstation at the front lobby of a business creates both a perceived and a real observation potential. If a sign-in process is in place, the receptionist also serves as the gatekeeper. In schools and other facilities in which patterns of problems are associated with locations, faculty or staff may need to be relocated to offices near or overlooking the problem areas to monitor them.

In department stores, the placement of the customer service, or returns, desk is not usually arbitrary. Consider the observation opportunities created in this placement. At issue here often is that the employees have not been trained on what their duties are at the location and how they can best serve the establishment. Cash registers should be in intentionally open areas to enhance opportunity for observation of the register activity. Raise the registers, and the clerk will have more opportunities to be seen; this will also increase the difficulty of any potential snatch and run offenses when the cash drawer is open. Additionally, it has been stated by some practitioners that the increased height places the clerk at a psychological advantage.

In office environments, the original design may have been fine but practice, or even policy, has since created potential for problems in limiting casual surveillance. A complex with offices or cubicles equipped with windows overlooking the interior work area are often rendered useless by the installation of blinds or the intentional covering of the windows by some other means. If blinds are needed for an interview process, a simple policy indicating that when no interview is in progress the blinds are to remain open may reduce pilfering losses, office larcenies, workplace violence, or other problems.

Retail establishments can use two-way mirrors, closed circuit television (CCTV) monitoring, and store detectives to improve surveillance. Remember, sometimes it is not the actual observation that discourages the criminal but rather the perception of the potential for being observed.

Visibility. Create open visible areas outside the residence or facility by using see-through type fencing, avoiding privacy fencing, and maintaining vegetation by trimming tree canopies to a lowest branch height of 6–8 feet and maintaining shrubbery at a maximum height of 3 feet. Use vista pruning to thin thick foliage if needed to improve light passage and visibility. Avoid the use of evergreens in areas where visibility is important. Evergreens are often used as sound and visibility barriers.

Ensure that all potential rooms that could be used for concealment from observation inside and outside the facility are secure. These may be janitorial closets, supply rooms, storage sheds, and the like. These rooms, and all corridor recesses and design features that might be used for entrapment or loitering to await victims, should be addressed by some means, activity, or physical device.

Practitioners should address the observation potential at the jurisdiction's bus stops. Bus stops constructed of clear polycarbonate or glass materials should be recommended to ensure visibility all around the bus stop, as well as into the shelter from outside.

Stairwells and elevators are crime problems due to their relative isolation and the privacy they provide. The practitioner should encourage the use of open stairwells in parking garages and facilities where they are allowed. In fact, even the walls of parking garages and similar facilities should be considered for increasing visibility and space by using support posts or rail construction instead of solid walls. Elevators and interior fire-protected stairwells may be addressed by providing some type of glass panels to allow open observation of the activities within the elevator or stairwell.

Formal Surveillance

Use formal surveillance to its fullest potential. Although not necessarily part of the design of a structure, formal surveillance, sometimes referred to as organized surveillance, is still a very important step in increasing observation and the perception of observation. Some examples of this type of surveillance are police patrols, security guards, store detectives, parking attendants, citizen patrols, and Neighborhood Watch.

Consider "sound surveillance" techniques to enhance visual observation or when visual observation is not possible. What we can't see, we may still be able to hear. Sounds may alert casual space users to something odd, or at least heighten their awareness of a potential harm. Some sound applications or techniques include the following:

- Gravel surfacing, rumble strips, or speed bumps are valuable for indicating vehicular traffic.
- Crushed gravel or wooden sidewalks may be used in walkways and other pedestrian applications to alert users of persons approaching from behind.
- Removing doors and using privacy panels at restroom entrances allows for audio surveillance and prevents subjects from locking or otherwise barricading would-be victims in restrooms and locker rooms where visual surveillance is not adequate.
- The sound of alarms operating or glass breaking, as discussed in Chapter 11, serves as a deterrent because of the attention that it draws to a certain facility or area.
- Business door chimes, bells, or tones direct the store clerk's attention to the entrance because they indicate that someone has entered the business.
- Listening devices that filter certain sounds but activate on others such as screams or breaking glass may be an option for an area in which controls on such sounds are tight.

In this section, I attempted to scratch the surface of surveillance applications and to demonstrate the importance of surveillance in crime prevention. As mentioned before, often one CPTED principle will depend upon or complement another. The examples given should demonstrate that premise. As we move to the final principle of CPTED, access control, this fact should become even more obvious.

■ Access Control

The final principle associated with CPTED is that of access control. As previously mentioned, all of the principles are intrinsically connected; in the case of controlling access, one primary function is to direct individuals to locations where surveillance opportunities will be optimal. In other words, by policy, direction, or design we control the movements of people into and within structures so that they can be observed and, if need be, addressed. As with the other principles, access may be controlled by natural, mechanical, or organized means. Successful access control should be virtually invisible in most applications. Avoiding the fortress look should be a primary goal; however, in some high security applications this may be impossible, and may actually not be desired. In high security applications the fortress appearance may actually serve as a deterrent.

However, in most cases, good access control in most facilities should be unnoticed by the end users of the building. In other words, they should be unaware that their movements are being directed for a specific purpose. One simple refrain that all practitioners should memorize, as mentioned before, is to place legitimate activities in unclaimed or problematic space and to strengthen the new use control access to and from the space. Before delving into some actual tips and considerations for applying access control, you should understand why access control contributes to the reduction of opportunities for criminal activity.

Controlling access reduces the availability of crime targets. By controlling the movement of individuals to safer, more active areas that offer more surveillance, the criminal is put at a disadvantage and must choose from those few rare individuals who venture into the unprotected, unobserved areas. Remember, most criminals want an easy target and anonymity. Controlling the potential victim denies the criminal the advantage.

Proper placement and design of access controls is cost-effective. When access controls are used properly, entrances are limited, thus allowing for better resource allocation to the areas of concern. For instance, if a business has two security guards working, they can be much more effective in monitoring and protecting the facility and individuals if they are monitoring one main entrance instead of several. A guard patrolling the premises is much more apt to notice a suspicious person in an unauthorized area because the excuse for his or her presence has been removed and therefore the criminal risk factor increases, as does the effort to be successful.

Controlling the movement of individuals to a more populated, better monitored area reduces users' fears and consequently increases the area's use, which is apt to lower the fear level even more. This is one of the most impressive things to watch happen when one first implements a successful access control technique. Even a controlled access without organized or mechanical surveillance is safer, simply by virtue of the increased usage.

Access Control Strategies

Access control strategies may be as simple as installing locks on doors or as complex as using biometric electronic access devices. Many of these types of security devices were outlined in Chapter 11. Some common methods of controlling access are:

- Install fences and gates.
- Signage can direct users to entry locations.
- Kiosks with maps to locations can graphically direct users.
- Create decorative paths and sidewalks leading from the parking area to the desired entrance; ground lighting along paths ensures their usage during hours of darkness.
- Barricades and Jersey barriers are used in some cases to control vehicular access. These are frequently used when a more hardened approach is necessary or desired.
- Spike sticks and tire shredders are another means of controlling access as related to vehicular traffic.
- Permanent or removable bollards are used to control access and are often also used to prevent vehicular attacks on a facility. A bollard may be permanently installed in concrete or affixed and removable via a sleeve or locking mechanism (see **FIGURE 12.1**).

FIGURE 12.1
Notice the effective use of the bollards to control traffic. The addition of a chain between bollards discourages pedestrians from cutting through.

- Strategic tree planting is another vehicle control, but one that avoids a fortress appearance.
- Placement of large landscaping boulders, sculptures, statues, or kiosk stands is another means of aesthetically controlling vehicular access to an area.
- Selective and strategic shrub planting is an excellent way of controlling both vehicular and pedestrian access. By concentrating on sensory reactions, pedestrians may be discouraged from assemblage or "cutting through," and are guided to a safer entrance or location. Tall shrubbery is discouraged for surveillance concerns but low shrub rows are an excellent treatment for guiding pedestrian traffic.
- Large planters, flower boxes, and site furniture are another attractive way to move vehicles and people to a certain desired entrance. Frequently, malls and government buildings will use this aesthetic approach to block certain areas.
- Use of raised berms and various unpleasant surfacing or ground treatments may deter shortcuts and loitering. One method that has been employed is creating a floral or rock garden surrounded by a deep layer of small, colored pebbles. The surface is very difficult to walk on but allows for beautification of the area.
- Assign placement of street vendors and carts, market stalls, and the like. Mobile types are especially beneficial in blocking areas, creating gatherings in desired areas, and improving surveillance.
- Using a design that naturally draws the eye of the user to the focal point as the desired entrance should always be considered in new construction (see **FIGURE 12.2**).
- Lighting of structures and areas of activity to improve surveillance is desired, but occasionally lighting is not a desired tool. Lighting encourages gathering, and likewise the lack of lighting tends to discourage the use of an area.

FIGURE 12.2
The large window, double doors of a different color, and overhanging roof naturally draw the eye to this entrance.

- Whether a school, an office building, or a manufacturer of classified equipment, visitor identification programs are recommended.
- Controlling vehicle speed is an important aspect of preventing crime, especially in this age of domestic and international terrorism. The higher the speed of a vehicle crashing into a bollard, tree, barrier, or other access control device, the more damage and probability of defeating the protective effect of the device. Traffic calming is not generally recommended for high volume streets, but rather is intended for feeder or secondary streets.

■ Other Related Issues

Retrofitting a design feature after the structure has been built is more costly than incorporating it into the design, and in some cases is quite difficult to accomplish. Retrofits are generally necessary when changes in the structures or environment are made. Improvements to an existing building, add-on structures, and even a change in the general use of the structure and community may necessitate retrofitting crime prevention techniques to make the built environment safer. With changes to the structure made, the practitioner should examine the building as though it was new and he or she was evaluating it for the first time. The practitioner will sometimes encounter the following issues.

Entrapment Areas

An entrapment area is a confined area that is not generally observable due to some barrier or concealment. It may be a dead space under a stairwell or a walkway that used to lead to a parking area but now leads to a new wall. As discussed earlier, the walkway actually directs persons to an area, but in this case it is to an area of entrapment.

Isolation Areas

Naturally, some sites are going to have isolation areas built into the environment—a greenway comes to mind. Obviously the most important thing that a law enforcement crime prevention practitioner can do is to be involved in giving input throughout the design stages in order to attempt to address these concerns. Law enforcement can rest assured that once the trail or facility is built, and crime becomes a problem, they will be called in to "fix it." There are stories of how the political powers became involved and ordered a regular patrol on a trail, posted a standing guard at an underpass, and otherwise expended untold hours of valuable police time protecting citizens from what may have been prevented by a few changes in the design stage. If, however, that ship has sailed and the practitioner is called upon to remedy such an issue, a useful method, short of expending police time, is to engage a local group that uses the facility regularly to schedule activities at the facility. Using trail runners or bicyclists as natural guardians of the trail or using a local parks and recreation department to schedule skate park activities accomplishes two of the CPTED principles, territoriality and surveillance. In isolated areas, installing solar-powered emergency telephones, allowing additional uses that may draw more persons to the area, and using police cadets or other volunteer patrols are a viable option to prevent expending police resources.

Conflicting Land Use

Occasionally a problem of conflicting design or land use may be encountered. This problem is created when two incompatible activities are located close to one another. This incompatibility is a recipe for police calls to increase substantially, at a minimum, with the possibility of a disaster being very real. Assume that a halfway house for drug users is placed in a neighborhood across the street from a teen club. Attendance at the teen club would certainly suffer, and those who continued to allow their teens to attend would be like a coiled snake ready to strike at the first rumor of impropriety by the halfway house members. The best prevention is to not allow the hostile environment to begin with. The practitioner should work with his or her zoning department to ensure that land use plans address the potential for such a mishap.

Street Crime

Street crime is sometimes seen as a crime that cannot be addressed by CPTED. Crimes such as street drug dealing and prostitution are the result of a natural selection process, as with other crimes. Some locations are simply more conducive to generating such activities. Understanding the needs and desires of the criminal is essential in addressing the problem. Narcotics officers know that the street drug dealer is interested in easy escape (melting into the community) and adequate drive-up traffic.

I addressed just such a problem in 1997 in a public housing development with a chronic street drug sales problem. The problem had been ongoing, and every effort of the police had failed to address it, resulting in officers "camping" out on the street when not otherwise tied up. The apartment complex was unable to rent an entire building due to the traffic. After meeting with a very cooperative management, we implemented several changes including improved lighting and a change in vehicular traffic patterns that, in essence, prevented quick in-and-out traffic. A few other minor changes were made, and some of the apartments were leased. Within 30 days the street drug traffic was gone from this area. Was it gone altogether? No—it was displaced to another location, which we then addressed, and so on. The point is that street crime can be addressed using CPTED principles; in the above case it was addressed using surveillance and access control. In order to address such problems, the particular crime to be addressed must be thoroughly studied to identify what design features are attractive to the criminal, and thus what techniques are most likely to be successfully in addressing the crime. Some techniques to consider are street closure, conversion to a one-way street (study should reveal which way is the most advantageous), parking restrictions, traffic calming, lighting and surveillance enhancements or deterrents, and conversion of illegitimately used space to a legitimate use.

■ Security Assessment—Target Hardening, CPTED, and Practice

An assessment is a method of determining value or importance based on an evaluation. A survey examines condition or value. An audit is a methodical examination and review. Crime prevention practitioners may refer to the practice of evaluating a site for vulnerabilities and making recommendations to address those vulnerabilities as any of these three terms. Regardless of what you choose to call it, the focus remains the same—review a site and identify the vulnerabilities, analyze possible solutions, and recommend the best possible solution to reduce the potential risk.

Some agencies are passive in their approach and wait for a business or resident to contact them with a request. While this limits the time spent engaged in conducting such assessments, it fails to use a valuable and proven technique for preventing crime.

The practitioner preparing to conduct the assessment should identify the contact person of the business or residence that is most knowledgeable about the site and its operation. Much of the assessment will be based on an interview with the contact person.

After the interview has been completed, the contact person should be asked to accompany the assessor on the physical inspection of the site. The assessor, drawing on his training and knowledge of crime risks for that specific facility, will methodically examine the facility as though he were the criminal planning to commit the crime. This aids the practitioner in identifying vulnerabilities.

Once the actual on-site inspection is complete and the notes are reviewed, the arduous task of completing a written report of your findings should be prepared. All written reports should contain a disclaimer that no guarantee of crime proofing the facility is made.

You may find that some businesses do not want a written report or may state that they "just want you to conduct a walk-through of one area." Some will request that only verbal recommendations be given. Because recommendations and findings may be used in future litigation, I recommend in these cases that the merchant be advised that you will still prepare a written report for retention in your files in case it is needed in the future, and that all assessments must be accompanied by a written report.

Regardless of the format chosen, the assessor should always endeavor to meet with the executive of the facility in person to deliver the report and to discuss recommendations, specifically emphasizing the priority items. As mentioned earlier, the assessor must develop a thick skin and realize that not all of the recommendations will be implemented; however, any vulnerability addressed makes the business, facility, or residence safer and should be considered a positive step.

See Appendixes 12.1 and 12.2 for sample formats of Home and General Business surveys.

■ Advancing CPTED Through Partnerships

CPTED is a very effective process when used by the knowledgeable practitioner in conjunction with other prevention measures. More and more trained CPTED practitioners are taking part in plan review for new construction projects to ensure the safe design of buildings. Law enforcement should never fail to take advantage of the expertise that is available to assist in building safer places. To this end, the practitioner should develop relationships with planners, architects, lighting engineers, horticulturists or arborists, and fire and building officials. I am proud to be associated with a state that has been actively involved in moving the premise and practice of CPTED forward since 1983. As part of its effort, the Virginia CPTED Committee, a committee of the Virginia Crime Prevention Association, has formally engaged the various disciplines listed as partners to address safety through their own organizations. In 2004, the committee published a document entitled *CPTED Guidelines, Safety by Design*. This document, endorsed by the Virginia Department of Housing and Community Development and the Virginia chapter of the American Planning Association, contains a wealth of information for those interested in more information about CPTED, and I highly recommend it. Copies may be obtained through the Virginia Crime Prevention Association.

Other contacts of interest are the American Planners Association, the National Fire Protection Association, your local chapter of the American Institute of Architects, the American Society of Landscape Architects, and the Illuminating Engineer Society of North America. Each of these groups are made up of professionals with vastly more knowledge in their specialties than any one CPTED practitioner might possess. They may be able to provide the practitioner with educational opportunities related to landscaping materials and facts related to them such as mature height and recommended uses, blueprint and plan reading, fire codes specific to an issue, and lighting particulars and drawbacks.

■ Chapter Summary

Having scratched the surface of CPTED in this chapter, one might say you have sufficient information to graduate kindergarten. That is, you know the basic facts and how CPTED works. Now, you must obtain other sources, and study and apply what you have learned to grow in knowledge. The physical environment not only helps to protect, but also can direct potential victims and criminals. Understanding criminal psychology and criminals' favored environments is essential in creating safer places to work, live, and play.

■ Review Questions

1. What does the acronym CPTED represent?
2. What are the three main principles of CPTED?
3. Which of the CPTED principles encourages ownership of an area in order to address crime?
4. A confined area that is not generally observable due to some barrier or concealment is referred to by what term?

■ References

Jacobs, Jane. 1961. *The Death and Life of Great American Cities*. New York: Vintage Books.

Newman, Oscar. 1972. *Defensible Space: Crime Prevention Through Urban Design*. New York: Macmillan.

Jeffrey, C. Ray. 1971. *Crime Prevention Through Environmental Design*. Beverly Hills, CA: Sage Publications.

Wilson, J. Q., and Kelling, G. L. March 1982. "Broken windows." *Atlantic Monthly*, 29–38.

Prevention for the Future

CHAPTER 13

"The years teach much which the days never knew."

—Ralph Waldo Emerson

■ Introduction

As our society changes, crime changes with it. In the 1970s we taught our children to beware of unknown people approaching them on the playground, on the street, and while walking home from school. Those lessons still apply, but now we also must concern ourselves with the predator who we invite into our homes by way of the Internet.

We practitioners used to educate our citizens on ways to protect themselves from thieves stealing items from their car; for businesses our prevention techniques related to credit cards and shoplifting. Now high technology allows anonymous criminals to steal something much more valuable than items from your car—your identity. Armed with your personal information they are free to steal repeatedly. Criminals have become increasingly sophisticated in their techniques, and the reason is simple in my mind—crime prevention works! If crime prevention techniques did not work, the criminal would feel free to continue using the same tried and true methods. Because of the dedication of crime prevention practitioners the information is getting out and being heeded, forcing the criminal to change methods, locations, and even crimes of choice. Such changes are a testament to the success of crime prevention and community policing. We must now endeavor to stay current with the trends that are emerging from the criminal world, while being ever vigilant in educating our customers about existing prevention techniques. Crime prevention practitioners and community police officers are innovative creatures, and once the new crime trends are recognized, studied, and understood, they will develop prevention programs or problem-solving techniques to address them.

■ Current Trends

Current trends that are particularly of concern are those associated with high tech crime. Criminals are using newly developed technology to perpetrate crimes. The Internet is being used to commit personal and business fraud. Criminals are accessing business databases, setting up false companies to receive credit card and bank account information, and bilking consumers out of their hard-earned cash. High tech crime prevention is a must, and we need to begin to develop strategies now. Any newly marketed gadget is apt to be used in committing crimes; for example, digital cameras, cellular telephones with photographic capabilities, listening devices, and micro-cameras are all being used to steal property or information or to invade privacy. The crime prevention practitioner of the present and of the future must stay in touch with his or her civilian counterparts and partner with them using preventative techniques as they are developed.

■ A Shifting Landscape

We must recognize that the landscape has changed as related to solving problems and addressing crimes, due to the movement toward a more global society. Law enforcement practitioners serve all citizens and businesses in their jurisdiction, whether they are from Appalachia or Afghanistan. Our approach to each must be tailored to their culture and the life experiences that they bring with them.

The truly successful practitioner is one who endeavors to understand his or her customers through study and open communication and who has developed resources to aid in that endeavor. The crime prevention practitioner/community police officer must be citizen, public servant, social worker, ambassador, and soldier in today's global society. For the peaceful refugee or immigrant, we must attempt to solve problems of hatred and isolation that may lead them down a road of retaliation and thus afoul of the law. To those who would attack our freedoms and the representations of such through terrorist acts, whether they are foreign-born or homegrown terrorists, we must endeavor to make their task more difficult by using the prevention techniques discussed in this text. Terrorism, domestic or international, is still a crime. We in the law enforcement community must do our duty to protect the homeland just as others are preventing attacks on our soil through their efforts abroad.

Many excellent seminars are being taught to assist the law enforcement community in preparing to meet the challenges of terrorism. I would simply reiterate that to understand the reward sought, whether cash, fame, or sexual gratification, is to take the first step toward prevention. Study, research, and analyze the techniques used to achieve the reward and then begin to plan ways to address the opportunities that allow the chosen techniques. A good starting point for your research is the U.S. Department of State and its literature on patterns of global terrorism.

The shifting landscape will undoubtedly be met head on by practitioners developing strategies to combat new crime trends. Perhaps the most difficult aspect of this development will be paying for the programs. Crime prevention is rarely heavily funded in local budgets. Practitioners find it difficult to prove that something was prevented from happening, and local governments tend to fund programs with solid examples of success. Grant funding has long been the mainstay for the crime prevention and community policing world. With national funding being diverted to the war on terror and homeland security, much of the grant funding is dwindling. In fact, most grant managers and grant writers recognize this fact and believe that it is only a matter of time before the majority of such funding opportunities are gone.

The good news is that the federal government is always looking for a new need to fund, and that new need is now homeland security. Protecting the homeland is already becoming the grant focus of the future, but that should not discourage crime prevention and community policing–oriented officers. Protecting the homeland is often accomplished by using the same tools that one would use in preventing or addressing crime. Consequently, grants may be applied for, and awarded, to achieve a homeland defense initiative and, if planned properly, may also address crime at its basic level. The same tools used to combat a terrorist attack, such as a new mobile command center, may be used in combating street drug crime in a high crime neighborhood. In-car computers used to provide immediate access to chemical spill and hazardous materials data may also be used to draft security assessments, and reverse 9-1-1 systems purchased to alert communities of terrorist attacks may also be used to alert specific communities of a scheduled Neighborhood Watch meeting.

In short, a planned use does not preclude additional uses. The primary goal of homeland security must be prevention before reaction. I believe that even our effort to fight the war on terrorism has at its core an understanding of crime prevention. President George W. Bush has often spoken of taking the fight to the terrorist where they are rather than waiting for them to bring it to us. The pressure caused by our doing so has caused the terrorists to change tactics and become desperate. World leaders in Great Britain, the United States, and elsewhere emphasize after an attack that we should continue to live our lives as normal. Each of these techniques—displacement, increasing the effort, and reducing the desired reward of crippling a society through fear—are nothing more than crime prevention.

■ Summary

To close, I will simplify crime prevention and community policing services with this easy to remember list based on this statement: Everything I needed to know about crime prevention I learned from the story of Noah's ark (from the Book of Genesis):

1. *Plan for the unexpected.* It wasn't raining when Noah began to build. Often there is not yet a crime problem, but the opportunities are there. Poor planning, lack of a comprehensive land use plan, or unaddressed design features may cause a scramble to retrofit a fix when all of the elements finally come together and a crime occurs.
2. *Everyone can be of use.* Noah was 600 years old when he was called upon to serve. Don't overlook those in the community willing to help.
3. *When the safe way is available, take it.* Many were in the valley being preached to but refused to hear of the impending problem. Get on the boat!
4. *Amateurs are often better equipped for the task at hand than are professionals.* Noah was not a professional boat builder but he had something that was needed—righteousness to follow.
5. *There is safety in numbers.* The animals came two by two, and we can find a great lesson in that—whether in personal safety or in working on problems in the community, two points of view are always better.
6. *Even enemies will tolerate one another when they are in the same boat.* If a community is plagued with burglaries or with assaults, people who would normally never speak to one another become bound together for the common cause. Use this tendency to develop community cohesiveness for the future to prevent future crimes.
7. *When the trouble subsides, each will go his or her own way.* Realizing this tendency, it is our duty to find ways to keep the community engaged with one another.
8. *When you are doing what is right, ignore the critics.* Noah was undoubtedly laughed at and ridiculed, but he was right, and because of it we are here today. Community policing and crime prevention have always had their detractors who claim that the tactics don't work, that it is feel good policing, and the like, but as mentioned earlier, the change in criminals' methods proves that the combination of proactive policing and reactive policing are a success.

■ References

Book of Genesis: *The Holy Bible.* King James version. Nashville, TN: Thomas Nelson Publishers.

Problem Solving Project

Location: _____ Date of initiation: _____

Initiating complaint: _____
(Note name of person initiating complaint and the nature of the complaint)

Supervisor approving the initiation of this project: _____

■ SCANNING   Date scanning began: _____

Check scanning techniques used and place copies of any documents related to the scanning in the problem file.

- ☐ Calls for service data   ☐ Direct knowledge/observation
- ☐ Citizen comments or survey   ☐ Informant
- ☐ Media coverage   ☐ Property owner files
- ☐ Other source, list

■ ANALYSIS   Date analysis began: _____

What conditions preceded or accompanied the problem?

How frequently does the problem occur?

Is there a pattern to the times, days, or dates associated with the problem?

How long has this problem been going on?

What harm has this issue caused?

What potential harm is there?

What is the citizen involvement currently in addressing the problem?

What contributing factors were identified leading up to this problem?

What do neighborhood residents/businesses attribute the problem to?

■ SUMMARIZE THE UNDERLYING ISSUE(S) THAT CREATED THIS PROBLEM

What resources are available to address this problem?

Community resources: _____

City resources: _____

Police Dept. resources: _____

Other resources: _____

■ RESPONSE   Date response began: _____

Explain your planned response. (*Include specific actions and how long you anticipate conducting the response and why you are taking that step. For example: In order to send the message that the police are going to work this area for 2 weeks beginning June 1; utilize bicycle patrols to enforce a zero tolerance step 2 beginning the week of . . . etc.*)

What are your goals? *What do you want to accomplish? That is, lower fear of crime, decrease number of serious calls for service, etc.*

How are citizens involved in your response? Be specific.

Date	Actions or Activity on Project

■ ASSESSMENT   Date of assessment: _____

What problems did you encounter implementing your response?

What impact did your response have on the problem? Check one.

☐ Eliminated the problem   ☐ Displaced the problem
☐ Reduced the problem   ☐ Equipped the community to address the problem

Explain _____

Will your response require an ongoing effort to sustain the results?

What is the effort required and of whom will it be required?

Are citizens in the community equipped to maintain the solution?

Date to be re-checked for recurrence of same problem:

PROBLEM CLOSED BY RECOMMENDATION OF OFFICER: _____

DATE CLOSED: _____

SUPERVISOR APPROVING CLOSURE: _____

Civil Nuisance Petition

This is an example of the format used in some Virginia cases to file a civil nuisance petition.

Virginia: In the Circuit Court for the City of _____

Complaint and Petition

Section 48.1 Code of Virginia 1950, as amended

Come now the petitioners, who are all citizens of the City of _____, Virginia, and request this Court to summon a special grand jury for the purpose of specially investigating the following matter. The petitioners verily believe that a public nuisance is being caused or permitted by the (principals or residents of) _____.

Specifically, _____ produces _____

(Cite the nuisance here)_____

Moreover, the location from which the nuisance is originating is designated as
No. _____ on the City of _____ Map. The subject property is owned
by _____ to the best of the knowledge and belief
of the petitioners.

Respectfully submitted,

Petitioners' names _____   Petitioners' addresses _____

Trespassing Enforcement Authorization

This is an example of the content of the Trespassing Enforcement Authorization Letter currently used in some jurisdictions in Virginia.

I/We authorize sworn law enforcement personnel of the City of _____ to serve as the person(s) lawfully in charge of my/our property located in the City of _____ to wit: (*address of property*) for the purpose of enforcing trespassing laws of the Commonwealth of Virginia and the City of _____, Virginia, pursuant to Section 15.2–1717.1, Code of Virginia and City Code Section XX–XXX.

By my/our signature(s), we authorize sworn law enforcement personnel of the City of _____ to serve as the person(s) lawfully in charge of my/our property for purposes of serving written notice of barrment and enforcement of the trespassing laws of the Commonwealth of Virginia and the City of _____, Virginia on my/our property pursuant to the Landlord Tenant Act, Code of Virginia, Section 55-248.31:01.

By virtue of my/our signature(s) on this document, I/we agree to post the affected property with "No Trespassing" signs, clearly visible from all points of access/egress into the designated property. I understand that it is my responsibility to notify the _____ Police Department if the listed property should change ownership. I further understand that this authorization to act as my/our agent may be rescinded at anytime by my/our providing a written and dated request to the Chief of Police for such a rescission.

Address of Property _____

Owner's signatures and address _____

Witness _____

Trespass Bar Letter

This is an example of a bar letter used by agencies with authorization to act on behalf of property owners in Virginia.

TRESPASS BAR LETTER   DATE: _____

This shall serve as written notice that _____ is barred from the property, located at _____, City of _____, Virginia.

This action is taken pursuant to the written permission of the landowner of said property to effect such actions, as filed with the _____ Police Department (55-248.31:01 Code of Virginia).

Acts leading to this barrment: _____
(A copy of this notice shall be served on the tenant describing the above acts of the invitee or guest, which are the basis for this barrment action. The tenant is notified of his/her right pursuant to 55-248.27 Code of Virginia to file a "Tenant's Assertion" within 15 days from the date of this action in the General District Court, to protest this action.

Name of person barred: _____

Age _____ DOB _____ Race _____ Ht _____ Wt _____

Vehicle description _____

You are formally notified that your continued or subsequent presence on the premises named above will subject you to arrest for trespassing as authorized by the Code of Virginia and the ordinances of the City of _____.

Signature of barred person _____

Signature of officer _____

Original—PD
Copy 1—Barred Subject
Copy 2—Tenant, if applicable
Copy 3—Property Owner/Manager

APPENDIX

7.1

Property Check
Registration Form

■ EXTENDED ABSENCE PROPERTY CHECK

Property may be checked for a period of no more than 3 months. Properties may be checked for extended absences due to vacation (more than 1 week), deaths, or extended hospital stays.

Address to be checked: _____

Resident's name: _____

Friend or other person also checking residence: _____

Emergency contact (*If same as resident list, check here* ☐): _____

Emergency contact telephone #: _____ Departure date: _____

Return date: _____ Expected time: _____ a.m./p.m.

■ IMPORTANT PROPERTY NOTES

List any notes that might indicate a change in the norm (For example: lights on timer to activate 6 p.m. until 11 p.m. in front room; cars parked on property should be described; pets being cared for in home should be included as well as person caring for pets).

_____

_____

List any alarm or security service information: _____

Date checked: _____

Time checked: _____

Checked by: _____

Condition: If good, check here ☐

Comments/notes: _____

_____

_____

Confidential School Assessment

■ SAFETY TEAM REPRESENTATIVES

Faculty Representative _____

Student Representative _____

Administration Representative _____

Custodial/Building Maintenance Representative _____

Parent Representative _____

Law Enforcement Representative _____

School Security Representative _____

Others _____

■ SCHOOL EXTERIOR

	Y	N

1. Are school grounds fenced?

    All grounds fenced   ☐   ☐

    Only playground fenced   ☐   ☐

     No fencing but border definition exists   ☐   ☐

    Explain border definition type _____

    List height of any fencing _____

Fencing of school grounds clearly identifies the boundaries of the school grounds in which certain behaviors are expected. Fences protect small children and others from roaming off or darting from the play area into traffic, as well as creating an obstacle for truants to overcome.

    Fencing of the play area is desirable in an elementary setting at minimum. A middle or high school setting are recommended to have border definition at a minimum and partial fencing in secluded areas that cannot be easily monitored. By applying such fencing or border treatments the school directs pedestrians to the proper entry locations and discourages undetected unauthorized entry.

    Consideration to fencing material should be decided based on the use and location of the fence. When at all possible fencing should be wrought iron, chain link, cable, corral, separated pickets, or other see-through construction. The fence's purpose should not be to conceal but to protect and to reveal. Generally a 5–6 foot fence is more than adequate to accomplish the goals but if there is a high-security area being considered, a 7 foot fence topped with a strand of barbed wire may be employed. Finally, consideration must be given to entry/exit points of fenced areas. Entry/exits should be kept at a minimum and located in highly observable locations. Material of at least the quality as the fences should be used on all gates with special consideration given to the latches or locks, if required.

2. Are gates secured by quality heavy-duty padlocks after hours?   ☐   ☐

Padlocks that are not constructed of heavy gauge metal are easily defeated. When padlocks are used they should be quality padlocks and every effort should be made to ensure that the padlocked area is patrolled and checked by police or school security.

3. Is the school designated as a "drug free zone" with signage?   ☐   ☐

It is recommended that all schools be designated as a "Drug Free School Zone" and posted as such. The enhanced punishment associated with this designation usually requires that the area be posted. Posting of the area at the least put drug dealers on notice that the school is concerned enough to watch for drug activity.

4. Are signs posted on all exterior doors and coming from the parking lots, directing all visitors to report to the office through a single entrance?   ☐   ☐

   Is the office entrance identified by signage?   ☐   ☐

   Are other exterior doors exit only and secured from being used as an entrance?   ☐   ☐

In order to control access to the school and to control who is moving about within the school, it is recommended that one entrance only be designated as the public access entrance. Each other door should be secured from entry and exit only allowed through use of exit bar hardware. On the exterior of all doors not designated as the main entrance, it should be posted that all visitors must enter through the main entrance, designate where that entrance is and state that they must report to the office. For example, "All visitors must enter through the main entrance under the front awning, and report to the office." Once such a policy is put in place all teachers or faculty with work stations near an exit door should be given the responsibility to ensure that the door is kept secure and not propped open at any time.

5. Do trees and shrubbery permit visibility and discourage crime?

   Are all shrubs trimmed to a maximum of 3 feet?   ☐   ☐

   Are all trees trimmed up to 8 feet to the lowest branch?   ☐   ☐

   Are all trees at least 10 feet from any buildings?   ☐   ☐

   Are prickly or thorn shrubs used to discourage pedestrian traffic?   ☐   ☐

Trees and shrubs serve many purposes and are desirable on the school grounds, however, when not trimmed properly they may become concealment or tools for facilitators for criminal activity. In order to ensure patrols and those passing by have the opportunity to view and report any suspicious activity it is recommended that all shrubs be trimmed to a maximum of 3 feet height, especially shrubs in close proximity to the school windows and doors. Trees should be trimmed from the ground up to the first branch at a height of 8 feet and should be at least 10 feet from its closest branch to the school buildings. It is recommended that prickly or thorn shrubs be planted in areas that cannot easily be observed, to discourage undesirable assembly or concealment in that location.

6. Do the parking lot design and markings encourage safe driving? Are driving lanes marked with directional markings?   ☐   ☐

   Directional markings limit confusion and conflict and ensure orderly flow of vehicles within the parking lot. It is recommended that entry/exit locations be limited to discourage the perception of public access and to discourage cut through traffic. Do faculty and driving students park in the same lot?   ☐   ☐

   It is recommended that faculty and students share the same parking area. While many would argue that combining parking of faculty and students endangers the faculty member's vehicles, in most cases just the opposite is true. By having faculty share the parking lot with students ownership is taken of that space by the faculty who have a interest in the activity there and therefore more natural surveillance is achieved. Students, on the other hand, see the faculty members frequently in the parking lot and are much less likely to use the parking lot for illegitimate activity.

7. Is there a designated parking area for students arriving and leaving at abnormal times?   ☐   ☐

   In order to ensure that the parking lot may adequately be monitored for truants, thefts, and other illegitimate activity, it is important ensure that persons are only in the parking lot legitimately at designated times. It is therefore recommended that students with unusual class times park in a separate area within the parking lot or a separate parking area altogether.

8. Are there signs designating the speed limit?   ☐   ☐

   It is important that notice be given at all entrances to the campus of the expected behavior. Speed limits are a behavior that must be adhered to in order to ensure safety of all users.

9. Are there speed bumps?   ☐   ☐

   In order to ensure compliance with the speed restrictions, speed bumps should be placed within the driving lanes of the parking lot.

10. Are student drop-off points located away from high-traffic areas?   ☐   ☐

    In designing any safe traffic environment it is important that potential hazards be limited. Conflicting uses created from bicycles and pedestrians pose an unnecessary hazard. It is recommended that student drop-off locations be designated away from the private vehicle parking lot and the bus loading area. Work with the local traffic engineer may be necessary to designate such a location on the public street.

11. Are bus loading areas clearly marked and restricted to other vehicles during use?   ☐   ☐

    Loading and off-loading large numbers of students moving in and out of the bus area is chaotic enough without adding any additional drivers, let alone inexperienced drivers, to the mix. All bus loading areas should be used only by the buses, at least during specified loading and unloading times.

12. Are staff assigned to monitor bus area?   □   □

Due to the mass movement of students during loading and unloading of school buses, extra eyes and ears are a necessity in preventing accidents. Parents, teachers, faculty, or volunteers may serve in this capacity of monitor, but it is crucial that monitors be assigned to aid in these duties.

13. Is visitor parking close to the main entrance?   □   □

Visitors come to a school for any number of reasons, some legitimate and some illegitimate. In order to protect the students, faculty, and staff from those with illegitimate plans, it is important to restrict the movement of all visitors to certain locations that might be observed. Visitors must not be allowed to enter the grounds undetected or unobserved any more than they would be allowed to enter the school unobserved. It is recommended that all visitor parking be designed in the main entrance area, within view of the office and that signage specifying that all visitors must park in designated visitor parking be erected.

14. Are parking lots clearly observable from the school?   □   □

When possible all schools should be designed with parking lots well within the site of the school. Designs that isolate parking areas away from the school are flirting with danger. All lots should be clearly visible from some location occupied within the school. Closed Circuit Television (CCTV) may become necessary to monitor some school parking lots that are isolated.

15. Are parking lots monitored during the day?   □   □

While parking lots may be visible and jointly used by students and faculty, some monitoring via a walk-through is recommended at varying intervals throughout the day.

16. Is parking controlled by a decal system?   □   □

In order to ensure that parking lots on school grounds are used by legitimate students or employees, it is recommended that a vehicle decal system be initiated. If more than one parking area is used this process could ensure that students park in the proper lot. Decal systems also provide faculty a quick means of identifying the student or faculty member responsible for the vehicle. Use of the lot could be contingent on the driver signing an agreement of proper safe use and completing a vehicle descriptor card.

17. Are parking spaces assigned by number?   □   □

By assigning parking space numbers as part of an organized parking plan school administration is able to place potential problem students in locations that they might more closely observed. Assigned spaces reduce the potential for conflict over inadequate parking and may require turning some student parkers away.

18. Is student access to parking area restricted to times of arrival and dismissal? (No access during school day)   □   □

It is important that the parking are be used for its purpose, parking. By disallowing visits to personal vehicles throughout the school day the potential for students retrieving contraband such as weapons or drugs is greatly reduced. With a policy prohibiting visits to the parking lot, the monitor is empowered to question any student found there at improper times and to request to see a sign-out pass.

19. Are there designated bicycle parking areas?   ☐   ☐

Are there observable bike racks?   ☐   ☐

Bicycles are in wide use in urban environments and they should be encouraged by providing ˆthe riders a designated safe place to secure their bicycles. It is suggested that the designated bicycle parking area be apart from the vehicle and/or bus entrances.

Are all areas accessible to patrol vehicles?   ☐   ☐

School administration should ensure that any gate-controlled parking areas, bicycle trails, and all lots are accessible to police and security patrols.

20. Are exterior lights adequate?   ☐   ☐

Lighting of a facility is dependent upon a number of factors including the desired effect and use of the illumination, size of the area to be lighted, and the amount of ambient light in the area from other sources. For protective use in a school, the minimum lighting levels that are expected are at major entrances and the periphery of the school, when it can be reasonably expected that at least some occasional surveillance of the school by passing observers occurs.

21. Is there lighting at all entrances?   ☐   ☐

Is there lighting of all potential intrusion sites?   ☐   ☐

Understanding that the favored site for intrusion by burglars is the ground-level doors and windows, it is recommended that these areas be lighted with sufficient light to allow a passer by at the nearest point of observation to recognize a figure to be a person at the lighted site. Since each school is different, the type of lighting and fixture may vary but generally fluorescent lighting should not be used for exterior use.

22. Are all lights mounted at 12–14 feet height?   ☐   ☐

In order to reduce the opportunity for intruders to disable and/or prevent lights from performing their intended function of illuminating the intruder, it is recommended that lights be mounted 10–14 feet above the ground level.

23. Do exterior lights reduce shadowed areas near the school?   ☐   ☐

Shadows provide burglars a place to hide and to the extent possible lighting applications should be uniform and every effort should be made to reduce shadowing.

24. Do lights have break-resistant lenses?   ☐   ☐

By installing break-resistant lenses on all lighting the school ensures the lighting to be functional when it is needed. Installation of break-resistant lenses is not only recommended to prevent the burglar from disabling the light but also to prevent the vandal from damaging the light and thus inviting other criminal activity, due to the inoperability of the light.

25. Are light lenses cleaned at least annually?   ☐   ☐

Lighting lenses that accumulate insects and dirt and are not maintained are operating at a limited capacity. The expected illumination is reduced by poorly maintained lenses. It is recommended that an annual lens cleaning and bulb changing schedule be developed and adhered to. By changing the bulbs and cleaning the lenses on a regular schedule the lighting remains uniform and operates as initially planned.

26. Are lights checked monthly for inoperative fixtures or burned-out bulbs and repaired?   ☐   ☐

It is recommended that a monthly walk-through of the premises be conducted to ensure that all lights are functional.

27. Are the buildings and grounds generally safe? Are ladders and roof access secure?   ☐   ☐

Are dumpsters and other equipment a minimum of 10 feet from buuildings?   ☐   ☐

While second-story entry is not a frequent occurrence some simple precautions are in order to prevent the opportunist from choosing to vandalize or burglarize school property via the second-story access. Precautions include limiting access by items left unsecured and man-made access by poor placement of items. All ladders should be secured and all dumpsters or items that might provide access to the roof are positioned or secured at a minimum of 10 feet from the buildings.

28. Are all electrical, maintenance, and mechanical rooms kept locked?   ☐   ☐

Curious students, smokers, or truants have a knack for locating unlocked doors or places that provide them a site to conceal themselves. Needless to say persons accessing electrical or mechanical rooms can harm themselves and create a potential fire hazard. It is essential that these areas be kept locked.

29. Are trashcans secured to posts or anchors?   ☐   ☐

Are trashcans emptied at the end of each school day?   ☐   ☐

Trash receptacles that are not secured to posts may be turned over, used as weapons or used to damage the facility. Likewise unemptied containers provide a good place for hiding weapons or drugs. It is recommended that all trash receptacles on the exterior of the building be emptied several times during the day and at the end of the school day. This is recommended in order to reduce the possibility that contraband be concealed there prior to school and retrieved later.

30. Are the school grounds kept free of trash, large rocks, and debris?   ☐   ☐

Rocks and other debris may be used as weapons and as such should be removed when observed.

31. Is there a schedule for inspection and repair of locks, lockers, out-buildings, electrical plates, playground equipment, and fire alarms?   ☐   ☐

Schools are not immune to wear and tear, which is why professional maintenance persons are on staff at all schools. Equipment failure does not only lead to losses due to theft but may also be the cause of injury. It is essential that all equipment be inspected and repaired regularly to avoid such mishaps. The best means in which to achieve that goal is to develop a maintenance inspection schedule.

32. Are fire drills conducted as required by statute? ☐ ☐

Fire drills are required to ensure that all students and staff are familiar with escape routes and procedures set forth to protect and account for all present. Fire drills are mandated by statute.

33. Is there a security alarm system? ☐ ☐

Does the system have a power failure backup? ☐ ☐

Are security alarms tested at a minimum once every 6 months? ☐ ☐

A central alarm system is recommended for all school facilities. At a minimum the rooms that contain valuable equipment and/or files should be alarmed with a good centrally monitored system. Rooms such as the main office, cafeteria office, computer lab, music room, and audiovisual storage might be considered as "high risk." Due to the size and difficulty in locating intruders, a zoned alarm system is suggested in order to track the movement of the intruder. Ideally any alarm system should have a battery backup for power failures and all alarms should be tested at least every 6 months.

34. Are all keys assigned and physically inventoried at the beginning and end of the school year? ☐ ☐

Key control is a huge problem is most large facilities. Without a key control policy and annual inventory the security of any building is in dire jeopardy. In a school environment distribution of keys should be limited. One or two persons should be the only persons with exterior door access keys and should be given the responsibility of opening the facility and closing it. Individual office or classroom keys may be required but all keys should be distributed and signed for at the first of the year and collected at the end of the year. Lost or unaccounted for keys should require a lock change.

35. Is all vandalism reported? ☐ ☐

Is all graffiti photographed, reported, and removed immediately? ☐ ☐

Graffiti and vandalism of the school not only represent the destruction of property but may represent gang presence and or challenges to others. It is imperative that all such vandalism be reported to the police, photographed, and removed as quickly as possible to prevent retaliation and publicizing the group.

36. Is any pattern of vandalism, violence, or other problem reported to school administration? ☐ ☐

Any and all patterns represent a need to look closer at the perpetrator, the location, or the cause. If patterns are recognized, they should be reported to the school administration and/or police for further investigation.

37. Is playground equipment connected with tamper-resistant fasteners? ☐ ☐

In order to maintain a safe playground, tamper-resistant fasteners should be employed.

38. Has exterior hardware been removed from exterior doors not to be used as entrances? ☐ ☐

By removing the exterior hardware from no-entry doors, the administration can be sure that even if doors are inadvertently unlocked, the possibility of them being used for entry is reduced.

39. Are doors constructed of steel, aluminum alloy, or solid core hardwood? ☐ ☐

    Are glass doors framed and made of tempered glass? ☐ ☐

    Are double doors secured with multiple point flush bolts? ☐ ☐

    Are exposed door hinges equipped with non-removable hinges? ☐ ☐

    Are door frames made of heavy metal? ☐ ☐

    Are fire doors provided in stairwells and other appropriate locations? ☐ ☐

Door systems for schools should meet the minimum requirements that are set out for commercial establishments. All exterior doors should be constructed in a metal frame of steel, aluminum alloy, or solid hardwood core. All glazing should be of tempered safety glass or polycarbonate sheeting. Any exposed hinges must be of the non-removable pin hinge type. Where specified by fire code, such as in stairwells, a minimum 1 hour burn-rated fire door should be installed.

40. Is lexan, polycarbonate, or other scratch-proof break-resistant coating
used for windows? ☐ ☐

    Are all ground-floor window locks functional? ☐ ☐

    Are all windows intact? ☐ ☐

    Are all basement windows secured with grating or well covers? ☐ ☐

Window systems for the school environment should ensure that glazing is of scratch-proof lexan, polycarbonate, or other break-resistant coated material. All ground-level window should have functioning latches capable of securing the window and not being slipped. All glazing should be in good repair, free from cracks, and/or breaks. It is recommended that all basement windows be secured with grating or well covers and that all air ducts have steel grilles installed.

41. Are modular classrooms locked when not in use? ☐ ☐

With schools outgrowing space many schools have turned to the temporary use of modular classrooms set apart from the main school facility. Modular class rooms are not always in use and should be secured at all times when not in use to protect from vandalism and/or use of the vacant building for illegitimate activity.

42. Is there two-way communication between all classrooms, work
stations, and the office? ☐ ☐

Emergencies can occur in any classroom at any time. Teachers may observe activities that they need to report and, due to many studies revealing that disruptive behavior often occurs when the teacher is absent from the classroom, it is essential that all classrooms be equipped with some means of two-way communications. Modular classrooms should not be ignored when implementing a two-way communications system. Options include use of intercom systems, wire telephones, cellular digital telephones, and two-way radios.

	Y	N

43. Is there a central alarm system in the school? ☐ ☐

Are high-risk areas (where expensive items are stored, such as music room or computer lab) equipped with high-security locks and an alarm? ☐ ☐

Are high-risk areas intentionally not identified by signs? ☐ ☐

All schools should at least be partially alarmed in key high-risk areas. Such areas as the computer lab or areas in which valuable equipment is stored should be alarmed with a quality alarm system monitored by a central monitoring company or the local law enforcement agency. Area in which student files are stored, such as the guidance and main office should also be alarmed. In addition to alarms these areas should be equipped with locks rated by the Underwriters Laboratory (UL) as "high security locks." It is recommended that the computer lab, audiovisual closet, and other areas associated with high-dollar equipment should not be marked with signage. This is in order to reduce the opportunity of the burglar that is unfamiliar with the school from quickly selecting those sites to target.

■ SCHOOL INTERIOR   Y   N

1. Is the entrance lobby visible form the main office? ☐ ☐

2. Are visitors notified by signage the requirement to sign in? ☐ ☐

   By ensuring that the main entrance is visible from the office, natural surveillance of the entrance is achieved. Since sign-in by visitors should occur at the office and signage should be posted notifying visitors of the sign-in requirement, all visitors will recognize that they are being monitored from the time they enter the school.

3. Are all visitors required to enter through one designated entrance? ☐ ☐

4. If multiple buildings, is there one main entrance per building? ☐ ☐

5. If multiple buildings, is the entrance visible to the building office and other doors are secured? ☐ ☐

   It is specifically recommended that all schools require visitors to enter via one designated entrance. In a campus style school, each building should have a designated entrance that can be monitored by the building principal or administrator. All doors other than the designated entrance door should be secure from entrance and treated only as an exit door.

6. Are bathrooms monitored by staff? ☐ ☐

7. Are bathroom doors secured open and privacy panels installed at the entrance? ☐ ☐

   Due to the private nature of restrooms, they are frequently the location of choice for illicit activity. Use and sale of drugs, smoking of cigarettes, and violent acts all occur behind the private closed doors of the restroom. Therefore, it is prudent and necessary that restrooms be regularly checked by school staff for such activity. In order to remove some of the opportunity for the activities mentioned, entrance doors may be secured open or removed altogether. In order to maintain the visual privacy required, privacy walls or panels may be installed. By taking this step the student is never sure who is outside the door hearing the conversation, smoke tends to float through the open door and alert passers of the activity within the restroom, and any violent commotion will easily be heard outside the restroom.

8. Are bathroom and other privacy areas equipped with fixed (not dropped) ceiling panels?   ☐   ☐

Due to restrooms being a private location they may be used as a place for concealing contraband to be retrieved later at a more opportune time. It is recommended that all privacy areas be equipped with fixed ceiling panels to avoid such use.

9. Are all exit signs and emergency lights functional and properly mounted?   ☐   ☐

Students may vandalize exit signs and emergency lighting never realizing the importance that these devices play in an emergency situation. The exit signs and emergency lights should frequently be checked to ensure they are functional and all arrows are mounted to designate the intended direction for exit. Should a pattern of damage to one location be recognized, it should immediately be reported to school administrators.

10. Are all rooms, stairwells, and halls properly lighted?   ☐   ☐

Adequate lighting prevents falls and injuries, as well as creating a better environment in which to study. Poor lighting should be addressed immediately.

11. Are all custodian closets and mechanical rooms kept locked?   ☐   ☐

Students seeking private locations to conduct illicit activities may seek doors known to be open and not occupied, such as custodian closets and mechanical rooms. Not only does this present an opportunity for intentional harm but unintentional harm may occur by students smoking unknowingly around dangerous chemicals or playing with electrical panels. These doors must be kept locked.

12. Are students issued school ID badges?   ☐   ☐

13. Are all staff (full- or part-time) issued ID badges?   ☐   ☐

Identification badges are a precaution that businesses, government, and schools are all finding necessary to keep unauthorized persons from entering the facilities. Student ID badges are a recommended precaution for all middle and high schools, even if the student is only required to display it when asked by a staff member. Middle and high school students may have been suspended or expelled or even be from another school altogether and this simple requirement may avert disaster.

It is highly recommended that all schools institute a photo ID system for all full- and part-time staff that includes the requirement to wear such an ID on the outermost garment of clothing while on school property. Substitutes may be given a separate ID badge that is unique and numbered and must be picked up each day substituting and turned in at the end of the day.

14. Are restricted areas marked as such?   ☐   ☐

In order to eliminate excuses for persons found in restricted areas, it is essential that those areas be clearly identified as restricted.

15. Are school files and records maintained in locked vandal-proof
    containers or cabinets?   ☐   ☐

   The private records of students and personnel should be treated in accordance with
   Privacy Act guidelines and as such secured in locked files or cabinets. Access should
   be in accordance with the standards set forth by this act and the Commonwealth of
   Virginia Department of Education.

16. Are building emergency contacts provided to the local police?   ☐   ☐

   Each year a new listing of emergency contacts, and their telephone numbers, for each
   building on the school campus should be supplied to the local law enforcement
   agency and fire department. These emergency contacts should list in order who should
   be called first in the event of an emergency at the building. The list should also list
   subsequent second and third contacts if the primary contact cannot be made. In a
   school environment it is not advisable to post the contact and home telephone
   numbers on the doors.

17. Is all audiovisual, computers, and other valuable school property
    marked with an identifiable number and an inventory of such items
    maintained in then office?   ☐   ☐

   In order to discourage theft and pilferage and increase the possibility of recovery if
   lost or stolen, all valuable school property should be marked with an identifiable
   marking or number. At a minimum, all items valued at more than $250.00 should
   be inventoried including a complete description of the item, any school applied
   numbers, and the location of the item. If the item is placed in the care of an individual
   that person should sign verifying their responsibility for the item. It is recommended
   that, at least annually, a physical verification of all inventoried item's presence be
   conducted and any new items be updated to the inventory within thirty (30) days
   of receipt.

18. Are walkway cover, ledge, or other roof access, from second-story
    windows restricted?   ☐   ☐

   Any easy access to walkway covers, lower roofs, awnings, or ledges from second-story
   windows must be addressed through securing or alarming the windows.

■ POLICIES   Y   N

1. Are all policies distributed in written form to any group or individual
   the policy concerns?   ☐   ☐

   In order for policies to be followed it is essential that those concerned are aware of the
   policy and have at their disposal a quick reference to such policies. It is recommended
   that when policies are drafted, input from the concerned party be sought and all
   concerned parties receive a written copy of the policy to review. The concerned parties
   may later be required to sign that they have read and understood the policy. If a school
   system has its own network or a secure Internet access, they may wish to post all
   policies for personnel to review.

2. Is proper ID required of unknown vendors or repairmen? ☐   ☐

While often a policy that visitors sign in and receive a visitor's pass is in place, vendors or unknown repairmen are excluded. It is recommended that these visitors be required to identify themselves with proper ID and sign in as others.

3. Must all visitors sign in the office and be issued a visitor pass? ☐   ☐

This policy is a must to ensure that only authorized persons with legitimate reasons for being in the school are allowed to move within the school.

4. Is there one designated person to conduct a security walk-through of the building and ensure no persons remain, proper doors are locked, and alarms are activated at the close of the school? ☐   ☐

Frequently intruders do not break into the school, they simply never leave. Each school should have a designated person(s) to physically conduct a walk-through at the end of the school day to ensure that no person is secreting themselves within the school. This designee, should also be briefed to ensure that certain interior doors and sites that are required to be locked are secured daily. The policy should specify what actions the designee should take if he/she detects a person within the school.

5. Is the student conduct policy reviewed and updated annually? ☐   ☐

Due to the many changes that occur through legislation, administrative policies, and personnel, it is necessary that the student conduct policy be reviewed annually prior to the school year and that updates or changes be included in the new policy distributed to all parents, faculty, and students.

6. Does the school have a Crisis Management Plan that includes a coordinated effort with law enforcement and other emergency agencies? ☐   ☐

Does it cover:

Acts of violence? ☐   ☐

Natural disaster? ☐   ☐

Accidents? ☐   ☐

Death? ☐   ☐

Bomb threats? ☐   ☐

All Virginia schools are required by statute to have in place a Crisis Management Plan. Such a crisis plan as defined by statute generally means the essential procedures, operations, and assignments required to prevent, manage, and respond to a critical event or emergency. Section 22.1–279.8 of the Code of Virginia defines further what is included in such a plan. Generally acts of violence, disasters, loss of power, student or faculty death, hostage situation, and bomb threats are mentioned but any incident that poses a threat of harm to the school buildings, students, or personnel should be addressed. It is recommended that if, you do not have such a coordinated plan prepared that the school administration contact the local law enforcement agency, emergency management agency and fire department to develop a plan. Additionally, technical assistance is available through the Department of Criminal Justice Services, School Safety Center.

	Y	N

7. Is the Crisis Management Plan reviewed with staff and updated annually? ☐ ☐

Like all policies and plans, the Crisis Plan will be rendered useless unless it is reviewed and updated and all involved parties train concerning its content. While other policies may briefly touched on and reviewed through distribution of written copies, the Crisis Plan must be openly discussed and reviewed annually to ensure that all responsible parties understand their role in a crisis.

8. Has the school established a "chain of command" for when administrators are away from the building? ☐ ☐

It is not sufficient that only the principal or vice principal be familiar with school policy and plans but it is important that an established "chain of command" be known to all in the event a critical incident requires a decision. To ensure quick reaction time, this chain of command should be established in advance and made known prior to any incident creating the need.

9. Must written permission be given for a student to be picked up at school by anyone other than a custodial parent? ☐ ☐

A clear policy stating that only persons identified by a custodial parent in writing may pick up their child should be adopted. Signed permission cards should be filed and verified each time a non-custodial parent or other person requests to pick up a child from the school. While a person may have had permission at the beginning of the school year, the permission may have been withdrawn without knowledge and the permission card verification would alert the staff to that fact.

10. Are there regulations and/or policies concerning school personnel using the school after hours? ☐ ☐

Teachers may request to remain in their classroom or access their classroom late to work on projects. If such access is allowed a policy should be in place governing the hours, requirements for signing out and returning an exterior door key, responsibility to secure the door upon entering and leaving and other pertinent liability issues. In most cases long after hours work should be discouraged.

11. Are staff remaining after hours required to sign out? ☐ ☐

Occasionally it may be necessary for staff to work over for a short period. It is recommended that a policy requiring the staff member to exit via a designated self-locking door and to sign out the time of departure be implemented. By requiring staff to exit a designated door, exit most visible to natural surveillance or CCTV cameras may be chosen, which contributes to the safety of the staff member and protects from pilferage. The sign out documents a record of who is working over and how often and if placed near the designated exit door makes it less convenient to use another door.

12. Is audiovisual and other equipment signed out by the user? ☐ ☐

To ensure accountability for the annual inventory and to ensure inoperative equipment is reported as needing repair, all audiovisual and other equipment should be signed out.

Y N

13. Is there a policy for depositing and handling all cash received? ☐ ☐

As with any business taking in cash, a policy specifying cash handling and deposits should be implemented. At a minimum it is recommended that each position handling cash be required to verify the beginning amount, and receipts written or printed via a cash register checked against the ending balance. Only one person should handle the cash once it is received at the beginning of the day and all cash except the required beginning amount be deposited daily. Petty cash funds should always be kept separate from other cash and receipts should always be required to account for any authorized expenditures.

14. Is discipline consistently enforced? ☐ ☐

In that the code of conduct for each school specifies expected behavior, it is imperative that the discipline for infractions and violations be consistent and uniform for all. Feelings of inequity may lead to violence against others students, faculty, or the school building. It is recommended that a disciplinary review policy be implemented to ensure consistent equitable discipline.

15. Are parents considered an integral part of student discipline? ☐ ☐

Parents must be informed and the cause for any discipline be discussed. Often issues contributing to the student misbehavior are unknown to the administrator and such insight is essential in equitable effective discipline.

16. Have alternatives to expulsion and suspension been built into the discipline policy? ☐ ☐

Discipline is designed to bring the student into compliance and to ensure that they conform to the behavioral standards set forth in the Code of Conduct. While ensuring conformity to behavioral standards, every effort must be made to avoid harming the student academically. Therefore alternatives to expulsion and suspension should be built into the discipline policy.

17. Are behavioral expectations and consequences for violations clearly outlined in the Code of Conduct provided to all students? ☐ ☐

One cannot be held accountable for standards that they are unaware of and that is why it is necessary that clear concise behavioral expectations must be presented to all student in writing. Reading and understanding the Code of Conduct should be required and indicated by the student's or parent's signature on a document returned to the school. While this does not ensure that the Code of Conduct was read, it does indicate that they at least were aware of the document and their requirement to read it.

18. Is there a policy and a means for students and staff to report problems or criminal activity anonymously? ☐ ☐

Most students have a great deal of pride in their school and want to do what is right concerning dangerous or harmful activities. They are often aware of violent and criminal acts before they occur and want to report the activity, but for the peer pressure of being labeled a "snitch." It is recommended that every school have a means established for students to report such activities anonymously. This may be done by a telephone answering machine dedicated to receiving such tips, Internet tip address, or a School Crime Stopper program implemented in accordance with Code of Virginia Section 22.1–280.2.

19. Are the responsibilities of faculty and staff for monitoring and supervising students in the classroom, hallways, and all school grounds or functions clearly specified? ☐ ☐

Often teachers consider their area of responsibility as their classroom and the adjacent hall only. As such there are often pockets of areas that are essentially unsupervised at all. It is strongly suggested that clear responsibilities be identified to all faculty and staff. At the least a policy stating what area will be monitored and by whom should be adopted.

20. Has an incident reporting procedure for disruptive behavior been established? ☐ ☐

A policy specifying when a documented report is required is a must to ensure that the much needed documentation be available as severe discipline becomes necessary. Each school must identify what will be reported. Section 22.1–280.1 of the Code of Virginia mandates that certain violent crimes must be reported to the superintendent of schools. It is recommended that a central repository for these reports be identified in order that the data may be analyzed.

21. Are the incidents categorized and analyzed to identify recurring problems or patterns with regard to locations, times, students involved, etc.? ☐ ☐

Evaluate where and when assaults occur.

Where: __ Classrooms   When: __ Before school
       __ Hallways   __ After school
       __ Toilets   __ Change of class
       __ Locker rooms   __ Lunch period
       __ Play areas   __ During gym
       __ Parking lots   __ During class
       __ Other

Evaluate where and when vandalism occurs.

Where: __ Classrooms   When: __ Before school
       __ Hallways   __ After school
       __ Toilets   __ During school hours
       __ Locker rooms   __ Weekends
       __ Play areas
       __ Parking lots
       __ Other

Compilation of reported incidents into a data base for analysis is crucial to developing solutions to prevent recurrence of problems. All school systems should endeavor to mandate reporting and designate a staff person for such analysis. If a school is unable designate a staff person to complete the analysis, it is recommended that they seek assistance from the local law enforcement crime analyst or local university. Student identity may be protected by designating a staff person to assign a number to student (for tracking) and redact the name from the document. Recidivism may be tracked this way while not identifying the student.

22. Have steps been taken to address the patterns? ☐ ☐

Explain.

If patterns have been identified, some response to address the pattern must be taken. Typically the pattern will point to a contributing factor, such as lack of supervision in the area, conflicting class scheduled, or overcrowding during a certain time. Once steps have been taken to address the contributing factor some effort to monitor the pattern for continued problem or eliminations should be undertaken.

23. Are violations of state and federal law reported to law enforcement? ☐   ☐

In order to avoid liability issues and ensure a trusted working relationship guidelines must be developed on what is required to be reported to law enforcement.

24. Is all seized evidence and/or contraband photographed and turned over immediately to law enforcement? ☐   ☐

School administrators, security staff, and faculty may intervene in situations in which they seize contraband or evidence. The school should enter into an agreement with the local law enforcement agency to receive and store any evidence taken from a student. The law enforcement agency is aware of chain of custody issues and protection of evidence required to maintain the integrity of said evidence. Certain items found but not associated with any incident such as switchblade knives should also be turned over to law enforcement for destruction. Many of these items are illegal to possess and may subject an unknowing administrator to charges. Usually a photograph of the item is sufficient for any administrative hearing.

25. Is law enforcement consulted when school construction projects are being planned? ☐   ☐

The proper design and effective use of the built environment can lead to the reduction in the opportunity for crime to occur. This sentence describes a concept known as "Crime Prevention Through Environmental Design (CPTED)." Many law enforcement have personnel trained in CPTED and are willing to review plans and offer suggestions on how the environment might be made safer in new construction projects. The implementations of the suggestions are not required but are invaluable in bringing in the crime prevention perspective. Plan review is recommended at the conceptual stage, before final plans are drawn. If the local law enforcement agency does not have a CPTED trained staff member, the Department of Criminal Justice Services, School Safety Center, may offer this service as technical assistance.

■ COLLABORATION AND DEVELOPMENT   Y   N

1. Are all of the following offered representation on the safety team for this audit?

   Faculty ☐   ☐
   Student ☐   ☐
   Administration ☐   ☐
   Custodial/Building Maintenance ☐   ☐
   Parent ☐   ☐
   Law Enforcement ☐   ☐
   School Security ☐   ☐

School safety audits are mandated by statute in Virginia. The statute recommends that the audit committee consists of members from the faculty, student body, administration, building maintenance, parents, law enforcement, and school security.

2. Does the school offer adequate recognition opportunities for students? □   □

Positive reinforcement and recognition are essential ingredients in producing confident students who are willing to ignore peer pressure to do what is right. All schools should have recognition opportunities as related to good character and citizenship.

3. Are students encouraged to establish clubs with a safety focus? □   □

Students should not only be encouraged to be good citizens in their various clubs but should take an active role to make their school safe. If a School Crime Stoppers program is in place, a student board may play an active role in the success of the program. Youth Crime Watch, Safety Alert, and other programs teach students how they may assist in making their school and their community safer.

4. Are students offered instruction in how to avoid becoming the victim of violence and the hazards of illicit drug use? □   □

While the DARE and GREAT programs are well known they are not the only programs that educate students about the hazards of drugs and violence. Every school should have some type of educational opportunity to assist students in avoiding the situations that lead to drug use or violence.

5. Does the school include the neighborhood when planning safety programs or addressing hazardous conditions? □   □

The school is not an island unto itself and as such it should always give the neighborhood an opportunity to be included and developing safety plans. If a local civic group or neighborhood watch exists, the occasional attendance of their meeting will go a long way in fostering good neighborly relationships. It is recommended that all schools contact their local government to identify any community organizations active in their area.

6. Are the principal and administration accessible to students, staff, and parents? □   □

School administrators should make every effort to be available to students, parents, and staff to discuss issues that may lead to problems. It is recommended that time be set aside each week for such meetings and that parent, students, and staff are aware of the times.

7. Are administrators a visible presence throughout the school? □   □

Nothing builds the confidence in the school environment like seeing the top administrators in the halls, classes, and at school activities. Administrators should attempt to interact with faculty and students in a positive non-authoritarian role as much as possible. By so doing when it becomes necessary to speak to them in an official capacity a more open dialogue is likely.

	Y	N
8. Are staff trained in personal safety?	☐	☐

All teachers and support staff should be trained in conflict resolution techniques and in ways to avoid the creation of dangerous situations by reacting to anger or violence in an improper manner. Since they have the responsibility to handle such situations, training to ensure their safety should be made available to them.

	Y	N
9. Are there school security officers in this school?	☐	☐
Are pre-employment background checks conducted for security guards?	☐	☐
Do school security officers receive basic and in-service training for their responsibilities?	☐	☐
Are their roles clearly defined?	☐	☐
Are they involved in the safe school planning process?	☐	☐

A school security officer is defined as an individual who is employed by the local school board for the singular purpose of maintaining order and discipline, preventing crime, investigating violations of school board policy, and detaining students violating the law or school board policies on school property or at school-sponsored events and who is responsible for ensuring the safety, security, and welfare of all students, faculty, staff, and visitors at the assigned school.

Should a school chose to employ a school security officer they should have a pre-employment background check conducted. When a school employs school security officers it is mandated under Section 9.1–102 Code of Virginia that such officers be certified as meeting the minimum standards for a school security officer which includes liability, responsibilities, law, security awareness, conflict resolution, emergency response, and students behavioral issues.

	Y	N
10. Does this school have a full-time school resource officer (SRO)?	☐	☐
Does this school have a part time SRO?	☐	☐
Has the SRO attended a SRO training and received in-service training for their responsibilities in the school?	☐	☐
Do SROs participate in after school activities?	☐	☐

The SRO is a certified law enforcement officer hired by the local law enforcement agency to provide law enforcement services to the school. The SRO is a positive role model to students and stresses positive rapport building with students. The SRO teaches various classes related to prevention, police interaction, and safe habits and frequently counsels students related to laws and behavioral norms. All schools are encouraged to have a full- or part-time SRO in the school. The SRO should participate in after school activities to enhance the positive interaction of student and officer.

	Y	N
11. Do school volunteers receive training pertaining to their duties?	☐	☐

It is recommended that all volunteers be trained as to their specific duties to ensure that no improper action be taken by the volunteer in a duty for which they are not responsible or capable.

	Y	N
12. Do students have access to conflict resolution programs?	☐	☐

Conflict resolution programs, student-guided peer groups, and the like are quite successful in resolving problems before they escalate to violence. Students should have access to some type of conflict resolution program in the school.

13. Are students assisted in developing anger management skills? □   □

Students that are identified through discipline records or recommendations as being unable to manage their anger appropriately should be assisted by the school through offering of an anger management program and/or counseling. By training the student in techniques that assist him/her with coping skills, the student and the student body is rewarded.

14. Is diversity awareness emphasized? □   □

Students should be taught the value of all people's contributions to society. As such, emphasis of not only accepting diversity, but valuing our differences should be expressed in multi-cultural programs, field trips, and experiences. Such emphasis leads to better understanding of our differences and less conflict related to prejudice.

15. Are programs available for students who are academically at risk? □   □

Programs to assist students who may be at risk academically and to develop their confidence in themselves are important to ensuring their continuance in school and ultimate success. All schools should have at their core the ultimate goal of pushing the student to accomplish all that they can and to provide them with the resources to do so.

16. Are truancy programs in place? □   □

Some means of addressing truants should be in place in all school systems. A comprehensive approach including cooperative efforts with other agencies in identifying truants and ensuring their attendance in school is recommended.

Confidential Home Security Survey

■ HOME SECURITY CHECKLIST Y N

Any question answered with a "No" identifies vulnerability for the residence. Below are recommendations for a solution followed by explanations of the importance of the solution.

1. Are address numbers visible from the street? ☐ ☐

   Although house numbering doesn't seem like a prevention technique, it may be the reason a house is burglarized. Most burglars seek targets that offer them a reduced risk of capture. Any delay in officers responding to the property is an opportunity for escape.

   Depending upon the proximity of your home or numbers to the street, a minimum of a 4–6 inch letter is recommended. The numbers should be clearly contrasted to the mounting surface and visible at night.

2. Street or other lighting working? ☐ ☐

   Street and other lighting have been proven in studies to be responsible for crime reduction. Lighting deters criminals intent on concealment and operating under the cover of darkness.

   Additional lighting should be added in shadowed areas not typically covered by street lighting such as alleyways. When adding lighting it is important to place the lighting where it will have the most affect, where someone may see the area lighted in passing. It does little good to light a building when there is nobody to see the criminal activity.

3. Does lighting illuminate entrances? ☐ ☐

   Lighting of entrances, especially when the resident is away, is extremely important. The light not only illuminates the major location of most burglaries to passersby but also ensures the resident that no intruder is lurking nearby. It also provides the resident reaction time to leave and call the police if they discover the door ajar.

4. Is all glare minimized? ☐ ☐

   Glare is nothing more than horizontal light. Lights that illuminate horizontally temporarily blind the viewer and defeat the purpose of the light, which is to reveal whatever it falls upon. If the glare is toward your home, you are unable to see any prowlers outside. If it is from your home, you prevent patrolling officers and passers that are potential witnesses from seeing your home.

All glare should be reduced by readjustment, directing, or shielding of lighting.

5. Are all shrubs near the house less than 3 feet in height?   ☐   ☐

Controlling shrubbery near the home is important in several ways. First, a home that looks well-cared for is less likely to fall victim to a burglar. Second and most important is that tall shrubbery near the home offer quick and easy concealment for burglars. By keeping the shrubbery trimmed to 3 feet it is much less likely to conceal a grown criminal.

6. Do border shrubs block view from the street?   ☐   ☐

Natural surveillance afforded by casual passers is perhaps one of the best and least expensive deterrents to criminal activity there is. If border definition is the goal, it is recommended that shrubbery with a mature height of less than that of the sidewalk or road-grade height be used. Other options are to define the property with fencing that has visual acuity, burms with ground plantings, or trees kept trimmed up to a height of 6 feet.

7. Is tree canopy trimmed up to a height of 6 feet from the ground?   ☐   ☐

Special consideration should be given to trees surrounding the property, especially at night. It is recommended that all trees be trimmed up to a height of 6–8 feet to afford visible surveillance and to discourage use of the trees as concealment.

8. Are all fences of see-through construction? (Not privacy fencing)   ☐   ☐

Fencing is typically used to define the property boundary, to keep domesticated animals from roaming, to protect children and to afford a sense of privacy. Unfortunately by providing privacy for yourself you also provide privacy for the burglar and or prowler to work undetected.

Privacy fences are not recommended and if already installed may be altered to create a safe environment by removing every other board. It is recommended that fencing be of a material that allows visual acuity. Picket, corral, wrought iron, or chain-link are all good examples of such fencing.

9. Are all doors solid wood core or metal?   ☐   ☐

Hollow core door offers little protection. These doors are constructed of two thin panels of wood attached to a 2 × 2 frame and are never suitable for exterior doors or for doors leading to any space where security is a concern.

It is recommended that all exterior doors, and interior doors leading from a basement or outbuilding, be constructed of solid wood core or metal and be a minimum of 1¾ inch thickness.

10. Are doors hinged inside or protected from being removed?   ☐   ☐

Exposed unsecured hinges offer easy access to the criminal by simply removing the hinge pins and opening the removing or opening the door. All exterior doors should be hinged on the inside.

Doors that are hinged outside may be removed and re-hinged. Other options are to spot weld the hinge pins to the hinge, replace the hinges with factory hinges specially constructed to prevent hinge removal or pin the door to the frame. Pinning the door to the frame may be done by inserting a screw into the edge of the door in which the hinges are affixed and drilling a coinciding hole across from the screw on the doorframe of sufficient size to accommodate the screw when the door is closed.

11. Is there glass within 40 inches of the door lock?

Doors that contain glass sidelights or windowing present the intruder with easy access by breaking the glass and reaching through to unlock the door. Although an easy recommendation would be to install double-keyed deadbolt locks, fire or building code in many places forbid the installation of these locks due to fire escape concerns. If a person has this type of lock and insists on keeping it, it is recommended that they be cautioned to keep the key concealed somewhere close to the door, preferably low to the floor in case of fire.

A similar lock that meets the code and is recommended is a captive deadbolt lock in which the interior key acts as a thumb latch and in order to remove it a special operation of the key set is required. This provides the protection of a double cylinder (keyed) deadbolt, when the resident is away from home, with the fire safe means of escape while at home. Other options to address this problem are the installation of tightly designed (to prevent reaching through) grating on the inside of the window, replacing the glass with lexan or polycarbonate, replace the door with a solid core or metal door and installation of a second deadbolt near the floor out of reach from the glass.

12. Are there deadbolt locks on exterior doors?

A good quality deadbolt lock is recommended for all exterior or any door in which security is a concern. The lock should have a 1 inch case-hardened bolt and, when properly installed, should completely engage into the strike plate, or the lock is not secure. A deadbolt should not be able to be pushed back into the lockset when engaged. The quality of deadbolt depends on the level of security you wish to enjoy. At a minimum a lock with a good housing and bolt is recommended. High-security locks rated by the Underwriters Laboratory for being pick and jimmy resistant are available at a locksmith for a substantially increased price.

Spring or key in the knob latches are not recommended for exterior doors and any auxiliary or secondary locks such as chain locks should be considered as little protection and are discouraged due to the false sense of security that is presented by having them.

13. Is there a peephole or other means of viewing the exterior of the door?

We have always taught our children not to open the door to strangers, yet that is what we do each time we answer to an unknown person. Home intrusion attacks are becoming more frequent as the criminal becomes bolder. A seemingly innocent visitor may be a front for others concealing themselves around the entrance awaiting their chance to rush in when the door is opened. We recommend that you not only speak though a locked door to unknown visitors but also that all exterior doors have some means of visibly seeing 160 degrees around them. It is recommended that a wide-angle peephole viewer be installed in solid doors to meet this recommendation.

14. Are all strike plates secured with minimal 2½–3 inch screws?   ☐   ☐

A door kicked or forced will give at its weakest point. If a proper deadbolt and door are used this weak area is typically the strike plate. The reason is that most locksets come with screws that are inadequate for the common door construction today. Pre-hung doors are typically hung in a 1 inch frame, which is shimmed to the door stud leaving anywhere from 1–2 inches of nothing between the frame and the stud. The locksets usually come with a ¾–1½ inch screw for mounting the strike plate. Thus your deadbolt is seated in a strike plate held in place by a 1 inch board with the screws in the board only or the board and air.

   We recommend installation of a high-security strike plate mounted with a minimum of 2½ inch screws. Even if the strike plate is not replaced the screws should be changed to ensure strengthening of the locking system. One may strengthen the doorframe further by adding screws of 3–4 inch length above and below the strike plate.

15. Are all sliding doors secured with a Charley Bar or similar device?   ☐   ☐

The average sliding door and/or window have poor locking mechanisms and require reinforcement. In addition, the construction of the unaltered sliding door frequently allows an intruder to simply lift the door up and out of the frame.

   It is recommended that at a minimum a dowel rod or metal bar be placed in the track behind the slider to prevent easy sliding of the door. Although this only offers a little better protection and doesn't strengthen the top of the door, which might tilt. A commercially offered device, commonly referred to as a Charley Bar, that operates on the same premise, preventing the door from being opened, but mounts midway the door is the better solution. To prevent the door from being lifted from the track it is recommended that all adjustment screws be tightened and several screws be inserted into the top of the track but left protruding ¼ inch or more, depending upon the gap in the track. This will create an obstacle for the door if lifted. Finally, we recommend that an inexpensive commercially offered lock for sliders be added as an auxiliary to the factory set.

16. Are all sliders protected from being lifted from the track?   ☐   ☐

See explanation above.

17. Is the lock on the slider adequate?   ☐   ☐

See explanation above.

18. Are all glass swinging doors protected with adequate locks or bars?   ☐   ☐

Glass-hinged doors offer no more problem than other doors. Doors with glass panes offer more of a dilemma due to the ability to silence the panes when breakage occurs. Larger (all one pane) doors make a substantial sound and the shards pose a threat of falling to the criminal. The major problem with these doors is their location, usually in the back of the house, where they are less likely to be observed.

   Glass doors should be treated as any door that has glass within reach of the lock. Due to fire and building code often forbidding it, we cannot make the obvious recommendation to install double-keyed deadbolt locks. If a person has this type of lock and insists on keeping it, it is recommended that they be cautioned to keep the key concealed somewhere close to the door, preferably low to the floor in case of fire.

A similar lock that meets the code and is recommended is a captive deadbolt lock, in which the interior key acts as a thumb latch and in order to remove it a special operation of the key set is required. This provides the protection of a double cylinder (keyed) deadbolt, when the resident is away from home, with the fire safe means of escape while at home. Other options to address this problem are the installation of tightly designed (to prevent reaching through) grating on the inside of the glass, replacing the glass with lexan or polycarbonate or replace the door with a solid core or metal door.

19. Are all double doors protected with extra security on the stationary leaf?   ☐   ☐

Double doors weakest point is the slide latch that secures the inactive leaf. The active leaf secures to this therefore making the entire system a risk. The typical problem is that the latch is of cheap grade material and may be shaken to loosen the top latch, leaving only the thin bottom latch and the active leaf–keyed latch to secure the door.

It is recommended that a new extension latch that protruded deeper into the top and bottom of the frame be installed. The latch should secure in place and not be able to be forced or shaken down. The bolt plate in which the bolt extends should be reinforced with $2\frac{1}{2}$ inch screws. A deadbolt lock with a minimum 1 inch throw is recommended.

20. Are all garage bay doors capable of being locked?   ☐   ☐

Locks that come with most garage or bay doors are poor. Even when adequate locks are installed, the panel construction and installed windows complicate securing the garage.

Windows in garage doors are rarely the point of entry but they may be secured by changing them to lexan or by installing grating inside. The panels may be reinforced by securing a bar or boar across the panels. While the above are rarely implemented it is recommended that a good case-hardened hasp and padlock be installed on either side of the garage door. At a minimum a padlock should be used in the track of the door.

21. Is the garage kept locked?   ☐   ☐

It seems elementary but a favorite location for entry is the door into the house from a concealed location. By leaving the garage door open, a concealment location is created for the intruder who enters the garage, closes the door, and, usually using tools inside the garage, forces entry undetected.

It is recommended that the garage be kept locked at all times that it is not in use.

22. Is the home entrance from the garage and/or any basement treated as an exterior door?   ☐   ☐

Doors leading from a basement or garage are easy concealment for the criminal and in order to deter and delay his action, these doors should be treated as exterior doors with the same recommendations for construction, reinforcement, and locks.

23. Are all easily accessible windows secured with a keyed lock or other lock and pinned?   ☐   ☐

Statistics show that following a ground-level door, burglars enter most often through a ground-level window. Many of these burglaries are preventable by the use of an effective locking device. The locks on such windows are most frequently defeated rather than breaking the glass.

It is recommended that all-ground level windows be secured with a quality key lock or additional lock rather than with just a typical sheet metal crescent latch that can easily be slipped. In addition, the window may be reinforced by drilling at a downward angle through the window frame of the first window and partially through the second on double hung windows. Care must be taken to clear the glass that is inside the framing. A nail or metal pin may then be inserted into the hole to create extra security. By drilling downward the pin is not apt to be vibrated out by tapping on the frame.

24. Are accessible windows kept locked? □ □

Although it should go without saying, each year many homes are entered while the resident is working in the yard or visiting a neighbor. This is especially true of the gypsy burglars who may even use one person to distract the resident in the yard while another clean out the house. It is recommended that locks be used when you cannot see the door from where you are visiting or working.

25. Are all second-story windows protected from access by ladders, trees, etc.? □ □

While second stories are not as frequent a means of entry into a home as ground-level entrances, they do, nonetheless, pose a problem. In most cases that a second-story entrance is made it is by use of means readily available at or near the scene. That is to say it is by natural climbing devices near the home such as trellises, trees, or trashcans near a low roof or even a ladder left outside or in an opened garage or outbuilding.

It is recommended that all ladders and such items be eliminated as potential access to the second story, trees be kept thinned, and second-story windows be secured with effective locking devices as well as ground level windows.

26. Are all sheds and tools kept secure? □ □

Many jurisdictions have statutes that allow officers to charge persons with possession of burglar's tools. Therefore, many burglars, rather than risk the charge or be seen as suspicious, find the tools they need at or near the victim's home. There are any number of garages, tool sheds, and open truck toolboxes with just the right tools for the job along the way.

We recommend that, through your neighborhood watch or civic group, or even through door-to-door contact with neighbors, you attempt to educate them to secure their tools. Most importantly, you should secure all tools that you have around your own home.

27. Is there an alarm? □ □

While alarms are not prevention tools per se, if they are an audible type they may alert neighbors and frighten the suspect intruder away.

Should you opt to have an alarm installed it is recommended that you choose a reputable company and ensure that the technician is a Department of Criminal Justice Services–certified technician by asking to see his card or certification. A quality audible alarm is preferred for prevention as opposed to an alarm that is monitored by a monitoring company and which may take some time to verify an entry. The bell or siren should be positioned so as to alert a neighbor that is frequently home and agrees to call the police. Finally, care should be taken to ensure that users are educated in the use of the alarm, since operator error is the largest cause of false activations and some jurisdictions charge fees for such false alarm activations.

28. Can neighbors see the ground exterior of the house?   ☐   ☐

Burglars, rapists, and other intruders target residences in which they may work undetected or concealed from view. One of the least expensive but most effective crime prevention measures is to ensure that passing vehicles, pedestrians, and neighbors have a clear view of your home ground-level windows and entrances.

It is recommended that shrubs near the home not be permitted to reach a height of more than 3 feet and that trees be trimmed up from the ground to at least 6 feet height. This will prevent persons from concealing themselves near the home and ensure a open view from neighboring homes.

29. Have the locks been used by previous residents or contractors?   ☐   ☐

When purchasing a previously owned home or moving into a residential unit, it is recommended that the locks be changed, for obvious reasons. The previous residents may have been involved in criminal activity, loaned keys to friends, or there may be any number of other problems that make changing the locks a sound practice.

30. When leaving home for several days do you ensure the home looks
lived in?   ☐   ☐

Burglars look for certain telling signs that the home is a safe target. Signs such as overflowing mailboxes, trash that is not put out with others in the neighborhood, and newspapers and periodicals piling up, give the burglar a easy indication that the resident may be out for several days. It is recommended that you have a trusted neighbor watch after your home by picking up your mail and newspapers and taking other steps to indicate that someone is home. If no neighbors are available, a quick telephone call to your post office and/or newspaper to stop delivery is better than taking no steps.

Confidential Business Security Survey

■ STATEMENT OF PURPOSE

The definition of crime prevention that is generally accepted across the United States and abroad is, "the anticipation, recognition and appraisal of a crime risk and the initiation of some action to remove or reduce it." A critical means of preventing crime is the security survey.

A security survey is a critical look at a business, facility, or home to evaluate the existing security status and potential vulnerabilities. The individual conducting the security survey must have the cooperation of the property user to completely evaluate the premises. After examination of the premises the assessor applies proven techniques and acquired knowledge to recommendations that are known to reduce or remove the opportunity for crime and criminal activity.

Preventing crime is dependent upon the application of the recommendations of the assessor. To delineate from the recommendation or to apply partially the recommendation reduces the potential for success. Nevertheless, even partial implementation of the recommendation should reduce the vulnerabilities of crime to a degree.

The following security survey and recommendations should not be viewed as being capable of making the facility/business burglar proof, robbery proof, or theft proof. They will, however, reduce the probability of losses occurring if properly applied and maintained.

Crime opportunity prevention, like all management responsibilities, will require constant upgrading and attention to keep abreast of changing operational needs of security.

Many times the implementation of one phase of the recommended actions is linked to, and dependent on, the implementation of other recommendations. Therefore, the enclosed recommendations should not be fragmented, in order to avoid breaching of the security elements recommended.

On behalf of my agency, I want to thank you for demonstrating your interest in improving the safe working conditions of your business and your community.

■ ROBBERY VULNERABILITIES

Business History and Policies

The crime prevention practitioner should obtain the following information from their crime analyst and through an interview with the business management, owner, or designated employees.

1. Has the business been robbery free or attempted robbery free over the last 12 months?   ☐   ☐

   Perhaps the best indicator of vulnerability is the history of the business. While absence of robbery incidents does not indicate lack of vulnerabilities, just the opposite is true of past robberies. Businesses that have been robbed within the past 12 months have a significantly higher chance of being robbed again. By examining the crime history we are able to gain a better understanding of what measures may need to be implemented, and to what degree, in order to reduce the potential for criminal acts.

2. Is the business located in a high-crime area or area with known crime generators?   ☐   ☐

   Retail establishments are needed in all communities. The fact that a business is located in a high-crime neighborhood, or one that is associated with increased crime simply means that the business has to take additional steps to protect its employees and itself from loss.

3. Is there a policy prohibiting opening any non-public access door to unauthorized persons?   ☐   ☐

   Robbers are not limited to public access when perpetrating their crimes. They may attempt entry to the back office area of a business using some ruse of injury or delivery. In addition, employee theft may be conducted by use of a back or delivery door.

   It is recommended that back door use be kept to a minimum and whenever possible, deliveries be made through the public access in convenience store businesses. When deliveries are accepted at loading docks or back doors, specific hours for deliveries should be coordinated with the vendor to ensure delivery is during slow times. This will enable the business to have a designated person check the delivery, preventing delivery person theft, as well reduce the potential for a robber to gain access by this means.

4. Is the business in a populated area, visible to other businesses, and/or homes?   ☐   ☐

   Robbers are apt to weigh their effort for success, their reward, and the potential for detection or capture. Being isolated is directly related to the amount of effort and their risk factor. Businesses located in populated areas should take advantage of their neighbors and offer every opportunity for their natural surveillance to the business. Businesses that are located in isolated areas need to ensure that they strengthen their security by always having at least two clerks on duty and implement most of the strategies identified in this report.

5. Is the business located near access to interstates or major highways?   ☐   ☐

   As mentioned above the potential for success is key in the selection of a target, therefore, businesses near quick escape routes such as interstate ramps and major highways have a higher potential for victimization, absent adequate prevention steps. Parking lot exit designs that require traffic to exit indirectly go a long way toward making the business a less attractive target.

6. Does the business have a reputation for being busy frequently?   ☐   ☐

Robbers rarely rob a business with lots of patrons. Each patron represents a witness, which limits the probability of success. Whatever steps can be taken to increase potential witnesses are steps well worth taking. Allowing charities to sell cookies or conduct a car wash are not only ways to build a good reputation in the community; it also decreases the potential for crime.

7. Is the business frequented by police patrols? ☐ ☐

Obviously where police patrols frequent, there is a much less likely potential for problems of all kinds. Any incentive to draw officers to the business is encouraged. This may be done by offering use of the office, telephone, restroom facility, or simply making a request of the beat officers in the area.

8. Is there a policy against making change after dark? ☐ ☐

Each time that the cash register opens is an opportunity for loss. Many robbers use the premise of requesting change to get the register open and expedite their crime. There should be a policy prohibiting changing large bills anytime, and prohibiting the making of change after hours.

9. Does the business prohibit cashing of payroll checks? ☐ ☐

While this convenience may encourage customers to spend their money in your establishment, it also reveals that you have large amounts of cash on hand. The reward of such a bounty greatly increases the probability of your being selected as a target. It is recommended that payroll checks not be cashed and that signage stating that no payroll checks are cashed because only a minimum amount of cash is kept on hand at any time be posted.

10. Are cash totals recorded throughout the business day? ☐ ☐

By totaling cash at various times throughout the day, internal theft is discouraged and relocating the cash to a safe or deposit is encouraged. Limiting the amount of cash is limiting the amount of loss in the event of a robbery.

11. Are store hours posted and strictly followed? ☐ ☐

Posting of store hours may seem to be an unlikely tool of prevention, however, with regular hours posted and strict adherence being mandated, the employee does not inadvertently offend customers by not opening the door at their requests. Employees should be made aware that the opening and closing times are particularly vulnerable times and that under what circumstances they should vary from store times. Employees should be made aware that they can help stranded motorists or persons claiming a need for police or medical personnel best by calling help for them, not by letting them in the business.

12. Are all cash or till transfers made at irregular (non-routine) times? ☐ ☐

Routine allows for patterning and planning and it is discouraged. Irregular till transfers at non-specific times are recommended whenever possible.

13. Are there standardized procedures for reporting incidents to the police? ☐ ☐

All employees should be aware of when to call the police and what is to be reported. They should be trained in what should be considered suspicious and when in doubt to call. The law enforcement community would much rather respond to a call in which they were not needed than to later respond because of an actual past robbery.

14. Does the business use a recorded serial number bill, marked money, or other technique for identifying the money stolen in a robbery? ☐ ☐

An investigative tool, the use of bait money or traceable bills could serve as a deterrent indirectly by ensuring the capture of the robber. The reputation of quick apprehension is bound to deter other criminals from seeing your business as an easy mark. We recommend that each till be prepared to include bills in which the serial number has been recorded or the bills have been marked.

15. Is there a policy/procedure addressing how employees are to react during a robbery or other violent incident? ☐ ☐

All retail establishments should have a policy concerning robberies and what specific action their employees should take during and after the robbery. Training should be based on this policy and the policy reviewed regularly to ensure that all employees are aware of what is expected.

16. Is robbery prevention/response training provided to employees? ☐ ☐

Robbery prevention training should be provided in order to ensure that the employee recognized the potential for a robbery and takes steps to head off the robbery. Once the robbery begins the employee is at the mercy of the criminal but several steps may be taken that possibly may thwart the robbers intent. Employees should be trained to make eye contact and greet customers in order alert them that you have noticed them. Cashiers should be trained to remove themselves from the area of the cash register when not actually ringing up merchandise and to increase the effort of robbing the register that is closed.

    All employees should be trained concerning specific hazards that they might encounter. Employees should be trained that once a robbery begins they should assist the robber with whatever is requested, do or say nothing to upset the robber and to cooperate fully. The ultimate goal of the employee should be to give the robber what they demand in order that the incident may end quickly and without harm to the employee. They should also be trained to lock the door as soon as the robber departs, call the police and to touch nothing until law enforcement arrives.

17. Does the business have a publicized policy of prosecuting all thefts? ☐ ☐

Any business that is known for having little tolerance for theft is less likely to be seen as an easy mark for any criminal act. If a policy of prosecution of all shoplifters is posted and backed up through actual prosecutions, it is likely that the robber will be aware of the increased risk of prosecution if caught, which may act as a deterrent.

18. Is there a policy limiting the amount of cash left in the register at all times? ☐ ☐

It is recommended that the minimal amount of cash needed for operation of the business be kept on hand. In addition, the fact that only a minimal amount is kept on hand should be advertised by posting a sign to that fact prominently near the cashier.

19. Is there a policy to ensure safe opening and closing procedures? ☐ ☐

Perhaps one of the most susceptible times for robbery is at opening and closing. It is therefore imperative that solid procedures for opening the store and closing is written and trained on to ensure compliance. Each store policy will be different—dependent on their location, hours, the number of employees, and other factors—but essential to the procedures is a requirement that no one individual open or close alone. Another common denominator is the check of the business at closing to ensure no hiding "lock in" burglars are left behind.

20. Is there a procedure or policy for depositing the day's receipts that includes non-routine deposits? ☐ ☐

Routine is unhealthy when making bank runs for deposits. Unfortunately, many businesses fall into a routine of holding all the day's receipts until the manager leaves or the business closes. The robber is looking for just this pattern. Deposits being made at varying times during the day reduce the potential loss of a robbery, as well as reduce the possibility that the robber will follow and pattern the depositor. Deposits should be made in an inconspicuous manner.

21. Does the store present a neat well-kept appearance? ☐ ☐

A well-kept store or business is indicative of an organized business. From the criminal perspective, an organized business is much more likely to have security measures in place that protect it from crime. Likewise, a cluttered chaotic business presents the potential of being more apt to keep large sums of money on the premises, not have a safe, and not make frequent deposits

22. If Closed Circuit Television (CCTV) is used, is there a policy for retention periods and cataloging of tapes? ☐ ☐

While CCTV has more of an investigative role than preventative, it can assist officers in identifying robbers. Robbers frequently will visit their target to evaluate the risk and effort and as such may be identified from tapes that are catalogued by date and retained for a minimal period, such as thirty days. Tapes that are reused over and over tend to lose their quality and the CCTV policy should limit the number of times a tape may be reused. Policies should address if the CCTV will be monitored, where is the most strategic location for the camera and where will the monitor and tape deck be secured?

23. Does your business belong to a local business watch or crime prevention association? ☐ ☐

Business watch programs are designed to provide a wide variety of crime prevention services to local businesses. Training and model policies may be available from your local law enforcement agency or crime prevention association. Membership in such organizations also provides potential for co-op buying and knowledge of the most recent in prevention techniques.

24. Does the business encourage employees to identify crime problems and theft opportunities and offer incentives for doing so? ☐ ☐

Newly hired employees should be trained as to the value of their role with the business. They should be educated that the success of the business and future wage increases for employees are dependant on keeping losses down. Since employees are being asked to prevent losses they should be given training in how to prevent thefts and losses. In order to ensure that employees realize that the business really does recognize their ability to prevent crime and reduce losses a recognition program is recommended. A recognition program that may include special discounts, gifts, days off with pay, and other incentives paid out for identifying causes of loss are likely to cost much less than the losses disregarded by a disgruntled or uncaring employee. In the event recognition programs are unsuccessful, the business might consider deductions to a department for losses incurred.

25. Does the business have a policy of securing outside items in some means and locking up tools? ☐   ☐

Securing outside items of value via chains, cables, or other means is essential if these items are to remain stored outside the business while closed. Not only does the business stand to experience losses from theft of these items but also many of these items may be used to facilitate a burglary of the business. Pallets can become makeshift ladders, landscaping tools may become instruments for prying locks, and wheelbarrows may become the easy means to carry away a large supply of items.

26. Does the business record cash movements and inventories? ☐   ☐

While the persons handling cash and deposits should be our most trusted employees, that is not always the case. The best way to prevent problems is to have a good cash handling system and to make it clear that all levels of the procedure are checked. An example of a good procedure would be to ensure first that the person handling accounts payable is not the same person handling accounts receivable or daily deposits. Secondly, the person cashing the till should be checked by the person responsible for deposit. Three deposit slips should document the deposit procedure. One would be retained by the bank, one returned to the employee making the deposit and the third mailed to the company auditors or designated party.

Any good system of checks and balances is still dependent upon obedience to the procedure and ensuring that all involved are knowledgeable concerning it.

27. Is an annual audit of the books done by an independent firm, stressing critical review? ☐   ☐

Outside auditing of accounting practices are essential to ensuring employees remain honest and to identifying holes in the audit trail that may need to be repaired. A critical look at the books, procedures, and actual operations is recommended.

28. Is there a policy of periodically monitoring employee's transactions and work? ☐   ☐

A policy stating that management may periodically monitor employees, work practices, e-mail and other work-related activities should be part of an employee packet given to all employees when first hired. The policy not only serves as protection should the monitoring reveal problems, but it is also a deterrent for selling of trade secrets, sweetheart cashiering, and others.

29. Is there a policy allowing for the random inspection of any parcels, coats, or containers being removed by employees? ☐   ☐

A typical procedure allowing inspection of parcels, coats, baggage, and large containers is recommended. In a retail sales environment the business may wish to require that all purchases made on work time be stored in a central location with a receipt attached and initialed by management until the employee's shift ends.

30. Is there a zero tolerance policy for employee theft that involves measures to deter such theft? ☐ ☐

Policy is the deterrent and the tool for prosecution, if need be. A well-stated employee theft policy identifying actions that may, or will, be taken is at the center of any such deterrence. Management should support the policy by learning how to read the register receipt for indication of cashier theft, read the employee behavior for signs of embezzlement or selling of trade secrets, and listen for clues that employees in such situations are in dire financial straights.

31. Is the person responsible for accounts payable different from the one responsible for accounts payable? ☐ ☐

Dual responsibility in such a financial environment is a recipe for disaster. The person in such a position can easily conceal losses and in some cases may make such adjustments, not to steal but to make the books balance. A close scrutiny of the books by a professional auditor often reveals the discrepancy, but only after it has cost the business substantial losses.

Exterior   Y   N

1. Does the parking area have spaces not visible to employees? ☐ ☐

As much as is possible the employees should be able to view the entire parking lot for any vehicle. If the lot has blind spots that are close to the building they may be controlled by designating them as handicapped parking or even police patrol parking, if appropriate, or by relocating some other legitimate use there.

2. Are all concealment locations around the business limited or reduced through design, use, or other means? ☐ ☐

Reducing the concealment locations around the business not only discourages robbers from waiting for an opportune moment to don a mask and enter the business but it also protects customers from attack. Concealment locations can be limited by removal of foliage, large items, and/or solid fencing. By removing concealment the business is open to observation from passersby and the robber's goal is much more difficult.

3. Is lighting sufficient to ensure facial recognition and provide visual surveillance both into and out of the business? ☐ ☐

Rather than consider lighting by the foot-candle measure and recommended industry standard for a parking lot, we want to consider the sufficiency of the lighting to the task. In the case of the convenience store, the measure is does it provide uniformity for two-way surveillance into the store and out of the store and does it provide adequate illumination for facial recognition from a typical distance of 35 feet? Lighting that is not uniform will present the problem of eye adjustment, glare, and in fact contribute to the criminal act rather than aid in preventing it.

4. Are parking area entrances/exits limited to the minimum necessary to ensure safe travel?   ☐   ☐

The quick and easy entrance onto the main highway or several ways to exit the lot present the criminal with quick escape routes, which when combined with other attractive factors makes the business a good target. A number of entrance/exits to businesses have also been found to contribute to loitering by youth. If the business is closed during certain hours, "No Trespassing" signs identifying the specified closed times should be posted to avoid loitering and vandalism. If the business experiences a high volume of traffic during a patterned 1 or 2 hours daily, it might be recommended that after the busy time, the extra entrance be closed with a cable or gate.

5. Are all exterior windows kept free of posters and other items, which would limit visibility into the business?   ☐   ☐

Natural surveillance is an excellent deterrent to robbery and other crimes. Anything that can create the "fishbowl effect" of allowing passing vehicles, pedestrians, and customers to view inside the store is helpful in making the business unattractive to criminals. It does little good to have excellent uniform lighting only to cover the windows with posters and adds or displays stacked to ceiling height.

6. Are all pay telephone stations located away from the periphery of the business and within view of the cashier?   ☐   ☐

Pay telephone stations are a convenience to the public that have the potential to create problems for the store. Pay telephones located on the periphery of a business lot are considered by many judges to be "public" and therefore accessible to any and all who wish to use them. Pay stations create a legitimate reason for loitering at the location. The loiterer may be selling narcotics, "casing" the store, or awaiting to victimize your customers. With the station located on the fringes of the lot, it is less likely to be monitored by employees and less likely considered to be controlled by the criminal.

Businesses should request that the pay telephones receive no incoming calls. This is usually provided by the telephone company at no charge. Pay stations are best located within view of the cashier, close, or attached to the building. In a community where the phone may be used in illegal activity, it might even be located inside, within close proximity of the cashier to ensure legitimate use.

7. Are there signs and/or street numbers that allow for quick location of the business?   ☐   ☐

In order to ensure quick response to calls for assistance, all businesses and residences should be identified with their street address in numbers over the door or placed according to local ordinance. All businesses can ensure quick response by identifying their business with appropriate signage.

8. Do exterior door locks on business entrances require a key to lock from the inside?   ☐   ☐

Since the business entrance, open to the public, is not secured while occupied by customers, it is proper and recommended that the exterior front doors be equipped with commercial grade double cylinder deadbolt locks. In the event of the clerk observing suspicious activity indicating a robbery is imminent or just after a robbery they can secure the door but, due to the absence of a thumb lock, the robber is prevented from locking the door during a robbery.

9. Are all non-public access doors equipped with a wide-angle viewer? ☐   ☐

   All back doors in which shipments might be received or trash might be removed should be equipped with a wide-angle viewer that allows for a minimum of 160-degree vision. Policies concerning when this door might be accessed and requiring that the user check prior to opening to ensure there is no person loitering outside should be part of the overall security procedures for the business.

10. Are public-access exterior doors designed to only open one way? ☐   ☐

    One of the key premises behind crime prevention is to delay the criminal is to deter the criminal. Two-way swinging doors make for an easy escape and should be avoided.

11. Can doors be secured to allow only one door to be accessed? ☐   ☐

    It is typical in a retail setting to have a double door in which one of the doors may be secured with a flush or surface bolt. This gives the store clerk an option of restricting access egress and therefore delaying the quick exit of shoplifters, robbers, and other criminals. It is recommended that during night hours or during times when the retail business is especially susceptible to theft that one of the doors be secured in this fashion.

12. Are fences or other means employed to direct persons to more visible areas? ☐   ☐

    The strategic placement of fences, dumpsters, and other items on a parking lot, entrance way, or sidewalk to direct customers, vehicles, and pedestrians to a visible location is yet another way that natural surveillance can be accomplished. Any area that is not visible to neighbors or employees should be addressed by some such manner.

13. Is all shrubbery near the building maintained at a height of 3 feet or less? ☐   ☐

    By maintaining the shrubbery at the recommended 3 feet height, the potential for concealment by robbers or others and attack of persons leaving the business is greatly reduced. While protecting persons with well-trimmed shrubs, the business protects the building as well from burglars.

14. Have trees been trimmed up to a 6 foot canopy? ☐   ☐

    Like the above recommendation, keeping tree canopies trimmed up to at least 6 feet provide good visual surveillance to persons and patrols passing the business as well as employees and customers leaving the business.

15. Are the boundaries clearly defined with signage, fencing, or landscaping? ☐   ☐

    Property boundaries should clearly be defined by treatment that demonstrates a transition from one property to another. Low fencing, a change in sidewalk color or texture, fences, and a variety of other means may be employed to accomplish this. It is important that property be defined in order to specify that a different behavior is expected. Private property does not have to tolerate the same behaviors that public property does. Boundary definition makes clear that private property behavior is expected.

Interior

	Y	N

1. Is the cash register(s) located near the front of the store? ☐ ☐

   By locating the cash register at the front of the store, the business forces all persons to pass by the last point of payment and be observed as they leave. This deters shoplifting. In addition this locations allows the clerk to observe patrons and greet them as they enter the store, putting any criminal at a psychological disadvantage and allowing the clerk to look for suspicious activities.

2. Is the register and surrounding area visible from the exterior of the business? ☐ ☐

   The cash register and area behind is the primary target of robbers and thus it is important that, of all places the fishbowl effect be created here. Robbers may force a clerk down in the floor behind the register counter during a robbery and any observation of this area is encouraged. Open observation of this area also proves that no cash is kept in bags or under the counter and thus reduces the potential reward to the observant robber.

3. Are customers visible at all locations within the store or business by employees? ☐ ☐

   The store design should encourage observation of customers in most, if not all locations in the store. Shorter shelving, aisles open toward the cashier, and use of observation mirrors are means of accomplishing this goal. Increasing the effort and risk that they will be caught discourages all sorts of criminals. The robber may wait in the store until he sees an opportunity to pull his gun or mask from concealment and by opening the observation of the store this action is possibly eliminated while the reaction time for the clerk is enhanced.

4. Are store displays located and designed so as to not obstruct the view from outside or from within the business? ☐ ☐

   Surveillance by passing vehicles, pedestrians, and customers to view inside the store is helpful in making the business unattractive to criminals. Displays and anything that obstructs that view make the business more likely to be targeted by robbers.

5. Does the business have a drop safe or other safe? ☐ ☐

   The U.S. Department of Labor, Occupational Safety and Health Administration recommend that late-night retail establishments use drop safes to limit the availability of cash to robbers. Signs indicating that the clerk cannot access the cash in the drop safe should be conspicuously posted. If drop safes are not available, some other type of drop system in an area located in the office away from the public access may be used. After being dropped the cash should not be accessible to the clerk. All safes should be anchored to the building floor.

6. Is the safe access limited to management and/or specific accounting staff? ☐ ☐

   A limited number of persons with access to the safe is recommended. A procedure that the combination be changed when any of the employees with the business having safe access terminates employment should be the norm.

7. Is there a requirement that at least two employees be present when the safe is opened? □ □

In order to build in accountability for the contents of the safe and those having last secured the contents, it is recommended that there always be two persons present during the opening of the safe to retrieve the deposits or start-up money. With two persons present, the opportunity for theft is greatly reduced.

8. Is access to the cash register(s) difficult for the public? □ □

In order to avoid a person reaching across and grabbing cash while the register is open or robbing the store by such a manner, steps should be taken to limit the easy access to the register. Such steps might be raising the cash register area by several inches. This creates a psychological advantage for the employee as well. Installing a wider counter is another measure that might achieve this effect.

9. If CCTV is employed, is the tape access secure? □ □

Videotape for CCTV should not be located under the counter or in the same area of the camera but should be in a locked room or cabinet to protect the tape.

10. Can the CCTV be monitored from another room within the business? □ □

The usefulness of CCTV is enhanced when it is not only used after the fact of an incident but also used as a means of monitoring the business, the employees in the cash handling areas and the grounds in real time. A secure room with limited access is recommended for one of the sites of the monitors.

11. Can the CCTV pan and tilt to various angles around the register area? □ □

CCTV is a real prevention tool when it is located near the register and employees are aware that it is capable of panning, zooming, and monitoring cash transactions.

12. Are height markers affixed at exits? □ □

Employees should be trained that their primary role in a robbery is to cooperate with the robber so that he may quickly vacate the premises and to concentrate on his description. During such stressful situations suspects often appear larger to the victim. By placing height markers on the doorposts, the employee has an accurate gauge of height.

13. Are customer service desks/returns desks located immediately within the entrance doors? □ □

Returns should be received as customers enter the doors to prevent the use of store or business bags to conceal merchandise from within. It is recommended that the customer service desk handling such returns be located immediately inside the retail environment and check parcels in as customers arrive. The customer service personnel or others should greet every customer with eye contact to ensure they know that they have been seen and may be identified.

14. Are there multiple sets of doors to exit the business? □ □

Multiple entrances/exits pose a control problem for the office environment in which the criminal may slip in and commit crimes. Such entrances pose a theft problem for the retail environment where the thief may simply be seeking a quick grab and escape route. In both cases the problem is real and can easily be remedied by either reducing the entrances/exits or, when such action is not permissible, design work space near the entrance/exits to act as natural guardians of the problem area.

15. Are any robbery alarms of the silent activation type? ☐ ☐

Businesses equipped with robbery or panic alarms are encouraged to utilize the silent type to avoid panicking the robber into harming employees and/or taking them as a hostage. Careful consideration should be given when deciding upon the installation of and potential use of such alarms.

16. Are there walk-in coolers, safes, or offices that can be locked? ☐ ☐

If there are locations that may be used by a robber to secure employees while the business is being robbed some preparation is recommended. Such locations should be equipped with a first aid kit and some form of emergency communications such as a telephone, radio with batteries kept fresh, or an intercom system.

■ BURGLARY VULNERABILITIES

Criminals committing burglaries are often attracted to businesses by the same weaknesses that those committing robberies are, therefore, many of the questions listed will be similar but not always identical. Burglars are often driven by a different reward, if the risks and effort outweigh the reward, the burglar will most likely choose a target elsewhere.

Exterior   Y   N

1. Does a full or partial fence protect the business? ☐ ☐

While fencing is not essential, it can be of protection to certain vulnerable areas of the store while closed. If fencing is employed, it is recommended that a minimum 6 foot height chain-link or other see-through fencing be used to allow for police patrol surveillance. Angled stands of barbed wire may be used to reinforce the fence from climbing.

2. If fenced, are all boxes and containers kept away from the fences? ☐ ☐

Fences are designed to restrict access to certain areas and in order to ensure their effective use it is imperative that all containers, trees, and other items that might assist in climbing the fence be removed.

3. Is concealment next to the building eliminated? ☐ ☐

Reducing the concealment locations around the business reduces the opportunity for burglars to force entry undetected. Concealment locations can be limited by removal of foliage, large items, and/or solid fencing. By removing concealment, the business is open to observation from passers.

4. Are there surveillance opportunities for the business from streets, homes, or other businesses? ☐ ☐

Natural surveillance by neighboring residents, businesses, and vehicles should be encouraged by removal of concealment and ensuring that burglary-vulnerable areas are well lighted.

5. If there is roof access to the business, are all potential means of access secured?   ☐   ☐

Building-attached roof-access ladders should be gated off and locked with case-hardened padlocks. Any loose materials that might be used for climbing, such as shipping pallets, ladders, and trees within 10 feet of the building should be addressed to remove their potential use.

6. Is the business exterior alarmed?   ☐   ☐

Unlike a robbery alarm, the purpose of the burglar alarm is to alert the burglar that he/she has been detected and to draw attention to the facility. A combination monitored/audible alarm is ideal to achieve this goal and prevent the burglar from remaining on the scene for a prolonged period.

7. Are all openings to the building secure by some means?   ☐   ☐

Any ventilation ducts, skylights, and windows should be protected with bars or grating and locked.

8. Are all exterior locks quality deadbolt locks?   ☐   ☐

All doors should be equipped with commercial grade quality deadbolt locks with a minimum 1 inch throw. Any second door should have flush bolts that lock into place at the top and bottom of the non-active (lock-equipped) door.

9. Are all exterior non-public access doors constructed of solid wood core or metal construction?   ☐   ☐

The nature of many businesses demands glass doors for public access. However, other doors that are used by staff or for receiving shipments should be of metal or solid wood core and a minimum of $1\frac{3}{4}$ inch thickness. The strike plate should be reinforced with extra long screws and the door fit snugly in the frame.

10. Are all door hinge pins protected from access or removal?   ☐   ☐

All hinge pins should be non-removable, welded, constructed with an anti-removal stud, or located on the inside of the doors.

11. Are all non-stationary or display windows equipped with suitable locking devices?   ☐   ☐

It is rare that a display window in a retail establishment may have non-stationary windows but in some office settings residential-style windows are used. If such is the case, they should be secured with suitable locks other than the stock crescent latch frequently found or replaced with stationary windows.

12. Is cash stored on the premises limited to a minimum required for opening the business?   ☐   ☐

Linked to the cash handling policy, it is essential that only the minimum cash required for opening the business be stored on the site. The opening cash should be secured in the safe.

13. Are there signs visible to the public stating that cash is not retained on the premises?   ☐   ☐

Signs indicating that, "all cash is removed from the premises daily" should be clearly posted. Such simple techniques as this indicating the reduced reward for any burglar goes a long way to their not finding this store a attractive target worth the risk.

14. Are other potential targets visibly secured with a secondary security device, such as chaining or cabling beer-cooler doors?   □   □

Visible deterrents that indicate an increased effort would be required to succeed are an additional step that is recommended prior to closing. By chaining the cooler containing alcohol or padlocking the shelving containing cigarettes, the burglar must weigh the reward against effort and usually will opt to locate another target.

Interior

1. Are cash register drawers left empty and visible to the public on the counter when closed?   □   □

A visible empty cash drawer reinforces the signage indicating that no cash is retained on the premises and therefore making the burglar decide if the reward is worth the risk. Anything that can force the criminal to weigh the risk is a successful deterrent.

2. Are safes secured to the building and concealed from public view in a secured office area?   □   □

In most retail establishments safes should be well within the interior of the building, UL approved, and substantially secured to the floor within a lockable office. The delay involved in locating, getting to, and then having to open, as opposed to removing, the safe all act as a means of preventing safe related crime.

3. Are the office doors treated as an exterior door and secured with similar locks?   □   □

Typically the office will contain the safe, the next day till for opening, and other important items and should be secured using the same criteria of an exterior door. Dependent on the other items and amount of security desired in the office, one may even consider the installation of a UL-approved "high security lock."

4. Are offices locked when the business is closed?   □   □

Regardless of the fact that the safe is locked, offices should also be secured at closing. Any means of delaying access is considered to contribute greatly to the burglar's lack of resolve and perceived risk of capture.

5. Are all keys controlled and inventoried regularly?   □   □

While only trusted employees should have keys to open or close the business, terminated or disgruntled employees may make copies of the keys available to other disreputable persons. A lock or lock core replacement policy should be instituted that requires the changing of the locks each time a key holder employee leave the employ of the business. If an alarm code accompanies the opening process, replacement of the alarm access code may be all that is required.

■ WHITE-COLLAR THEFT/SHOPLIFTING

                                                                    Y   N

1. Are employees trained concerning handling of personal and other
   types of checks?   ☐   ☐

   It is recommended that all personnel receiving checks receive minimal training in
   preventing check-related crimes. Such training should include calling to the attention
   of management suspicious activity, including use of starter checks or low-numbered
   checks indicating a new account; use of an invalid or expired driver's license as
   identification; and altered writing. In addition to the training policies, documenting
   the handling of such problematic check cashing issues should be distributed to
   employees with such duties to ensure proper handling.

2. Is there a policy prohibiting the cashing of two-party checks?   ☐   ☐

   Another favorite technique of perpetrating check fraud is by way of the two-party
   check. While some businesses see this as a positive service to their customers, from a
   crime prevention standpoint it is generally discouraged. If two-party checks are
   accepted it is recommended that it become policy that two forms of identification be
   required, both reflecting the same address and that it should be a local verifiable
   address. In addition, a work and home telephone number should be required.

3. Is there a policy against cashing obviously altered checks?   ☐   ☐

   While training may prohibit the cashing of altered checks or may require a manager's
   approval, it is essential that a policy specify how these checks are to be processed.

4. Is there a policy concerning acceptance and handling of counter checks? ☐ ☐

   Like the other check-cashing areas of concern, accepting counter or start-up checks
   can be problematic but don't always imply dishonesty. It is important that the
   individual make clear to their employees in policy if they will be accepted, when and
   how they will be accepted.

5. Is there a written procedure for handling bad and/or returned checks? ☐ ☐

   All businesses that accept checks are bound to receive bad or returned checks. In
   order to ensure that criminals intent on passing bad checks do not target the business,
   policies concerning handling the checks must clarify the procedures for successful
   prosecution. Since not all returned checks are based on criminal intent, notice by way
   of registered mail should notify the individual and give them opportunity to tender
   payment and any processing fee. Signs notifying customers that the store charges a fee
   for returned checks and that the store prosecutes should be prominently posted at all
   areas of check receiving. The policy should address whether partial payment will be
   accepted since after acceptance of any payment the business is barred from criminal
   prosecution. Finally, the policy must address when the business will prosecute and
   when the loss will be written off.

6. Are employees trained in the acceptance of credit and/or debit cards? ☐ ☐

   Several favored ways of committing credit card crime might be prevented by simply
   training employees to watch for signs and follow procedures for use of the card, even
   when busy. Posting of authorization numbers near the cashiers for easy access serves
   as a reminder of the procedures to employees and speeds transactions. Other training

should include the verification of all information, including visually verifying the person with the card is the one presented on the photo ID and visually inspecting the card for any alterations and expiration date.

7. Does the business require employees to check for credit card signatures and require ID when appropriate, including when noted on the card? ☐ ☐

Many crime prevention educated credit card holders are practicing safe use of their card by noting in the signature line that the cashier should check for ID. Checking for ID should be done in all such transactions and at any other time that the individual business might note the need. Acceptance of a card that is not signed should not be allowed. Policy should require that the individual sign the card or produce identification in two forms.

8. Does the business enjoy a good relationship with the local law enforcement white-collar crime investigators? ☐ ☐

Businesses are encouraged to meet with investigators that will be following up on crimes in their business. Frequently these investigators can offer advice for preventing specific crimes in the business's unique problem area. They also may be willing to train employees or refer the business to the appropriate crime prevention office for training. Investigators have as much an interest in preventing crime in your business as you do. Crimes prevented are crimes that don't draw on the investigator's time.

9. Does the store have a refund/returned item policy? ☐ ☐

Refund fraud usually takes on one of two forms, a shoplifted item is offered for return or a purchase is made with a bad check and a cash refund requested before the check is returned from the bank. In order to combat refund fraud, these two areas should be addressed in your policy. They might be addressed by only offering cash refunds by mail or by only allowing equal exchange. Whatever the policy, it should be clearly posted at the refund desk to avoid problems and to give the employee a "crutch" to lean on with disorderly customers. Additionally the business should consider requiring the following: proof of purchase (original receipt), proper identification, and customer signature on the refund slip.

10. Are the policies followed and periodic checks made to ensure compliance by employees? ☐ ☐

Policies are of little value if they are in writing only and not in practice. Managers and supervisors should conduct spot checks periodically to ensure that the policies are being followed. Mean of ensuring compliance should be discussed and agreed upon by management.

11. Are all employees trained that good customer service is good shoplifting prevention? ☐ ☐

Good customer service and attention to customer needs is desired of all employees in a retail or business environment. This same customer attention is one of the best prevention tools a business has at its disposal. Area employees making eye contact and speaking to every customer entering their area puts the person on notice that they have been observed but also puts the legitimate customer on notice that he/she has been served. Multiply this by as many departments as your business has and it becomes easy to see how the potential shoplifter will quickly get the point as he moves through the business.

12. Is there a policy concerning items taken to fitting rooms or restrooms?   ☐   ☐

Fitting rooms frequently facilitate shoplifting by poor management practices. This legitimately private area, uncontrolled, offers shoplifters an easy means of concealing merchandise. Likewise, restrooms pose a similar problem. Policy, employee posting, and signage should address each of these two areas.

13. Are employees trained in shoplifting prevention and reporting?   ☐   ☐

All employees should be of any retail business should be educated as to the importance of reducing losses. It should be made clear that shoplifting prevention is every employee's responsibility and that losses will ultimately be passed on to the customer through higher prices but also to the employee by lost wage increases. Prevention takes on many forms in relation to shoplifting. In developing training, some areas that may be taught are control of the fitting rooms, greet customers, keep shelves "fronted" so that a quick glance reveals something missing to the department employee, keep display cases locked, staple the bags if rung up within a department inside the store, return out-of-place merchandise to its rightful location or return cart, and contact store management or security when suspicious activity is observed.

14. Are employees hired with the specific role of controlling theft?   ☐   ☐

Individuals hired with the specific role of security, loss prevention, or control are unable to handle all shoplifting and loss functions alone. Instead their role should be one of facilitator, loss policy draftsperson, and trainer, as well. Unless a loss prevention staff is available, the loss control employee must be supported by all other employees and concentrate on ensuring the employees are trained. This staff person, assisted by management, should handle internal theft.

15. Are store loss control employees trained in prevention techniques as well as apprehension?   ☐   ☐

While large businesses typically have an internal training program for their loss prevention/control personnel, many smaller businesses do not. Poorly trained employees in this capacity could lead to huge losses, not through theft but through litigation caused by erroneous apprehensions and accusations. Law enforcement agencies may assist the loss prevention employee in understanding how to protect the business and themselves in making apprehensions. Prevention is one way to avoid litigation. Solid prevention techniques avoid accusations, the need for arrests, and costly court attendance. Such training may be obtained from your law enforcement agency or contract security agencies. Free prevention training is often available from local and state crime prevention associations to their members. Additionally such memberships offer a network of crime prevention specialists, which are available for free consultations on resolving specific problems.

16. Are store security/loss control personnel members of organizations that specialize in the latest in prevention, laws, and apprehension?   ☐   ☐

Membership in organizations mentioned above is recommended for all loss prevention personnel regardless of the size of the business. Such trade organizations keep abreast of recent changes in prevention techniques, which are passed on to their members through training, newsletters, and an annual conference. The wide variety of prevention-related specialties of such an organization's membership provide an excellent resource to the small and large business alike.

17. Does the business employ video surveillance, mirrors, detection shields, and other means of detecting internal and other theft? □   □

If any of the above items are used, the business should consider strategic placement of the items where thefts are most likely to occur. In some cases signage stating that the business is monitored by a number of surveillance tools will enhance the prevention role desired by the business. Modern technologies designed at preventing theft are being developed daily. Dependent on the type of business, management may choose a detection shield that activates an alarm, explodes a dye, or locks down certain doors. All such devices are designed to reduce the reward to the potential criminal or increase the perceived effort and risk associated with carrying out the crime. While these instruments greatly enhance prevention, nothing can take the place of human opportunity reduction techniques.

Access control device   A card or other device carried by a user that is placed near or inserted into a device reader, which reads coded information and validates the access authorization of the device.

Alarm contact   A pair of electrical parts that complete a circuit when touching and that activate an alarm when the circuit is broken.

Alarm entrance delay   The time lapse between when an alarm sensor detects a change in the environment and when the alarm annunciates or alerts. This lapse is built-in to allow for entrance and deactivation of the system by authorized users when the keypad is located inside the facility.

Ambient   Existing without additions (e.g., ambient lighting, ambient sound).

Annunciator/enunciator   The component of an alarm system (e.g., bell, siren) that alerts people that it has detected a change in the environment.

Area sensor   An alarm sensor designed to monitor a certain area within a zone.

Asset   Any item of value (e.g., cash, equipment, inventory, information).

Astragal   A flat piece of molded metal between two doors or a door and frame.

Auto-pan CCTV   A surveillance camera that has the capability to automatically and continuously survey the covered area in a back and forth motion.

Ballast   A device that provides electrical current to start electric discharge lighting.

Balustrade   Decorative rail.

Battery back-up   A battery used as a secondary power source in the event of a primary source failure. Used in alarm, CCTV, and other electronic security systems.

Biometric access control   An access control system in which people are granted access based upon a personal human feature, such as a retinal scan, fingerprints, or voice identification.

Bollard   A post that may be permanent or removable; it is used to block access to vehicular traffic.

Buttress   A supporting structure built against a wall to strengthen it.

Camera dome   A plastic, or in some cases ballistic glass, dome that protects a surveillance camera from common view, the elements, or attack.

Card access   An access control device that uses a coded card for identification/authorization.

Card reader   The stationary device that reads the programmed information on a card access device.

Casement window   A window that is hinged and swings outward when opened. The window is usually opened by use of a hand crank.

Column   A vertical load-carrying structure.

Construction master key   A system of using a single key to access all doors during facility construction and allowing the removal and replacement of the lock core at the completion of construction.

Core key   A special key that is used to remove the core of a lock and replace it with another.

Cutoff luminaire   A fixture that provides a shield that blocks light to an area normally illuminated by the light.

Cylinder   The area of a mechanical lock that contains the mechanism and the keyway. A lock with a single keyway is a single cylinder; a lock with a keyway on both sides is a double cylinder.

Double hung window   A window consisting of two sashes, vertically moving in adjoining tracks.

Double key system   A system that requires two people to access an area. Each individual possesses one key, and access can be gained only by using both keys.

Dummy camera   A device that appears to be an actual CCTV camera but that was never designed to function as a camera.

Duress alarm   An alarm that is manually activated by a person and annunciates silently or calls for assistance. These alarms are used as robbery alarms and in situations in which an audible activation may endanger the user or create a hostage situation.

Electromagnetic lock   A locking mechanism that is activated by current flow to a magnetic device.

Electronic article alarm   An alarm system in which a sensor is attached to an article and activates when the sensor passes receivers placed at exits. This type of alarm is frequently used in theft prevention for expensive items.

Electronic fail safe   An electronic locking system that unlocks the doors when power is removed from the doors.

Electronic fail secure   An electronic locking system that locks the doors when power is removed from the doors.

Emergency plan   A documented plan of action steps to take in the event of an emergency to protect lives, protect property, and restore the normal activities and operations of a facility.

Façade   The front wall of a building.

Footcandle   Used as a measure of light, it is the amount of light on a 1 square foot area from a standard candle located 1 foot away.

French doors   A set of swinging doors, typically constructed of a large percentage of glass.

Glass breakage alarm   An alarm system that functions by way of a microphone detecting the sound of breaking glass.

Heat sensor   An alarm sensor that activates when the temperature in the protected area rises above or dips below a preset rate.

Interlock system   A system that can lock an individual into a certain area; commonly referred to as a "mantrap."

Jamb   The vertical sides of a door or window frame.

Keypad   The component of an alarm system that allows authorized users to enter a key code to activate or deactivate the alarm system.

Laminated safety glass   A type of glass constructed of two plates with a plastic layer between them. This construction prevents falling and flying glass when shattered; the glass is bonded to the plastic, which holds it together.

Load-bearing wall   A wall that supports more than its own weight in a structure.

Lumen   The measure used to evaluate the output of a bulb.

Lumens per watt   A measure of the efficiency of a light bulb. To determine a bulb's output, obtain the lumens per watt from the light bulb package and multiply the watts by the lumens per watt.

Luminaire   A light fixture and all of its components.

Master key system   A system in which a single key fits all locks in a facility or all locks in a certain area of a facility.

Money clip sensor   An alarm sensor placed in a cash drawer that activates an alarm when the money under the clip is removed from between the contacts.

Multiplex   A process by which more than one transmission is carried over the same wire, frequency, or channel. It is most commonly observed in CCTV applications with several cameras feeding to one monitor at once; the operator can enhance or isolate any one of the views.

Optical access control   A card device that evaluates authorization access via the use of light passing through a card perforated with a pattern of holes to form the access code.

Overhead door   A cargo or garage door.

Pan/tilt camera   A camera that is capable of moving left to right and up and down from an automated remote area.

Passive sensing device   A device that detects natural radiation without needing to emit radiation to function.

Perimeter   The outermost property boundary of a facility or area of concern.

Photoelectric sensor   An alarm sensor that functions by emitting a light beam which, when broken, annunciates an alarm.

Pinhole camera   A tiny camera with a small lens designed for surreptitious use.

PML   Term used by security specialists; refers to the *possible maximum loss* and *probable maximum loss*.

Pressure mat sensor   A rubber mat containing metal wiring or strips placed at strategic locations that annunciates an alarm when pressure or weight is applied to it.

Proximity device/card   A device or card that contains wire circuits that activate a reader when placed in "proximity" to or near the reader.

Risk acceptance   A process in which a facility or company identifies the potential for losses and risks and determines the risks to be acceptable. The acceptance is generally due to a cost analysis comparison determining that the costs for protection far outweigh the potential for loss.

Risk assessment   A critical examination of a facility to determine potential risk of attack, loss, or damage.

Risk avoidance   A means of essentially removing the target from all access by the potential criminal.

Risk reduction   A means of reducing the opportunity for the criminal to be successful in completing his or her crime against a target (e.g., crime prevention, loss prevention).

Risk transfer   A means of transferring or sharing some of the potential losses due to risks, generally through insurance or other protections.

Schematic design   Rough drawings of a planned structure.

Security fencing   Fencing used to enhance protection of an area while allowing visual observation of the area—the four accepted types are chain link, barbed tape, barbed wire, and concertina.

Sensor   A device that measures the norm for an environment and "senses" any change, which usually results in alarm activation.

Sill   The lowest part of a window frame.

Stud   The wall structure skeleton to which wallboard or other covering is nailed (may be metal or wood construction).

Tailgate entry   An unauthorized entry that closely follows an authorized entry.

Video motion sensor   A sensor that monitors and evaluates a video image; when it detects a change in the image it annunciates an alarm.

INDEX